Yemeni Arabic Reference Grammar

Hamdi A. Qafisheh

Dunwoody Press
1992

All questions and inquiries should be directed to:

Dunwoody Press, P.O. Box 400, Kensington, MD, 20895

Printed and bound in the United States of America
Library of Congress Catalog Number: 91 - 77058
ISBN: 0 - 931745 - 83 - 7

The research reported herein was performed persuant to a grant from the U.S. Department of Education under the International Research and Studies Program, authorized by Title VI of the Higher Education Act of 1965, as amended.

Table of Contents

The Nineteen Sections

PART ONE
The Phonology of Yemeni Arabic

Table I – CONSONANTS

Table II – VOWELS

PART THREE
THE SYNTAX OF YEMENI ARABIC

14. Major Sentence Types

15. CLAUSES

16. MAJOR PHRASE TYPES

PART FOUR
TEXTS

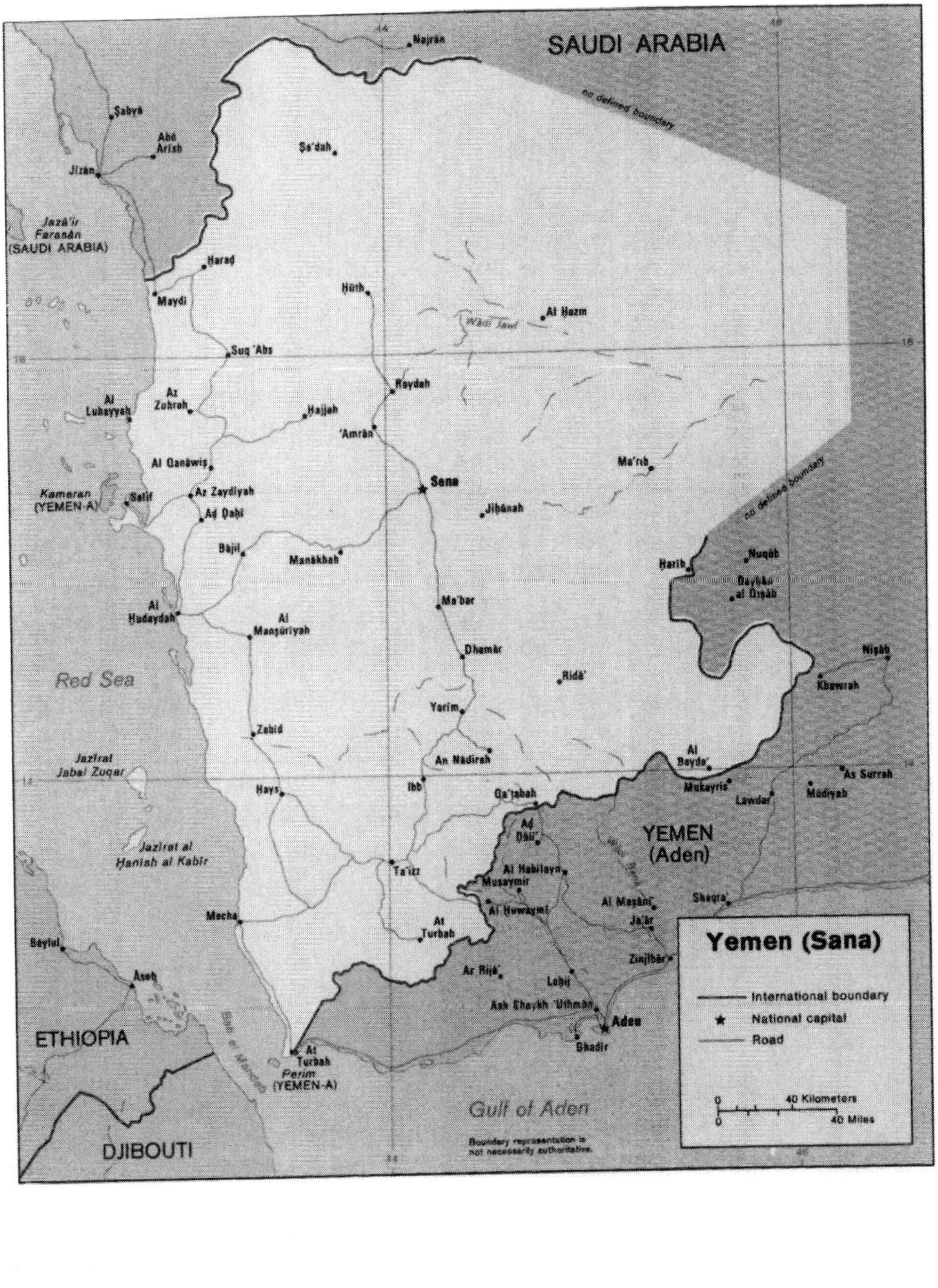
Yemen (Sana)
International boundary
National capital
Road
0 40 Kilometers
0 40 Miles
Boundary representation is not necessarily authoritative.
SAUDI ARABIA
no defined boundary
no defined boundary
YEMEN (Aden)
ETHIOPIA
DJIBOUTI
Red Sea
Gulf of Aden
Jazā'ir Farasān (SAUDI ARABIA)
Kameran (YEMEN-A)
Jazirat Jabal Zuqar
Jazirat al Ḥanish al Kabir
Perim (YEMEN-A)
Wādī Jawf
Najrān
Ṣabyā
Abū Arish
Jīzān
Ṣa'dah
Ḥaraḍ
Maydi
Ḥūth
Al Ḥazm
Suq 'Abs
Raydah
Az Zuhrah
Al Luhayyah
Ḥajjah
'Amrān
Al Qanāwiṣ
Ma'rib
Sana
Salif
Az Zaydiyah
Aḍ Ḍaḥi
Jiḥānah
Bājil
Manākhah
Ḥarīb
Nuqūb
Dayḥān al Ḍiṣāb
Ma'bar
Al Ḥudaydah
Al Manṣūriyah
Dhamār
Niṣāb
Riḍā'
Khawrah
Yarim
Zabid
An Nādirah
Al Bayḍā'
As Surrah
Ḥays
Ibb
Qa'ṭabah
Mukayris
Lawdar
Mūdiyah
Aḍ Ḍāli'
Al Habilayn
Ta'izz
Musaymir
Al Maṣḥni'
Shaqra'
Al Ḥuwaymī
Ja'ār
Mocha
At Turbah
Zinjibār
Beylul
Ar Rijā'
Lahij
Aseb
Ash Shaykh 'Uthmān
Aden
Shadir
At Turbah

Dedicated to
my wife, Kalida,
in affection and gratitude

Preface

The Yemen, or until very recently the Yemens (YAR or Yemen Arab Republic and PDRY, South Yemen, or People's Democratic Republic of Yemen, the first and only Marxist Arab nation), is one of the oldest inhabited areas of the world. The capital of SanՙSa, according to tradition, was founded by Shem, one of Noah's three sons. Arabic dialectologists have long recognized Yemen as a museum for the study of Arabic dialects since the Yemenite dialects have preserved very archaic grammatical and lexical usages. Consequently, this volume has much to offer specialists.

Dr. Hamdi A. Qafisheh, well known for his reference grammar and textbooks of Gulf Arabic among numerous other linguistic studies, has done extensive field work in Yemen and has written this clear, concise yet comprehensive reference grammar of colloquial Yemenite Arabic (based primarily on the dialect of the capital and the largest city). It is the first work of its kind. As such, travellers to Yemen, and to a certain extent other parts of the Arabian Peninsula as well, are well served by Qafisheh's fine prose and copious examples, but so too are general linguists wishing to check out something to do with Yemenite Arabic phonology, morphology, or syntax. Qafisheh's style is exemplary and straightforward as his explanatory descriptions offer clear-cut illustrations of the subject matter. The reader will instantly recognize that we have in this book an excellent and lasting contribution to Arabic dialectology which complements other recently published materials dealing with this important but rather neglected part of the Arab world, such as of Habaka Feghali's *Arabic Adeni Reader (Yemen)* and *Arabic Adeni Textbook (Yemen)* (Wheaton, Maryland: Dunwoody Press, 1990).

Alan S. Kaye
California State University
Fullerton, California

Introduction

1. Preliminary

The language that is described in this work is Arabic as it is used by semi-educated Yemenis in San'a, capital of the Republic of Yemen. Yemen is situated in the southwestern corner of the Arabian Peninsula, just north of the passage between the Red Sea and the Gulf of Aden. It enjoys a strategic position, being the gateway to the oil fields of Saudi Arabia and lying along the sea lanes carrying much of the noncommunist world's oil supply. It has a population of about twelve million people and the division and rivalries between the two major sects (Sunnis and Shiites) permit only limited ethnic cohesion. It has a tradition of religious tolerance, and until 1948 was the home of a Jewish community, estimated at 90,000. It was considered by the United Nations one of the 29 least developed countries in the world until the recent discovery of oil. The United States was one of the early donors of financial aid to the Yemen Arab Republic, known as North Yemen at that time, and between 1972 and 1990 the average U.S. aid was $6,000,000 a year. The Saudi annual assistance was $120,000 a year. Among other countries that still contribute financial assistance are Germany, China, the World Bank, and the Soviet Union. The Peace Corps volunteers are engaged in agricultural development, irrigation, nursing, and teaching English. Until September of 1990 the USIA operated YALI (the Yemen-America Language Institute) and a major agricultural program was being aided by seven American universities (The Consortium for International Development), of which the University of Arizona and the American University in Beirut are members. In the private sector, French, British, German, Italian, and Japanese companies have been aggressively seeking and getting businesses, especially since the discovery of oil.

San'a is the capital and seat of the government of the Republic of Yemen. It is situated on the high plateau of central Yemen, 7,500 feet above sea level. It is built at the foot of a high mountain at the southern end of a cultivated valley. The surrounding mountains are barren, except for cultivated terrace areas. Its climate is generally clear and mild. Night temperatures rarely drop below 32° F in winter, and midday temperatures range in the 70's and 80's. The old section of San'a, known as <u>Sanʕa l-gadiimah</u>, or simply the <u>madiinah</u>, is surrounded by a partially dismantled ancient city wall, and life within the city wall has changed little in the thousands of years since it was first settled.

2. Summary of Relevant Studies

Much has been written on the history and politics of Yemen; only a few fragmented linguistic studies have been made, but almost nothing of the scope of the present work has been previously attempted or published. *Yemeni Arabic I* (by this author), published by Librarie du Liban, 1990, is based on the dialect of San'a, the language used by unsophisticated Ṣanʕaanis for oral communication. It contains forty texts of dialogs and narratives, fifty conversations, approximately 2,000 vocabulary items, a Yemeni Arabic-English English-Yemeni Arabic glossary and an Index of Grammatical Terms. The dialogs and narratives cover a wide variety of interests, such as greetings, getting acquainted, directions, shopping, banking, mailing letters, atmospheric conditions, festivals, etc. *Yemeni Arabic I* was produced under the auspices of the International Studies and Research Program of the U.S. Department of Education. Yemeni Arabic II is in press.

Yemeni Arabic (mimeographed) prepared by David Critchfield (1979) for the American Peace Corps and *An Introduction to Yemeni Spoken Arabic* (unpublished) by Renaud (1977) are language texts. They adopt a grammar translation method or no method at all and require a knowledge of literary Arabic. The grammar notes are flimsy and sketchy; the grammar drills, if any, are limited in number and type and are unsuitable for classroom use. Not much use was made of Greenman (1979) or Diem (1973). The former is a description of the dialect of the central Yemeni Tihamah; the latter is a good book but it is not a study of Ṣanʕaani Arabic (SA). Sergeant and Lewcoct (1983) was used as background information on the City of San'a. A limited use was made of the glossary and index at the end of the book.

Rossi (1939) is quite useful; it is both a descriptive study and a textbook. It is based on the speech of San'a and the immediate vicinity. It presumes a knowledge of literary Arabic. There is a good selection of text materials in transcription, which covers a wide range of phrases and dialogs on common subjects, proverbs, stories, popular songs, and poetry. A lexicon lists words under various headings, followed by a vocabulary of about 1,000 items. The major drawback of the book is that it is too short; the grammar part is only forty-six pages long. Only eight pages are devoted to phonology. The phonology part does not discuss the following topics, which are essential features in any study of the phonology of Ṣanʕaani Arabic: phonological processes (such as pausal glottalization, pausal diphthongization, devoicing of voiced geminates, epenthesis, etc.), consonant clusters, diphthongs, and features of /r/, /l/, /g/ and /h/. His chart (on page 1) does not include the glides /w/ and /y/, labels /s/, /z/, and /ṣ/ as dentals, and the glottal stop, /h/, /ḥ/, and /ʕ/ as laryngeals. The morphology also suffers from an inadequate treatment of verb forms, derivation and inflection of nouns, noun modification, pronouns and particles. Moreover, the book does not include any description of syntax.

The Ṣanʕaani Arabic of today differs from that Rossi described. Rossi (1939) lacks a modern linguistic treatment and reflects theory and practice of some fifty years ago, in addition to its shortcomings. It is not a description of the present urban semi-educated Ṣanʕaanis.

Jastrow's *Zur Phonologie und Phonetik des Sanʕaanischen* (1984) is quite useful but it deals only with the phonological processes of geminate devoicing, pausal glottalization, pausal diphthongization, voicing of the stops /t/ and /ṭ/, and the morphological features of the feminine ending -eh/-ah and the third person singular pronominal suffixes. Among the phonological features that have not been dealt with are (1) the voiced velar stop /g/, the reflex of literary Arabic /q/, (2) the glottal stop /ʔ/, (3) the voiceless glottal fricative /h/, (4) the dental lateral /l/, (5) the flap /r/, (6) consonant clusters, and (7) imaalah. I might add that Jastrow's informants were university students of the Department of Philosophy of Ṣanʕa University, and he had personal contact with Dr. Yusif Abdalla and Ibrahim Aṣ-ṣilwi.

3. The Present Study

Yemeni Arabic Reference Grammar, based on the dialect of San'a, capital city of the Republic of Yemen, presents an explicit outline of the phonology, morphology, and syntax of Ṣanʕaani Arabic. It is the result of the author's field work in Yemen during the periods September 10, 1985-January 20, 1986, November 8, 1986-February 25, 1987, December 10, 1989-January 25, 1990, and June 10-August 18, 1990. Initially, a frequency word list of about 5,000 items for *Yemeni Arabic I* and *Yemeni Arabic II* was compiled from recordings which this author had made of spontaneous, unprepared narratives and conversations of unsophisticated Ṣanʕaanis in different situations, such as greetings, telephone conversations, comments, interviews, etc. Later on, there was an active search for tales, fables, anecdotes, and stories from storytellers, poets, and other native speakers.

The present work seeks to fill some of the important gaps that presently exist in linguistic and language studies of Peninsular Arabic, especially that of the Republic of Yemen. It is linguistically oriented and essentially synchronic. No attempt has been made to refer to any diachronic facts. However, some reference is made to other colloquial Arabic dialects to highlight certain features. The book is usable to students who have already acquired (or are acquiring) a knowledge of SA; to teachers who intend to use it as a checklist of grammatical points; and to Arabic linguists and dialectologists who will use it as a source of information about this dialect. It will also serve larger groups, namely, American personnel in Yemen, technical experts, and others who have communicative and linguistic interests in Yemen.

4. The Native Speakers

The native speakers ("informants") whose speech served as the basis for the language of the present work are semi-educated and unsophisticated speakers of SA. They are male and their ages range between twenty and forty. On most occasions the informants talked to each other either in their houses during qat sessions or in such places as coffeehouses, office buildings, etc. In informant interviews the question, "How do you say ...?" was avoided as much as possible for the sake of authenticity. Indeed, some of them had the tendency to emulate my dialect or other Arabic dialects, especially Egyptian and Palestinian. I have run across contrast of šagaayir," 'a package of cigarettes' on one occasion and "gafa šugaayir," on another occasion. The latter is the SA form. In instances such as this one, I would check with the informants again, or another informant would contribute saying, "We do not use this in our dialect."

It was almost impossible for me to carry on direct conversation with a female informant. Only on two occasions was I able to talk to a wife through her husband. She was very shy and conservative in her speech. Women in Yemen have their own qat chewing sessions.

Acknowledgements

I would like to express my thanks and appreciation to all those who helped in the preparation of this study. First, to the administrators of the International Studies and Research Program of the United States Department of Education, authorized by Title VI of the Higher Education Act of 1965 as amended, for the grant that made the present study possible. To Professor Ernest N. McCarus, Director of the Center for Near Eastern and North African Studies of the University of Michigan, for having carefully read the phonology and the morphology parts of the manuscript and made a number of corrections and instructive suggestions, and for having edited the English translation of the TEXTS; to Professor Alan S. Kaye, Department of Linguistics, California State University, Fullerton, for his comments and insightful suggestions on the phonology, the morphology, and the syntax parts; to my research assistants Abdalla Al-Ansi and Jamal Al-Yusfi of this University for their assistance and patience throughout; to my language informants, Mutahhar Abdulkadir, Abdulkadir Bin Abdalla and his relatives of San'a, for their intelligence, patience, humor, and warm hospitality; to Dr. Abdul-Aziz Al-Magalih, Rector, San'a University and Director of the Yemeni Center for Research and Studies, for having made it possible for me to meet with useful informants and helped in many other ways; to Ms. Barbara Cook of the Department of Near Eastern Studies of this University for an efficient production of the final copy of the manuscript. Last, but not least, my thanks go to Professor William G. Dever, Head, Department of Near Eastern Studies of this university, for his interest and for having provided adequate office facilities and released time needed for the completion of this project.

H.A.Q.
Tucson, Arizona
1992

Transcription

Consonants

Symbol	Approximate Sound	Symbol	Approximate Sound
ʔ	(glottal stop)	p	p in pen
b	b in big	q	
d	d in dog	r	Spanish r in caro
f	f in fan	s	s in sip
g	g in God	ṣ	s in sauce
ġ	Parisian r in Paris	š	sh in ship
h	h in hat	t	t in tall
ḥ	----------	ṭ	t in tot
j	j in jam	w	w in win
k	k in skim	x	German ch in Nacht
l	l in lathe	y	y in yet
ḷ	ḷ in bell	z	z in zeal
m	m in mat	θ	th in thin
n	n in nap	ð	th in this
		ð̣	th in thus
		ʕ	----------

Vowels

Short	Approximate Sound	Long	Approximate Sound
i	i in sit	ii	ea in seat
a	----------	aa	a in hat
e	e in bed	ee	----------
u	u in put	uu	oo in food
		oo	British aw in law

Symbols and Abbreviations

Symbols

→	item on the left is changed into item on the right
←	item on the right is derived from item on the left
*	indicates an ungrammatical utterance
AP	active participle
PP	passive participle
C	consonant
C1	first consonant
C2	second consonant
C3	third consonant
N	noun
<u>N</u>	noun head
SA	Ṣanʕaani Arabic
V	vowel
V-ed	passive participle
( )	item enclosed is optional, e.g., cup (of s. th.)can be cup or cup of s. th., or explanatory, e.g., (English) is from English, (m.s.) is masculine singular, (coll.) is collective, etc.

Abbreviations

adj.	adjective	neg.	negative
adv.	adverb	obj.	object
alt.	alternate	p.	plural
coll.	collective	s.	singular
dim	diminutive	s.th.	something
f.	feminine	s.o.	someone
imp.	imperative	subj.	subject
intra.	intransitive	tra.	transitive
lit.	literally	var.	variant
loc.	locative	vd	voiced
m.	masculine	vl	voiceless

Note: The abbreviations, e.g., (coll.), (m.), (f.), (m.s.), etc. are enclosed in the gloss and considered as part of the meaning of an item.

Part One

The Phonology of Yemeni Arabic

Table 1

Consonants

		Bilabial	Labiodental	Interdental	Dental	Alveolar	Alveo-Palatal	Velar	Uvular	Pharyngeal	Glottal
Stops	vl				t ṭ			k			ʔ
	vd	b			d			g			
Fricatives	vl		f	θ		s ṣ	š		x	ḥ	h
	vd			ð ḍ̄		z			ġ	ʕ	
Affricatives	vl										
	vd						j				
Nasals		m			n						
Laterals					l						
Flap						r					
Semivowel		w					y				

Table 2

Vowels

1. Short

	Front	Central	Back
High	i		u
Mid	e		
Low		a	

2. Long

	Front	Central	Back
High	ii		uu
Mid	ee		oo
Low		aa	

Section One

1. Consonants

The consonant sounds below are described in terms of point of articulation (e.g., bilabial, labiodental, etc.) and manner of articulation (e.g., stops, fricatives, etc.). Among the consonant sounds of Ṣanʕaani Arabic, the stops, fricatives, and affricates may be either voiceless or voiced. A voiceless sound is one which is produced without vibration in the vocal cords, e.g., the t̲ sound in English p̲a̲t̲. A voiced sound is produced with vibration in the vocal cords, e.g., the d̲ sound in English p̲a̲d̲. The voiceless-voiced pairs in American English are:

1. Stops: p-b, t-d, k-g
2. Fricatives: f-v, θ-ð, s-z, š-ž
3. Affricates: č-j

Those of SA are:

1. Stops: t-d, k-g
2. Fricatives: θ-ð, s-z, x-ġ, ḥ-ʕ

1.1 Stops: **b, t, d, ṭ, k, g, ʔ**

A stop is a sound which is produced by halting the passage of air by a complete closure at some point along the vocal tract, and then releasing the air.

b: voiced bilabial stop. Similar to English /b/

b-ḥasb	*according to*
baġl	*mule*
ʔibsir!	*Look (m.s.)!*
jallaab	*importer*

This phoneme becomes devoiced, i.e., it has the allophone [p] if it is doubled and if it occurs intervocalically.

sabbaak	→	[sæppææk]	*pipe fitter*
murabbiḥ	→	[murappiḥ]	*profitable*
xabbaaz	→	[xæppææz]	*baker*
musabbir	→	[musæppir]	*preparer; maker*
ðibbaal	→	[ðippææl]	*wedding celebration*

t: voiceless dental stop Similar to English /t/:

taaʕib	*tired*
matkeh	*cushion, pad*
ʔantayn	*you (f.p.)*
gaat	*qat*[1]

This phoneme is replaced by the phoneme /d/ in an intervocalic environment or in word-initial position followed by a vowel.

yitfil	*he spits*	but	dafal	*he spat*
matkeh	*cushion, pad*	but	madaaki	*cushions, pads*
bintih	*his daughter*	but	banaadi	*my daughters*
ʔiftadaḥ	*he inaugurated*	but	fadaḥ	*he opened*

In word-initial position followed by a vowel the phoneme /t/ is also heard, especially in the speech of educated Ṣaʕaanis; I have heard both tafal and dafal *he spat*, tirmi and dirmi *she throws; you (m.s.) throw*, etc.

d: voiced counterpart of /t/. Similar to English d

ʔidaareh	*office, bureau*
bardag	*glass (of s.th.); cup*
gadr	*scope, extent*
maḥḥad	*no one*

Like /b/, this phoneme becomes devoiced if it is doubled and if it occurs intervocalically.

ḥaddaad	→	[ḥættææd]	*blacksmith*
gaddar	→	[gættær]	*he appreciated*
muʔaddab	→	[muʔættæb]	*well-mannered*
ʔid-daktoor	→	[ʔittæktoor]	*the doctor*

(For dd → tt, see 4.3 below.)

ṭ: velarized counterpart of /t/

/t/ and /ṭ/ constitute the first pair of plain and velarized[2] consonants that we will take up. In the production of /t/, the tip of the tongue touches the back of the upper teeth; for the pharyngealized /ṭ/ the tongue, instead of remaining relaxed as for plain /t/, is tense and a little retracted. /t/ is a little aspirated, i.e., pronounced with a little burst of air, while /ṭ/ is unaspirated. /ṭ/, like any other pharyngealized consonant sound, takes the backed pronunciation of adjacent vowels, while /t/ takes the fronted variety.

Like /t/, the phoneme /ṭ/ has an allophone [ḍ] in an intervocalic environment (including geminates) or in word-initial position followed by a vowel.

ʕaṭš	*thirst*	but	[ʕaaḍiš]	*thirsty*
ʔusṭa	*craftsman*	but	[ʔaṣaaḍi]	*craftsmen*
maṭbax	*kitchen*	but	[maḍaabix]	*kitchens*

Other examples:

[muḍahhar]	*(mas. name)*
[maḍar]	*rain*
[salaḍah]	*salad*
[šaḍaleh]	*fork*
[ḍamaaḍiis]	*tomatoes*
[ḍali]	*lamb*
[ḍaageh]	*window*
[muʕaḍḍal]	*out of order*

Elsewhere, the allophone [ṭ] occurs:

[baṭn]	*belly*
[raṭl]	*pound (weight)*
[maṭʕam]	*restaurant*
[ʔaṭlag]	*he set free*

It should be pointed out that this allophone [ḍ] is semi-pharyngealized, i.e., the pharyngealization is not as pronounced as it is in colloquial Levantine or colloquial Egyptian Arabic. The tongue is less tense, lower in the middle, and less raised toward the back for the SA [ḍ].

k: voiceless velar stop. Similar to English k̲

kaawiyeh	*an iron*
(ʔi)ktasar	*it was broken*
mikannis	*sweeper*
sambuuk	*sailing boat*

g: voiced counterpart of /k/

The voiced velar stop /g/ is the reflex of original (early Arabic) /q/ in all environments, including proper names:

ʔal-gaahirah	*Cairo*
gafaṣ	*package*
ʔal-gurʔaan	*the Quran*
ġallag	*he shut, closed*
gaṭar	*Qatar*
ḥaggi	*mine*
gaat	*qat*
dagiigeh	*minute*
ḥadiigeh	*garden*
baggaal	*green grocer*

(For the devoicing of /g/, see 4.3 below.)

ʔ: glottal stop

This sound does not exist in English as a distinctive sound. It is not a full-fledged phoneme in English, and it is not represented in regular writing. It is produced by all speakers of English in vowel-initial isolated words, e.g., ice, uptown, ink, etc. It sometimes occurs as a variant of /t/ as in some dialects of English (e.g., bottle, button, etc., with the glottal stop instead of --tt-). It is also used, e.g., instead of /h/ in the English interjections: oh-oh! In SA /ʔ/ is a distinctive sound; it occurs in all positions:

Initially:

ʔayn	*where?*
ʔayš	*what?*
ʔal-gaahirah	*Cairo*
ʔamwaas	*razors*

Medially:

giraaʔah	*reading*
faʔs	*adz*
maʔdubeh	*banquet*
raaʔ iḥah	*smell (n.)*
raʔs	*head*
faʔr	*mouse, rat*

Finally:

garaʔ	*he read*
maaʔ	*water*
waraaʔ	*behind*
jubaaʔ	*ceiling; roof*
hamraaʔ	*red (f.)*
zargaaʔ	*blue (f.)*
ʕawraaʔ	*one-eyed (f.)*
latgaaʔ	*stammerer (f.)*

In word-final position the occurrence of the glottal stop is very rare in other Arabic dialects, e.g., in colloquial Gulf, Levantine, or Egyptian, the final glottal stop in the words above is dropped.

Sometimes, especially in rapid speech, word-initial /ʔ/ and preceding long /aa/ in final position in one-syllable words are dropped.

yaa ʔibni	→	y-ibni	*oh, my son*
yaa ʔummi	→	y-ummi	*oh, my mother*
maa ʔadri	→	m-adri	*I do not know*
(ʔi)laa ʔayn	→	l-ayn	*where to?*

1.2 Fricatives: **f, θ, ð, ð̣, s, z, ṣ, š, x, ġ, ḥ, ʕ, h**

f: voiceless labiodental fricative. Similar to English f in fat. The air stream is impeded between the lips and the teeth.

faariḥ	*cheerful*
fiisaʕ	*fast, quickly*
ftaš	*he inspected*
razfeh	*song, especially at a wedding*
mulaflaf	*wrapped*

θ: voiceless interdental fricative. Similar to English th in thin, and bath.

θawr	*bull*
θurayyah	*candelabra*
θaaliθ	*third*
wariiθ	*inheritor*
ġaθθ	*he irritated s.o.*

ð: voiced counterpart of /θ/. Similar to English th in this, rather, and lathe.

ðibbaal	*wedding celebration*
ðubbi	*fly (n.)*
gaðaf	*he threw up*
naðag	*he threw s.th. on the floor*
ḥaððar	*he warned*
faxð	*thigh*

ð̣: velarized counterpart of /ð/

The dot under /ð̣/ represents velarization, traditionally known as "emphasis". A velarized sound is pronounced with the tongue farther back in the mouth; the lips are rounded or protruded slightly. In producing the plain non-velarized /ð/ the tongue is relaxed and its tip protrudes a little beyond the edges of the upper and the lower teeth. For the velarized /ð̣/, on the other hand, the tongue is tense, lower in the middle, and more raised toward the back part. Note that this changes the quality of adjacent vowels, especially /a/ and /aa/, and gives a 'hollow' or 'backed' effect. (The aa sound in /ðaaʕ/ 'he broadcast,' for example, is similar to the a in English that, but it changes to a sound similar to the a sound in hard in the SA word /ð̣aaʕ/ 'he, it got lost.') /ð - ð̣/ is the second pair of plain and velarized consonants.

ð̣aaʔ	*he lit, illuminated s.th.*
ð̣amm	*he kept s.th. for himself; he embraced*
ʕað̣m	*(coll.) bones*
bagð̣ah	*hatred*
nað̣ð̣af	*he cleaned*
ġaliið̣	*dense; thick*

s: voiceless dental grooved fricative. Similar to English s in sip.

sabbar	*he made; he prepared*
(ʔi)staḥagg	*he deserved, was worthy of s.th.*
naafiseh	*midwife*
ʔibsir	*look (m.s.)!*
bisbaas	*(coll.) hot peppers*

z: voiced counterpart of /s/

zalaṭ	*money*
zaarathiin	*sometimes*
ʔajhizeh	*dagger holders*
xabbaaz	*baker*

ṣ: velarized counterpart of /s/

/s/ and /ṣ/ constitute the third pair of plain and velarized consonants. In the production of /ṣ/ the front part of the tongue is in the same position for /s/, but the central part is depressed and the back part raised toward the velum. Velarized /ṣ/ has a lower pitch than plain /s/.

ṣabuuḥ	*breakfast*
(ʔi)ṣṭabaḥ	*he had breakfast*
lagṣah	*reptile bite; a pinch*
gaṣgaṣ	*he cut up s.th. into little pieces*

š: voiceless alveopalatal grooved fricative. Similar to English sh in ship.

šaagi	*workman, laborer*
šamiiz	*shirt*
šuuʕ	*ugly (in shape)*
šta	*he liked; he wanted*
yištiy	*he wants*
(ʔi) mšann	*water filter*
bugaš	*p. of bugšeh*[3] *small unit of money*

x: voiceless uvular fricative

This sound is similar to Scottish ch in loch and German ch in Nacht. For the production of /x/ the tongue is in the same position as for /k/ but is allowed to move down just a little bit in order to let the air pass through.

xalas	*he undressed, took off his clothes*
xatan	*he circumcised*
xuṭiy	*he walked, went on foot*
nusxah	*copy*
m(i)xazzin	*having chewed qat*
waxxar	*he moved (s.th.) backwards or aside*
juux	*(coll.) broadcloth*

ġ: voiced counterpart of /x/. This sound is produced in gargling; it is close in quality to the Parisian (r) as in Paris, rien, etc. Examples:

ġaaliṭ	*mistaken, having made a mistake*
ġudweh	*tomorrow*
maġraf	*ladle, scoop*

ḥ: voiceless pharyngeal fricative

For the production of /ḥ/ the muscles of the throat are tense and the passageway at the back of the throat becomes constricted. /x/ has been described above as a voiceless uvular fricative. In producing /x/ the back of the tongue must come near the uvula: for /ḥ/ the tongue must not approach it.

From the writer's own experience in teaching Arabic, /ḥ/ is one of the two most difficult sounds for native speakers of English. The other sound is /ʕ/, which is described below. The following exercise has been tried with students in order to help them recognize and produce an acceptable /ḥ/ sound: whisper and repeat the phrase 'Hey you!' as loudly and as deep in your throat as you can; then say only 'Hey,' elongating the initial h̲ sound, "Hhhhhhhhhhhey." Repeat this with the muscles used in gagging tensed up. This would be an acceptable approximation of /ḥ/. An alternative suggestion is to start /ḥ/ with 'ah!', whispering it as loudly as you can. Now repeat it and narrow the pharynx by moving the root of the tongue back, and raising the larynx.

ḥareew	*bridegroom*
ḥaali	*beautiful; nice*
ḥuzwiyeh	*anecdote; fairy tale*
ḥuut	*(coll.) fish*
ṭawḥah	*dizziness*
baḥr	*sea*
maḥḥad	*no one, nobody*

ʕ: voiced counterpart of /ḥ/

ʕaaṭiš	*thirsty*
ʕala sibb	*because*
(ʔi)ʕtagad	*he believed; he thought*
magʕad	*sofa, couch*
madaaʕah	*waterpipe, hubble-bubble*
jaawiʕ	*hungry*

h: voiceless glottal fricative

Similar to English h in hat. Contrary to English the SA /h/ may occur in a pre-consonant position, a post-consonant position, or at the end of a word. In word-final position /h/ is distinctly heard in SA; it corresponds to the feminine marker /taaʔ marbuuṭa/ of literary Arabic[4] or the third-person masculine singular pronominal suffix; it usually drops in rapid speech:

matkeh	*cushion, pillow*
sagṭah	*epilepsy*
ṭaageh	*window*
ḥilbeh	*fenugreek*
bintih	*his daughter*
zarwaṭah	*swallowing*
b-saaʕatih	*in a hurry*
xaaʔiḍ̄ah	*menstruous (woman)*

The feminine marker /-eh/ ~ /-ah/[5] changes into /-at/ if the noun in which it occurs is the first term of an /ʔiḍaafa/ construction:

matkat ad-diiwaan	*the living room cushion*
ṭaagat ad-dayma	*the (old Yemeni) kitchen window*

1.3 Affricate: j

j: voiced alveopalatal affricate. Similar to English j in judge and dg in edge.

jaawiʕ	*hungry*
ʔal-jumʕah	*Friday*
jambiyeh	*dagger*
najjaar	*carpenter*
ʔaʕjam	*dumb, mute*
ʔal-ḥajj	*pilgrimage*

(For jj →čč, See 4.3 below.)

1.4 Nasals: **m, n**

Similar to the English sounds m and n in man and night, respectively.

m:

maaseh	*table;desk*
farmaleh	*brake*
ðimmeh	*conscience*
guddaam	*in front of*

n:

nawm	*sleep*
digneh	*chin*
nuxreh	*nose*
šann	*he filtered (water)*

1.5 Lateral l

l: dental lateral

While there is no similar sound in American English, there is an approximation of the SA/l/ in words like lean, lack, late, etc., where the l sound is initial and prevocalic. In other positions the American /l/ is more or less velarized, depending upon the dialects of the speakers. SA/l/ is a plain sound as opposed to the dark /l/ as in American English hill and belly. In the production of SA/l/ the tip of the tongue touches the tooth ridge (slightly farther forward than in English and in Gulf, Levantine or Egyptian Arabic), and the middle of the tongue is low.

ladaah	*personal effects, belongings*
lilma	*why?*
luḥuuḥ	*(coll.) pancake bread*
(ʔi)ltabaj	*he hit himself*
gišleh	*fortress*
(ʔi)stagall	*it, he became independent*

/l/ has a velarized allophone [ḷ] in the following environments:

(1) In a cluster with a velarized consonant.

xalṭ	*mixing*
raṭlayn	*two pounds*
faṣl	*season*
ʔaṣlak	*your origin*
faḍ̣l	*grace, favor*
šaṭaleh	*fork*

(2) After a long vowel other than /ii/which is in turn preceded by a velarized consonant. Examples:

ṭuul	*length*
ṣaaloon	*living room*
ṭaal	*it lingered long*
ð̣aall	*straying; lost*

In other environments the /l/ is a plain non-velarized phoneme, e.g.; /zalaṭ/ 'money', /saliiṭ/ 'motor oil', /ð̣alam/ 'he oppressed', /ṭalab/ 'application', and /galaṣ/ 'drinking glass'.

A velarized [ḷ] appears in certain forms of the word for "God", e.g., /ʔaḷḷaah/ 'God', /wallạah/ 'by God'. No minimal or near minimal pairs could be found to establish the presence of a velarized /ḷ/ phoneme in SA.

1.6 Flap: /r/

SA /r/ is not like American English /r/; the former is a consonant while the latter is more of a vowel than a consonant. For the production of /r/, most Americans curl the tongue up toward the roof of the mouth as in car, far, etc., and round their lips when the /r/ sound is word-initial or syllable-initial, as in ream, rock, marry, etc. SA /r/ is a tongue flap; it is produced by striking the tip of the tongue against the roof of the mouth, and unlike other dialects of Arabic, the tongue is flatter and the lips are less rounded:

raʔs	*head*
raʔiis	*director*
saarah	*Sarah*
faʔr	*rat, mouse*
ʔidaareh	*administration*
garaʔ	*he read*
maġraf	*ladle, scoop*
ḥaarr	*hot*

/r/ in all of the examples cited above is a plain /r/ in SA. It is a velarized allophone of /r/ in this environment in most other Arabic dialects, especially Levantine, Egyptian and Gulf Arabic.

/r/ has a velarized allophone [ṛ] only in the following environments in SA: /v-ç/, /-çv/, /çv-/ and /-vç/, where v is any vowel and /ç/ is a velarized consonant. In the following examples /r/ is velarized:

farḍ̣	*duty*
gaṭar	*Qatar*
gurṭ	*earring*
ʔagraaṭ	*earrings*
gaṭrah	*eyedrops*
maḥḍ̣ar	*official report*
ʔaxḍ̣ar	*green*
tamayraḍ̣	*he pretended to be ill*

1.7 Semivowels: **w** and **y**

w:

waaṭi	*low (not high)*
wigaayeh	*prevention*
zawaaj	*marriage*
ḥareeweh	*bride*

y:

yaabis	*dry (not humid)*
ðayyih	*this (f.)*
yurt	*yoghurt*
θintayn	*two (f.)*

/w/ and /y/ may replace the glottal stop /ʔ/ in a few isolated words, e.g., waniis instead of ʔaniis 'companion', mawaajil instead of maʔaajil 'basins', mistaysir instead of mistaʔsir 'having taken s.o. captive', muwaððin instead of muʔaððin 'muezzin', and muwaddab instead of muʔaddab 'well-behaved'. However, the forms with the glottal stop are more frequent. No other examples could be found and the environment in which /ʔ/ →/w/ or /y/ could not be determined. The choice of /ʔ/ versus /w/ or /y/ does not correlate with socioeconomic factors, such as class, education,etc.

Section Two

2. Vowels

Short and Long. Like literary Arabic and most other dialects of Arabic, SA has in its vowel system three short vowels and the corresponding three long vowels: i-ii, a-aa and u-uu. In addition SA has the short vowel e and the corresponding long vowel ee, plus a long vowell oo with no corresponding short vowel.

/i/: high front

Similar to English i in bit, though not so high and tense. This variant occurs when it is not word-final or preceded by semivowel /y/ or in the contiguity of velarized consonants. However, it occurs adjacent to pharyngeals /ḥ/ and /ʕ/:

biʔr	*a well*
kaawiyeh	*an iron*
ḥilbeh	*fenugreek*
mikayyis	*masseur*

Another variant of this sound is one between the i sound in bit and the u sound in club:

(ʔi)mbaarak (masculine name)
liʕib 'he played'

/i/ is often retracted and lowered in the environment of velarized consonants:

ḥiṣṣah	*share, portion*
mumarriḍ̣ah	*nurse (f.)*
ṣiḥḥah	*health*
ṭiʕiim	*delicious, tasty*
ḍ̣iig	*distress, hardship*

/ii/: long counterpart of /i/

This low vowel is approximately twice as long as /i/ and has a different quality. It is similar to the English sound i in machine, but is a monophthong and does not have any glide quality.

biibar	*(coll.) bell peppers*	girriiḥ	*(coll.) firecrackers*
dagiigeh	*minute; moment*	ʔiijaar	*rent, rent money*
zaarathiin	*sometimes*	miskiin	*poor; humble*

ii/ is deeper and more audible in the environment of velarized consonants:

mariið̣	*sick*
ṭabiineh	*second wife*
gaṣdiir	*aluminum*
basiiṭ	*simple; easy*

/a/: short low [front], central [or back] vowel.
The phoneme /a/ has three allophones:

(1) a low back unrounded sound [ɑ] in the environment of velarized consonants:

baṭn	*belly*
šaṭaleh	*fork*
fað̣l	*favor*
gaṣr	*palace*
gabṣah	*a pinch*
muṭabbin	*polygamist*

(2) a mid central [ə] allophone in unstressed word-final position and as the vowel of the definite article /ʔal-/ when preceded by another word:

waladha	*her son*
gaṣraha	*her palace*
maaʔ al-biʔr	*the well water*
baab ad-daar	*the house door*

(3) elsewhere, [æ] is farther front than the a in father:

kawa	*he cauterized*
samn	*shortening*

for example; its quality ranges between the e in pen and a in pan. Examples:

gatl	*killing*
sawd	*(coll.) charcoal*
gad	*already*
ḥawl	*(prep.) around*
samn	*shortening*
ʕasiib	*uncurved dagger*

/aa/: long counterpart of /a/:

Long /aa/ has a clear retracted and lowered quality in the contiguity of velarized consonants.

baal	*he urinated*
faarix	*coffee pot*
gaat	*qat*
haaðih	*this (f.)*
ṣaabuun	*(coll.) soap*
ʔasaaṭi	*craftsmen*
ṭaaseh	*cooking utensil*
ḍ̱aaʔ	*he illuminated*

/u/: short high back rounded

/u/: Close to the <u>oo</u> sound in <u>book</u>. It has a mid-back allophone[ɔ] in the environment of velarized consonants, the uvulars /x-ġ/ and the pharyngeals /ḥ-ʕ/; elsewhere it occurs interchangeably with a high (open) back [u] sound:

xuṭiy	*he walked*
ʕuṭuš	*he was thirsty*
ʕuṣyeh	*stick*
ḥuzwiyeh	*anecdote,tale*
ʕurs	*wedding*
xuzgi	*hole*
baytukum	*your house*
ḥaggukum	*yours (m.p.)*

/uu/: long counterpart of /u/

/uu/ is a monophthong. It is similar to English <u>oo</u> in moon. In <u>moon</u> the lips become more rounded toward the end of the vowel; but for SA /uu/ the lips maintain the same rounded position throughout:

ʔuubah	*he looked for s.th.*
barguug	*(coll.) apricots*
duulaab	*wardrobe; cupboard*
gataluuh	*they killed him*
jumhuuriy	*republican*

In addition to the vowels mentioned above SA has the short vowel /e/ and the corresponding long vowel /ee/. /e/ occurs only in a word-final position in nouns and as part of the feminine ending /eh/. Long /oo/ occurs only in loan words. Examples:

ḥilbeh	*fenugreek*
dubbaayeh	*a zucchini*
waršeh	*machine shop*
firsikeh	*a peach*
razfeh	*song*
ṭumṭuseh	*a tomato*
ʔasaaṭiyeh	*craftsmen*
ṣaʕbeh	*jenny ass*
ṣaaloon	*living room*
gaaloon	*gallon*
raadyoo	*radio*
talafizyoon	*television*

Similarly /ee/ occurs only in the word-final sequence /eeʔ/[6]. This will be not only in singular feminine adjectives of color or defect but also in any words that ended originally in /aaʔ/.

ḥamreeʔ	*red (f.)*
bayḏeeʔ	*white (f.)*
ʕamyeeʔ	*blind (f.)*
zargeeʔ	*blue (f.)*
latgeeʔ	*stammerer (f.)*
jeeʔ	*he came*
meeʔ	*water*
wareeʔ	*behind*

It should be pointed out that final /aaʔ/ in such words remains /aaʔ/ if they are not followed by pause, e.g., /maaʔ al-maṭar/ 'rain water', /jaaʔ al-wagt/ 'the time has come', /sawdaaʔ al-ʕuyuun/ 'black-eyed (f.)', etc.

Section Three

3. SOUND COMBINATIONS

3.1 Diphthongs

A diphthong may be defined as a vowel and a glide in the same syllable. There are two diphthongs in SA.

Diphthong /ay/

The diphthong /ay/ is very frequent in SA; it occurs in (1) the dual suffix of nouns, (2) primary nouns, including some proper names, (3) the first person singular and plural forms of weak and doubled perfect tense verbs, and in (4) the second and third person feminine plural verb suffixes:

(1)

baabayn	*two doors*
θintayn	*two (f.)*
ʔiθnayn	*two (m.)*
kalbatayn	*pair of pliers*
ʔalfayn	*two thousand*
bugšatayn	*two bugšas*

(2)

bayt	*house*
xaymeh	*tent*
layl	*night*
ʕayn	*eye*
bayʕ	*selling*
šayʔ	*thing*
xayš	*canvas*
jayš	*army*
bayruut	*Beirut*
ʔal-ḥudaydah	*Hudaida*

(3)

galayt	*I fried*
galayna	*we fried*
bagayt	*I stayed*
ḥamayna	*we defended*
ġaθθayt	*I irritated s.o.*
ḥaṭṭayna	*we put*

(4)

darastayn	*you (f.p.) studied.*
darasayn	*they (f.) studied*
tuktubayn	*you (f.p.) write*
yuktubayn	*they (f.) write*
?uktubayn	*write (f.p.)!*
?udrusayn	*study (f.p.)!*

In the examples above the diphthong /ay/ is in free variation with the long vowel /ee/ or the diphthong /ey/. Forms with /ay/, however, are more frequent. /ay/ does not have any variant in the sequence -ayy-, where syllable division is between the two y's. Examples:

?ayy(a)	*which (one)?*
?ayyin	*which one?*
θurayya	*candelabra*
tayyeh	*this (f.)*
ayya	*this (m.)*
mayyit	*dead*
mikayyis	*masseur*
mixayyiṭ	*tailor*
taḥiyyeh	*greeting*
baḥriyyeh	*sailors, seamen*

Diphthong /aw/

Similarly, but less frequently, the diphthong /aw/ is in free variation with the long vowel /oo/ or diphthong /ow/ in the following environment: -awc(v)(c) (where c is any consonant and v is any short vowel):

lawn	*color*
ð̣aw?	*light*
mawt	*death*
xawf	*fear*
ḥawl	*around*
bawl	*urine*
ðawla	*these*
?ad-dawḥa	*Doha?*
?ar-rawð̣ah	*Rawda*
dawleh	*state; government*
mawtar	*car; motor*
jaww	*weather*

The diphthong /aw/ is used in free variation with the long vowel /uu/ or the diphthong /uw/ in the second and third person masculine plural forms of weak and doubled verbs:

rað̣aw	*they (m.) were content, satisfied*
yirð̣aw	*they (m.) are content, satisfied*
tirð̣aw	*you (m.p.) are content, satisfied*
šallaw	*they (m.) carried, lifted s.th.*
tišillaw	*you (m.p.) carry, lift s.th.*
yišillaw	*they (p.) carry, lift s.th.*

3.2 Consonant Clusters

3.2.1 Double Consonants

In terms of length consonants in Arabic are referred to as single (i.e., short) or double (i.e., long) or doubled consonants. Clusters of two identical consonants, traditionally known as geminates, occur frequently in SA. Double consonants in English occur across word boundaries, e.g., straight to, hot tea, guess so, etc., and occasionally within compound words and words with prefixes or suffixes, e.g., cattail,unnamed, thinness, etc. Double consonants in SA occur initially, medially and finally.

Initial

Initially, double consonants are usually those formed by the combination of a prefix (the article prefix, or a conjunction, or a verb prefix) and the first stem consonant:

r-rajjaal	*the man*
d-dabbeh	*the gas cylinder*
n-najjaar	*the carpenter*
ṣ-ṣaddaam	*the (car) bumper*
w-wujid	*and it was found*
w-waršeh	*and a workshop*
d-darab	*he was hit*
d-dafaʕ	*it was paid*

Medial

Any double consonant may occur in an intervocalic position. -gg-, -dd- and -hh- are rare, however.

xabbaaz	*baker*
guṣṣah	*story*
ʔittifaag	*agreement*
zaṭṭah	*gulp of s.th*
ʔaθ-θaluuθ	*Tuesday*
naḍ̣ḍ̣af	*he cleaned*
rajjaal	*man*
tnaggaz	*he threw up*
maḥḥad	*no one*
bakkaʕ	*he lacerated*
muʔaððin	*muezzin*
ballayt	*I moistened*
waxxar	*he moved backwards*
sannab	*he stood up*
jaddiy	*my grandfather*
wannat	*she groaned*
ʔar-rawḍ̣ah	*Rawda*
jawwi	*atmospheric*
xazzan	*he chewed qat*
twassaʕ	*it was widened*
ʔas-sabt	*Saturday*
θurayyah	*candelabra*

Final

Any double consonant may occur finally except for /ġ/, /h/ and /ḏ̣/, which have not been noted. A final double consonant is not pronounced differently from a final single consonant, e.g., final /l/ in ʔagall 'less' is the same as final /l/ in tafal 'he spat' as far as the sound itself is concerned. The difference is in stress: ʔagáll and táfal or, rarely, tafál (see 5. STRESS, below). A few examples are given below:

sabb	*he cursed s.o.*
ʕadd	*he counted*
ḥaθθ	*he encouraged s.o.*
radd	*he returned s.th.*
kaḥḥ	*he coughed*
ġarr	*he deceived*
rizz	*(coll.) rice*
gazz	*he sheared sheep*
ʕass	*he touched*
rašš	*he sprinkled*
šaṭṭ	*he tore up s.th.*
šakk	*he doubted*
šall	*he took s.th. away*
laff	*he saved money*
ʔann	*he moaned*
ʔayy	*which, what?*
dubayy	*Dubai*
sadd	*dam*
ṣaḥḥ	*he became healthy; it was allowed, permissible*
ʔuff	*interj. expressing anger or displeasure*
ḥajj	*he went on pilgrimage*
sarr	*he cheered up s.o.; it pleased s.o.*
tamm	*it was completed*

3.2.2 Two-Consonant Clusters

A consonant cluster is here defined as any combination of two or more different consonants. Two-consonant clusters in SA are not very frequent initially.

Initial:

šta	*he wanted; he liked*
sfiih	*insolent, impudent*
kšaf	*he uncovered*
xfiif	*light, not heavy*
sfiif	*shelf, bookcase*
ṣḥiiḥ	*healthy*
kfuuf	*hand palms*
twaffa	*he died*
tka	*he reclined (on s.th.)*
ftaš	*he uncovered s.th.*
ksar	*he broke s.th.*
staʕfa	*he resigned*
ṣbuʕ	*finger*
traaya	*he dreamed*

Verb forms V, VI, VIII, and X (see 6.1) usually have initial two-consonant clusters. Forms V and VI may be heard with an intervening -a- between the two consonants and forms VIII and X may be heard with an initial /ʔi-/ in normal, not rapid speech.

t(a)ġassal	*he bathed*
t(a)bannan	*he stuffed himself with food*
t(a)waḏ̣ḏ̣aʔ	*he performed ablution before prayer*
t(a)ʕaafa	*he recuperated*
t(a)ṣaalaḥ	*he became reconciled with s.o.*
(ʔi)ltabaj	*he hit himself*
(ʔi)ṣṭabaḥ	*he had breakfast*
(ʔi)ktasar	*it was broken*
(ʔi)btasar	*it was viewed, seen*
(ʔi)gtaraʔ	*it was read*
(ʔi)staxbar	*he asked to be informed*

Medial and Final

Medially and finally two-consonant clusters are very common:

barʕah	*dance tune*
daymeh	*kitchen*
gambar	*he sat down*
ʔibsar	*he saw*
mabsareh	*eyeglasses*
booṣṭah	*mail, letters*
ġudweh	*tomorrow*
magbareh	*cemetery*
ṣalfaḥ	*he slapped*
lamlam	*he gathered*
faṣl	*season*
milḥ	*salt*
jayš	*army*
gaṣr	*castle*
ʕayn	*eye*
ʕumr	*age*
buxl	*stinginess*
ramayn	*they (f.) threw*
ramayt	*I threw*

3.2.3 Three-Consonant Clusters

Three-consonant clusters are rare in SA. Initially the following examples have been noted:

ftṣa: as in /ftṣa l-ʕamal/	*the work was completed*
štka	*he complained*
stkab	*it was spilled*
(ʔi)ʔtkal	*it was eaten*
(ʔi)btsar	*it was seen*

Medially the three-consonant clusters occur in the imperfect tense forms of /ftṣa/, /štka/, /stkab/, /(?i)?tkal/ and /(?i)btsar/. A medial three-consonant cluster may be encountered in a word that ends with a two-consonant cluster followed by a suffixed pronoun; however, an epenthetic vowel is usually used after the second consonant.

baytha	→	baytaha	*her house*
baytkum	→	baytukum	*your (m.p.) house*

Finally

Finally three-consonant clusters are encountered only in the negative form of the first or second person masculine singular perfect verb:

maa xazzantš	*I (or you) did not chew qat*
maa ṣṭabaḥtš	*I (or you) did not have breakfast*
maa ?ibsartš	*I (or you) did not see*

Between word boundaries three- or four-consonant clusters (usually with a helping vowel) are common (see 4.1 .)

Section Four

4. MAJOR SOUND CHANGES

4.1 Epenthesis

An epenthetic or helping vowel is sometimes inserted within consonant clusters. Its occurrence does not affect meaning: it is used only as an aid to pronunciation. This feature is known as epenthesis or anaptyxis.

Between word boundaries an epenthetic vowel is encountered in two cases:

A. When a word ends with a single consonant and is followed by a word beginning with a double consonant or two-consonant cluster. In such a case the helping vowel /i/ is inserted after the first of three consonants or between word boundaries.

man-i-ṣṭabaḥ?	*who had breakfast?*
gad-i-bsart	*I have already seen.*
hum-i-tġadduw?	*did they (m.) have lunch?*
hiy-i-ṣṭabaḥat?	*did she have breakfast?*
leeš-i-ktasar?	*why was it broken?*
gad-i-staʕfa	*he has already resigned*
law-i-tsawwag	*if he had gone shopping*
naʕam-i-stawfa θ-θaman	*yes, it was paid in full*
man-i-ṭṭalag?	*who was released, set free?*
laakin-i-xfiif.	*but it is light*
maaš-i-ṣḥiiḥ.	*he is not healthy*
lamman-i-ktasar	*when it was broken*
yištuun-i-yʕuumuun.	*they (m.) want to swim*

When a word ends with a two-consonant cluster or a double consonant and is followed by a word beginning with a single consonant. In such a case no helping vowel is used. Examples:

bank damm	*blood bank*
layl ṭawiil	*long night*
farg kabiir	*big difference*
gurṭ ðahab	*gold earring*
hagg ʕali	*belonging to Ali*
šall zalaṭi.	*he took away my money*
bi-yšinn mee?	*he filters water*

If the article prefix ?al- is used with the second noun, the glottal stop of the article prefix is dropped, and thus no helping vowel is needed:

bank ad-damm	*the blood bank*
gišr al-gahwah	*the skin of coffee beans*
gurṭ al-ḥareewah	*the bride's earring*
bayt ar-rajjaal	*the man's house*

B. When a word with a final two-consonant cluster or a double consonant is followed by a word with an initial two-consonant cluster or a double consonant, the helping vowel /i/ is inserted between the two words:

gurṭ-i-ktasar.	*an earring was broken*
ḥilm-i-ntasa.	*a dream was forgotten*
ʕumr-i-mammad	*Muhammad's age*
štarayt-i-kfuuf.	*I bought gloves*

4.2 Assimilation

4.2.1 Regressive Assimilation

Regressive assimilation in SA is frequent. The first consonant of a two-consonant cluster of stops or fricatives, excepting the pharyngeals /ḥ/ and /ʕ/, the glottal fricative /h/ and the dental stop /t/ assimilate to the second consonant in voicing. Examples:

b + k as in /yabki/	→	[yæpki]	*he weeps*
f + g as in /?afgar/	→	[?ævgar]	*poorer*
θ+ g as in /yiθgal/	→	[yiðgæl]	*It becomes heavy*
ð + k as in /yaðkur/	→	[yæθkur]	*he mentions*
k + b as in /?akbar/	→	[?ægbar]	*older; bigger*
ð̣ + ḥ as in /?að̣ḥak/	→	[?aθḥak]	*I laugh*
ṭ + l as in /raṭl/	→	[raḍl]	*pound(weight)*
s + j as in /masjuun/	→	[mæzjuun]	*imprisoned*
z + f as in /razfeh/	→	[ræsfeh]	*merry-making*
ġ + s as in /yiġsil/	→	[yixsil]	*he washes*
g +š as in /bugšeh/	→	[bukšeh]	*one bugša*

Regressive assimilation also appears across word boundaries. Examples:

/ʔab + kabiir/	→	[ʔæpkæbiir]	*old father*
/bas ġudweh/	→	[bæzgudweh]	*only tomorrow*
/ragad saalim/	→	[rægætsaalim]	*Salim fell asleep*

Total regressive assimilation occurs within words or across word boundaries in the following cases:

n + z as in /ʕan-zawwij/	→	[ʕæzzæwwij]	*we will marry off s.o.*
d + b as in /maa gad biš/	→	[maa gabbiš] [mææ gæppiš]	*there isn't any more* *(geminate devoicing)*
d + t as in /ragad + t/	→	[rægætt]	*I fell asleep*

4.2.2 Progressive Assimilation

Progressive assimilation is rare in SA. The following are the only examples of progressive assimilation that were found:

ḥ + d as in /waḥdi/	→	[wæḥti]	*alone, by myself*
h + b as in /ʔahbal/	→	[ʔæhpæl]	*weak-minded*
j + l as in /yijlis/	→	[yijjis]	*he sits down*
m + b as in /gambar/	→	[gæmmar]	*he sat down*
/gambaʕ/	→	[gammaʕ]	*he walked arrogantly*

4.3 Geminate Devoicing

An interesting characteristic of the SA sound system that most dialects of Arabic lack (e.g., Egyptian, Levantine and Gulf Arabic) is the devoicing of geminate stops as well as the affricate /j/.

It was mentioned in 1.1 above that /b/ has the allophone [p] if it is doubled and if it occurs intervocalically, e.g., sabbaak → sappaak 'pipe fitter'. This rule applies to the other voiced stops /d/, /g/ and the affricate /j/:

bb → pp:

xabbaaz	→	[xæppææz]	*baker*
dabbeh	→	[dæppeh]	*gas cylinder*
habbeh	→	[hæppeh]	*grain, seed*
ðubbi	→	[ðuppi]	*a fly*

dd → tt:

ʕaddaad	→	[ʕættææd]	*counter, meter*
jaddah	→	[jættæh]	*Jadda*
jaddi	→	[jætti]	*my grandfather*
ḥaddah	→	[ḥættæh]	*Hadda*
ḥaddaad	→	[ḥættææd]	*blacksmith*

gg → kk:

ḥaggi	→	[ḥækki]	*mine, belonging to me*
ḥaggak	→	[ḥækkæk]	*yours (m.s.)*
naggaar	→	[nækkaar]	*envious person*
ḥaggaar	→	[ḥækkaar]	*contemptuous, disdainful person*

jj → čč:

najjaar	→	[næččæær]	*carpenter*
dajjaal	→	[dæččææl]	*swindler*
rajjaal	→	[ræččææl]	*man*
fajjaar	→	[fæččæær]	*braggart*
ḥajji	→	[ḥæčči]	*pilgrim,; hadji*

This rule also applies to words in which the l̲ of the article prefix precedes a sun letter: a dental or a palatal with the exception of /j/ and /y/:

?ad-dabbeh	→	[?attæppeh]	*the gas cylinder*
?ad-dimm	→	[?attimm]	*the cat*

It also applies to words in which a /-t-/ assimilates to a following /d/. This is encountered in the third person feminine or the second person masculine singular form of the imperfect verb:

bitdaawim	→	biddaawim	→	[bittææwim]	*she goes to work, you (m.s.) go to work*
bitdawwir	→	biddawir	→	[bittæwwir]	*she is looking (for s.th.)* *you (m.s.) are looking (for s.th.)*
bitdallil	→	biddallil	→	[bittællil]	*she auctions (s.th.),you auction (s.th.)*

4.4 Pausal Diphthongization

Pausal diphthongization is another unique feature of SA. Verb forms ending with /-i/ or /-u/ in most other dialects of Arabic end with the diphthong /-iy/ ~ /-ey/ or /-uw/ ~ /-ow/, respectively in SA. /-iy/ and /-uw/ are more commonly heard than /-ey/ and /-ow/. /-i/ occurs in the following verb forms:

1. The second person feminine singular of the perfect and the imperfect aspects.
2. The second person feminine singular of the imperative.
3. The third person masculine singular of the perfect of final-weak verbs that end with /-i/.
4. The third person masculine singular of the imperfect of final-weak verbs whose perfect tense ends with /-a/.

/-u/ occurs in the following verb forms:

1. The second and third person masculine plural of the perfect and the imperfect tenses.
2. The second person masculine plural of the imperative.

katabti	→	katabtiy ~ katabtey	*you (f.s.) wrote*
tuktubi	→	tuktubiy ~ tuktubey	*you (f.s.) write*
?uktubi	→	?uktubiy ~ ?uktubey	*write (f.s.)!*
bigi	→	bigiy ~ bigey	*he stayed*
yisgi	→	yisgiy ~ yisgey	*he irrigates*

katabtu	→	katabtuw ~ katabtow	*you (m.p.) wrote*
tuktubu	→	tuktubuw ~ tuktubow	*you (m.p.) write*
katabu	→	katabuw ~ katabow	*they (m.) wrote*
yuktubu	→	yuktubuw ~ yuktubow	*they (m.) write*
ʔuktubu	→	ʔuktubuw ~ ʔuktubow	*write (m.p.)!*

Pausal diphthongization is also heard, but less frequently, in words ending with /-i/ or /-u/:

ʔahli	→	ʔahliy ~ ʔahley	*my folks*
naṣraani	→	narṣaaniy ~ naṣraaney	*Christian*
kitli	→	kitliy ~ kitley	*tea kettle*
mistaʕfi	→	mistaʕfiy ~ mistaʕfey	*having resigned (act.. part.)*
ʔantu	→	ʔantuw ~ ʔantow	*you (m.p.)*
hu	→	huw ~ how	*he*

In context, i.e., if the vowels /-i/ and /-u/ are not word-final, no diphthongization occurs:

maa xazzanuuš	*they (m.p.) did not chew qat*
maa xazzantiiš	*you (f.s.) did not chew qat*
ʔakaltuuha	*you (m.p.) ate it*
ʔaddaytuuni	*you (m.p.) gave me*
xuðiiha	*take (f.s.) it!*

4.5 Pausal Glottalization[7]

Pausal glottalization occurs in two cases:

1. After words ending with /-a/:

ʔadda	→	[ʔættæ]	→ [ættæʔ]	*he gave*
ʔaddayna	→	[ʔættaynæ]	→ [ættaynæʔ]	*we gave*
katabha	→	[kætæbhæʔ]		*he wrote it*
katabnaaha	→	[kætæbnææhæʔ]		*we wrote it*
rama	→	[ræmæʔ]		*he threw*
tka	→	[tkæʔ]		*he leaned*
hayya	→	[hæyyæʔ]		*come!, come here!*
lilma	→	[lilmæʔ]		*why?*
haana	→	[hæænæʔ]		*here*
katabna	→	[kætæbnæʔ]		*we wrote*

2. After a vowel preceded and followed by a consonant at the end of a word. If the vowel is long, it is usually shortened and if the last consonant is a voiced stop, fricative or affricate, it becomes voiceless due to the process of pausal glottalization:

ʔimaam	→	[ʔimæʔm]	*Imam*
ʔassas	→	[ʔœssœʔs]	*he built*
ʔaθ-θaluuθ	→	[ʔæθ-θæluʔθ]	*Tuesday*
diik	→	[diʔk]	*rooster*
balas	→	[bælæʔs]	*cactus fruit*
dimm	→	[diʔm]	*cat*
bunn	→	[buʔn]	*Yemeni coffee*
gaaloon	→	[gææloʔn]	*gallon*
mxazziniin	→	[mxæzziniʔn]	*having chewed (m.p.) qat*
raagid	→	[ræægiʔt]	*sleeping (m.s.)*
ġirig	→	[ġiriʔk]	*he drowned*
xabbaaz	→	[xæppæʔs]	*baker*
ġurraab	→	[ġurraˈp]	*(coll.) ravens*

If the last consonant is /-h/, /ḥ/ or /ʕ/, the glottal stop is not usually heard:

bih	*there is; there are*
luḥuuḥ	*pancake bread*
ḥlbeh	*fenugreek*
faṣiiḥ	*eloquent*
zalaṭeh	*his money*
ṣabuuḥ	*breakfast*
katabuuh	*they wrote it*
šaabiʕ	*not hungry*
katabtiih	*you (f.s.) wrote it*
šuʕšuuʕ	*elegant*
katabnaah	*we wrote it*
jaawiʕ	*hungry*

4.6 Imaalah[9]

It was mentioned in 2. VOWELS that /ee/ occurs only in the word final sequence /eeʔ/ and that this will be not only in singular feminine adjectives of color or defect but also in any words that ended originally in /aaʔ/. This feature which is characteristic of the speech of Sanʕaanis is known as /ʔimaalah/ 'deflection'. Imaalah is also present in personal proper names that end in /a/, e.g. /muuse/ 'Musa', /yaḥye/ 'Yahya', /layle/ 'Laila', etc. The use of imaalah in SA is optional.

4.7 Velarization

We have seen above (see the velarized consonants ṭ, ṣ,ð̣) that velarization is not limited only to a pharyngealized sound, but affects neighboring consonants and vowels and sometimes the whole word. Compare, e.g., /fatar/ 'it became warm' and /faṭar/ 'he broke s.th.'. /fa/ in /fatar/ is similar to English /f/ in /fat/, but in /faṭar/ the /fa/ sound is similar to that in /father/, i.e., it is backed and velarized. The quality of the vowel sound a̲ is different in /fatar/ from that in /faar/. In some analyses of Arabic f in /faar/, for example, would also be considered as a pharyngealized consonant. In this analysis, however, only /ṭ/, /ṣ/ and /ð̣/ are the velarized consonants and other sounds affected by these velarized consonants are considered plain and thus transcribed without subscript dots. In fact, velarization varies from one region to another and from speaker to speaker.

Section Five

5. STRESS

A stressed syllable in any given word is the one that is pronounced the loudest. In SA, stress is generally predictable, i.e., you can deduce which syllable in a word is stressed from the consonant-vowel sequence in that word. There are some exceptions, which will be pointed out as they occur. You should note the following general comments on syllable structure in SA:

1. Every syllable contains a vowel, short or long; it begins with a consonant and may end with a vowel.
2. An intervocalic consonant belongs in the syllable with the following vowel, as in ðaˑhab 'gold'.
3. If a word has an intervocalic two-consonant cluster, syllable division is between the two consonants, as in matˑkeh 'pillow'.
4. A long vowel may be followed by one consonant only (in the same syllable, as in maadˑdiin 'having stretched (m.p.) s.th.' The first or last syllable in a word may begin or end with a two- or three-consonant cluster:

trabba	*he was brought up*
tfallas	*he went bankrupt*
habs	*jail*
dimm	*cat*
štka	*he complained*
stkab	*it was poured*
maa ruḥtš	*I did not go*

A syllable in SA can be any of the following structures:

CV:	daˑras	*he studied*
CVC:	tiˑtin	*tobacco*
CVV:	baˑsaaˑtiin	*orchards*
CCV:	ttaˑfagu staˑbaḥ	*they came to an agreement* *he had breakfast*
CVVC:	ḥaˑreew	*bridegroom*
CVCC:	kayf šall ṣṭaˑbaḥt	*how* *he carried away s.th.* *I had breakfast*

	bayt·ha	*her house*
CCVC:	tkal·lam	*he spoke*
CCVVC:	šxaax	*urine*
	xfiif	*light*
	tmuut	*she dies; you (m.s.) die*
CCVV:	sxuu·neh	*temperature; heat*
	ftii·leh	*fuse; wick*
	traa·ya	*he dreamed*
	tʕaa·fa	*he recuperated*
CCVCC:	ltaff	*it was coiled*
	htazz	*it was shaken*
CCCV:	štka	*he complained*
	stkab	*it was poured*
	btsar	*it was seen*
CVCCC:	maa ʔib·sartš	*I did not see*
	maa da·rastš	*I did not study*

It should be noted that only CV, CVC, CVV, and CVVC occur in all positions: initially, medially, and finally. CCV, CCVC, CCVVC, and CCVV occur only initially, while CVCC occurs independently and finally. CCVCC and CCCV occur only independently. CVCCC occurs only finally.

There are two types of syllable in SA: short and long. Only CV and CVC are short syllables and the rest of the syllables are long.

Stress in SA is governed by the following rules:

1. In disyllabic words the ultima is stressed if it is long and if the penultima is short; otherwise the penultima is stressed:

rajjáal	*man*
ðalḥíin	*now*
ʔaddáyt	*I gave*
garráynʔ	*they (f.) taught*
máreh	*woman*
ʔáktub	*I write*
sánnab	*he stood up*
wúgaf	*he stopped*
dúulaab	*wardrobe*
ṭáabuur	*battalion*
fíisaʕ	*fast (adv.)*
máaši	*no; not*

2. In a three-syllable word the antepenultima is stressed if the penultima is short. However, if the penultima is long, it is stressed:

mádraseh	*school*
máktabeh	*library*
šáṭaleh	*fork*
gúnṭurah	*(pair of) shoes*
ʕállamayn	*they (f.) taught*
záwjatayn	*two wives*
ḥáṣṣaltayn	*you (f.p.) got*
dárrasuuh	*they (m.) taught him*
dakáakiin	*stores*
ʕammáariin	*masons*
garáagiiš	*scarves*
kaláamuh	*his words*
basáatiin	*orchards*
ḥaanúutak	*your (m.s.) store*
xabíireh	*girl friend*
šiigáarah	*cigarette*
wáaḥideh	*one (f.)*
máasathum	*their (m.) table*
záarathiin	*sometimes*
tkállamayn	*they (f.) spoke*
ʕáaʔilaat	*families*

3. In a four-syllable word stress falls on the antepenultima if the penultima is short and on the penultima if it is long:

madrásathum	*their (m.) school*
maktábatna	*our library*
takállamayn	*they (f.) spoke*
taʕállamuuh	*they (m.) learned it*
yahúudiyaat	*Jewesses*
baṭṭáaniyaat	*blankets*
xabáayirak	*your (m.s.) girl friends*
ganáaṭirak	*your (m.s.) shoes*
garaagíišiš	*your (f.s.) scarves*
ʔadawáatak	*your (m.s.) tools*

It should be pointed out that the above-mentioned stress rules are observed by Sanʕaani speakers under normal conditions. Thus, either the first syllable or the second syllable in disyllabic words can be stressed: /máreh/ or /maréh/ 'woman', /sánnab/ or /sannáb/ 'he stood up', /ʔáktub/ or /ʔaktúb/ 'I write', etc. In words of three or more syllables the rules mentioned above are generally observed. Five-syllable words are rare in SA.

FOOTNOTES

1. According to *Webster's Third New International Dictionary* (1971) qat is "a shrub (cathaedulis) cultivated by the Arabs for its leaves that act as a stimulant narcotic when chewed" (p.1233).

2. The feature of velarization is sometimes referred to as emphasis or pharyngealization. Velarization is probably a more satisfactory term since it does not suggest forceful articulation or features of the uvulars /x-ġ/ or the pharyngeals /ḥ-ʕ/. (See, for example, Wallace Erwin, *A Short Reference Grammar of Iraqi Arabic*, Georgetown University Press, Washington, D.C., 1963, pp. 13-14) and Mark C. Cowell, *A Reference Grammar of Syrian Arabic*, Georgetown University Press, Washington, D.C., 1964, pp. 6-7.

3. A bugšeh is approximately 1/40 of a Yemeni riyal.

4. Other names currently used are Contemporary Arabic, Modern Literary Arabic, Modern Standard Arabic, Modern Written Arabic, etc. The name Literary Arabic, however, is intended to represent the literary language in both its formal spoken and written forms.

5. For the occurrence of /-eh/ ~ /-ah/ see 9.4 below

6. See 4.6 below.

7. Glottalization is here defined as the insertion of a single glottal stop after the vowel. It is not a glottal feature imposed suprasegmentally over the vowel and coterminous with it.

8. This feature, traditionally known as ʔimaalah (deflection), is characteristic of the speech of Sanʕaanis. For a definition and discussion of ʔimaalah, see W.H.T. Gairdner, "The Arab Phoneticians on the Consonants and Vowels." Moslem World XXV, 1935, pp. 242-57, and W. Wright, *A Grammar of the Arabic Language*, 3rd Edition, Cambridge University Press, 1967, p. 9.

Part Two

The Morphology of Yemeni Arabic

Section Six

6. VERBS--DERIVATION

As far as derivational systems are concerned, SA verbs are based on either triliteral roots, i.e., having three radical consonants, or quadriliteral roots, i.e., having four radical consonants.

6.1 Simple Verbs

A simple verb, usually referred to as Form I or Class I, is the base-form from which all other forms or classes of the triliteral verb are derived. The other forms of the triliteral verb, i.e., Forms II through X are derived from Form I and they are sometimes referred to as Derived Verbs or Derived Themes[1] however, some verbs of forms II, III, IV and X are derived from other parts of speech.

6.1.1 Sound Verbs

Sound verbs are of four patterns, depending upon their stem vowels as will be explained later on: faʕal, fiʕil, fuʕil, and fuʕul.[2]

faʕal:

xatan	*he circumcised*
naðag	*he threw s.th.*
labaj	*he beat s.o.*
saʕal	*he coughed*
ragad	*he slept*
gaṭaʕ	*he cut off s.th.*
gaðaf	*he threw up*
galam	*he mowed*

fiʕil:

nikiʕ	*he fell down*
širib	*he drank*
ġirig	*he drowned*
zigim	*he grabbed s.th.*
yibis	*it became dry*
sikir	*he got drunk*

fuʕil:

wugif	*he stopped*
juwiʕ	*he was hungry*
wuriθ	*he inherited*
wugiʕ	*it took place*

fuʕul:

ʕuṭuš	*he was thirsty*
wuṣul	*he arrived*
kumul	*it was completed or finished*
muṭur	*he was drenched by rain*
kuθur	*it became abundant*
surug	*he was robbed*
xulug	*he, it was created*
ʕuṭus	*he sneezed*
ð̣uḥuk	*he laughed*

It should be pointed out that verbs of the fuʕil type are unstable in SA; they are sometimes of the pattern fuʕal, e.g., wugif/wugaf 'he stopped', wuriθ/wuraθ 'he inherited,' etc. Verbs of the fuʕul type usually have a velarized consonant. Those that do not have a velarized consonant are passive traces of Classical Arabic. There are a few verbs of the fʕal type in SA, e.g., ksar 'he broke,' fšar 'he bragged', kšaf 'he examined', kfad 'he spilled', ftaš 'he uncovered', etc.

6.1.2 Weak Verbs

Weak verbs have one or more unstable or weak radicals. Weak radicals in SA are the semivowels /w/ and /y/. Weak verbs are either defective or hollow. A defective verb is here defined as one with a weak final radical. Examples:

ligi	*he found*
diri	*he knew*
nisi	*he forgot*
xuṭi	*he walked*
riḏ̣i	*he was satisfied*
riwi	*it was irrigated*
ġili	*it boiled*
siṭi	*he could, was able*
ʕaṣa	*he rebelled*
ḥama	*he defended*
daʕa	*he invited*
bana	*he built*
jala	*he shined s.th.*
šaka	*he complained*
naʕa	*he cried over the dead*
dala	*he drew water from a well*

Hollow verbs are characterized by a medial long /aa/, with no radical /ʕ/:

ʕaam	*he swam*
šaar	*he advised*
baal	*he urinated*
ṭaaf	*he went around*
daam	*it lasted*
ṣaam	*he fasted*
ðaab	*it melted*
gaal	*he said*
kaal	*he weighed*

ṭaaʕ	*he obeyed*
baan	*it appeared*
saar	*he left*
faaš[3]	*it spread*
jaaʔ[4]	*he came*
zaad	*he increased s.th.*
baaḏ̣	*it laid eggs*
xaaf	*he became afraid*
naal	*he obtained*

6.1.3 Doubled Verbs

Simple doubled verbs are characterized by a final double consonant in the stem, i.e., the second and third radicals are identical.

xaṭṭ	*he drew a line*
šaṭṭ	*he tore s.th.*
ṭarr	*he drove away s.o.*
garr	*he confessed*
šann	*he filtered water*
mazz	*he squeezed*
ʕass	*he felt s.th.*
šall	*he took away, stole s.th.*

6.2 Derived Verbs

6.2.1 Form II

Form II verbs are characterized by a double middle radical. They are generally transitive and derived from Form I verbs, nouns, and adjectives. If they are derived from Form I verbs, they express the general meaning of 'to cause s.o. or s.th. to do s.th.' or undergo "an action expressed by the Form I verb.":

daras	*he studied*	darras	*he taught*
ð̣uḥuk	*he laughed*	ð̣aḥḥak	*he made s.o. laugh*
ragad	*he slept*	raggad	*he put s.o. to sleep*
faaš	*it spread*	fayyaš	*he spread, revealed s.th.*
ðaab	*it melted*	ðawwab	*he melted s.th.*
ṭaaf	*he went around*	ṭawwaf	*he took s.o. around*

If the Form I verb is transitive, then the corresponding Form II verb may be doubly transitive, i.e., with two objects:

darrashum ʕarabi.	*he taught them Arabic*
ṭawwafna ḥawl al-kaʕbah.	*he took us around the Kaba*

Some Form II verbs denote intensity or frequency of action:

kasar	*he broke s.th.*	kassar	*he smashed s.th.*
gatal	*he killed*	gattal	*he massacred*
zaad	*he increased s.th.*	zawwad	*he increased s.th. by a whole lot*

A few Form II verbs are derived from nouns:

xaymeh	*tent*	xayyam	*he camped*
šitaaʔ	*winter*	šatta	*he spent the winter*
ṣayf	*summer*	ṣayyaf	*he spent the summer*
magiil	*place where qat is chewed*	gayyal	*he chewed qat in a magiil*
ruxṣah	*license*	raxxaṣ	*he licensed*
ṣalaah	*prayer*	ṣalla	*he prayed*

Form II verbs derived from adjectives express the general meaning of 'to cause s.th. or s.o. to acquire the quality expressed by the adjective:

wasix	*dirty*	wassax	*he made s.th. dirty*
jadiid	*new*	jaddad	*he renewed*
gaṣiir	*short*	gaṣṣar	*he shortened*
raxiis	*cheap*	raxxas	*he lowered the price*
nað̣iif	*clean*	nað̣ð̣af	*he cleaned*

Form II verbs are also derived from adjectives of color:

Adjective		Form II	
ʔaḥmar	*red*	ḥammaar	*it turned red*
ʔaxð̣ar	*green*	xað̣ð̣ar	*it turned green*
ʔabyað̣	*white*	bayyað̣	*it turned white*
ʔaswad	*black*	sawwad	*it turned black*
ʔaṣfar	*yellow*	ṣaffar	*it turned yellow*

Some Form II verbs are not related to Form I verbs or nouns or adjectives:

bakkaʕ	*he tore off*
sannab[5]	*he stood up*
jarras[6]	*he insulted*
xazzan[7]	*he chewed qat*
ṭallab[8]	*he begged*
bawwa	*he shined shoes*

6.2.2 Form III

Form III verbs are generally derived from nouns; only one or two are derived from Form I verbs. They are derived by inserting the long vowel /aa/ between the first and the second radicals.

baarak	*he blessed*
xaalaf	*he violated*
gaayas	*he measured*
naada	*he called s.o.*
ḥaawal	*he tried*
ḥaaza	*he told an anecdote*
ʕaada	*he was at war with s.o.*
saafar	*he traveled*

Most Form III verbs are transitive; only a few are intransitive. As a class they do not have one meaning or closely related meanings associated with the words they are derived from. Only a few are "associative," i.e., they express the meaning of engaging or associating s.o. in an activity. Thus:

Form I		Form III	
saar	*he left*	saayar	*he engaged s.o. in leaving*
liʕib	*he played*	laaʕab	*he engaged s.o. in playing*
ḥaka	*he talked*	ḥaaka	*he engaged s.o. in conversation*

6.2.3 Form IV

This class of verbs is characterized by an optional prefix /ʔi-/ or /ʔa-/:

(ʔi)bsar	*he saw*
(ʔi)dxal	*he introduced s.th.*
(ʔi)xraj	*he excluded*
(ʔi)xlas	*he skinned (an animal)*
(ʔi)rbaš	*he mixed s.o. up*
(ʔi)xfa	*he concealed*

(ʔa)ḥsǎ	*he stuffed*
(ʔa)ṭlag	*he set free*
(ʔa)dda	*he gave*
(ʔa)ʕjab	*he pleased*
(ʔa)mḥa	*he destroyed*
(ʔa)mhal	*he delayed*
(ʔa)fham	*he informed s.o.*
(ʔa)mḍ̣a	*he signed*

6.2.4 Form V

Almost all Form V verbs are derived from Form II verbs by prefixing /t-/ to them. They are usually reflexive of Form II; they denote the state of an object as the result of the action of the Form II verb, i.e., the subject does something to himself.

Form II		Form V	
ġassal	*he gave s.o. a bath*	tġassal	*he bathed*
ġadda	*he gave lunch to s.o.*	tġadda	*he had lunch*
rabba	*he brought up*	trabba	*he was brought up*
ʕašša	*he gave dinner to s.o.*	tʕašša	*he had dinner*
gawwa	*he made s.o. or s.th. strong*	tgawwa	*he became strong*

Some Form V verbs have the meaning of Form I:

tbannan	*he stuffed himself with food*
twaḍ̣ḍ̣aʔ	*he performed ablution before prayer*
tšaggar	*he peeked*
tjammal	*he was thankful*
tfarraṭ	*he chattered in a /tafruṭa/*[9]

Some Form V verbs are passive in meaning:

Form II		Form V	
ġayyar	*he changed*	tġayyar	*it was changed*
θamman	*he priced s.th.*	θθamman	*it was priced*
waṭṭa	*he lowered s.th.*	twaṭṭa	*it was lowered*

Usually, the negative imperfect of Form V verbs denotes a passive-potential meaning:

haaðа ma yitġayyarš.	*This cannot be changed.*
yitgawwa walla maa yitgawwaaš?	*Can it be made stronger or not?*

6.2.5 Form VI

Most Form VI verbs are formed from Form III verbs by prefixing t(a):

Form III		Form VI	
ʕaafa	*he cured*	tʕaafa	*he recuperated*
gaabal	*he met s.o.*	tgaabal	*he met with s.o.; he had an interview with s.o.*
šaawar	*he consulted s.o.*	tšaawar	*he consulted (deliberated)with s.o.*
ḥaarab	*he fought s.o. or s.th.*	tḥaarab	*he was at war with s.o.*

A few Form VI verbs are derived from adjectives:

mariiḍ̌	*sick*
jaahil	*ignorant*
mayyit	*dead*
tmayraḍ̌[10]	*he pretended to be sick*
tajaahal	*he ignored s.o.*
tmaywat[11]	*he pretended to be dead*

Form VI verbs denote the following:

1. Reciprocity:

tšaawaruw	*they (m.) consulted (deliberated) with each other*
tgaabalayn	*they (f.) met with each other*
tḥaarabna	*we were at war with each other*

2. Pretense:

tajaahal	*he ignored s.o. or s.th.; he pretended to be ignorant of s.th.*
tmayraḍ̣	*he pretended to be sick*
tmaywat	*he pretended to be dead*

This meaning usually obtains with verbs derived from adjectives.

3. Other meanings:

tabaarak[12](aḷḷaah)	*(God), the blessed and the exalted*
traaya	*he dreamed*
tgaaʕad	*he retired*
tfaakah	*he ate fruit*

Some Form VI verbs are passive in meaning:

tʕaagab	*he was punished*
tʕaafa	*he recuperated, (i.e., he was cured)*

Some Form VI verbs are derived from nouns:

traaya	*he dreamed.* (from /ruʔyaa/ 'dream' in literary Arabic)
txaawayna	*we associated as brothers.* (from /ʔax/ 'brother')

Almost all Form VI verbs are derived from transitive Form III verbs as in the above examples and they have plural subjects except in a few cases as cited above: /tʕaafa/, /tmayrað/, /tajaahal/, /tmaywat/, /tabaarak/, /tgaaʕad/, and /traaya/. The subjects of all the Form VI verbs cited above are animate. In a few cases there may be inanimate subjects:

ʔas-sayyaaraat tsaabagayn.	*The cars had a race.*
ʔaṭ-ṭiigaan tgaabalayn.	*The windows faced each other.*
tsaawat al-ʔaaraaʔ.	*The opinions were the same.*

6.2.6 Form VII

There are no Form VII verbs in SA. The few Form VII verbs that may be heard are emulation of the speech of Arab immigrants.

6.2.7 Form VIII

Most Form VIII verbs are formed from Form I verbs by infixing /-t-/ after the first radical, i.e., between the first and the second radicals:

Form I		Form VIII	
labaj	*he hit s.o.*	ltabaj	*he was hit*
ball	*he wet s.th.*	btall	*he wet himself*
kasar	*he broke s.th.*	ktasar	*it was broken*
nagal	*he moved s.th.;he transferred s.o.*	ntagal	*it was moved; he was transferred*
rafaʕ	*he raised s.th.; he increased (e.g., the price)*	rtafaʕ	*it was raised; it (the price) was increased*
maḥag	*he ruined s.th.*	mtaḥag	*it was ruined*
faṭar	*he split s.th.*	ftaṭar	*it was split*
garaʔ	*he read*	gtaraʔ	*it was read*
ʔakal	*he ate s.th.*	(ʔi)ʔtkal	*it was eaten*

Most of Form VIII verbs denote the passive of Form I verbs. The object of a Form I verb becomes the subject of the corresponding Form VIII verb: /faṭar al-ʕajaleh/ 'he, it punctured the tire': /ftaṭarat al-ʕajaleh/ 'the tire was punctured'. Some Form VIII verbs have a reflexive or middle meaning; they are reflexive of Form I verbs, i.e., they have the meaning of doing s.th. to or for oneself:

Form I		Form VIII	
ball	*he made s.th. wet*	btall	*he wet himself*
jamaʕ	*he collected*	jtamaʕ	*he had a meeting*
madd	*he stretched s.th.*	mtadd	*it stretched*

A few Form VIII verbs are derived from Form IV verbs:

Form IV		Form VIII	
(ʔa)gnaʕ	*he convinced*	gtanaʕ	*he was convinced*
(ʔi)rbaš	*he mixed s.o. up*	rtabaš	*he was mixed up*

Some Form VIII verbs have no corresponding Form I or Form IV verbs; they are derived from nouns.

ḥtaaj	*he needed*
xtaar	*he selected*
ftajaʕ	*he was scared*
btaraʕ	*he danced*

The verb 'to want; to like, to have' /štha* → šta/ is not used in the past. /yišthi →yišti/ is used instead. However, the present tense is very commonly used.

Usually negative imperfect Form VIII verbs denote a passive-potential meaning:

haaði ʕajaleh maa tiftaṭarš.	*This is a tire that cannot be punctured.*
zijaaj maa yiktasarš	*unbreakable glass*
rajjaal maa yigtanaʕš	*man that cannot be convinced*

6.2.8 Form IX

Form IX verbs are not used in SA. While most other dialects of Arabic have the pattern /fʕall/ for Form IX verbs, SA has the pattern /faʕʕal/ or the pattern for Form II verbs instead. See 6.2 above.

6.2.9 Form X

Form X verbs are characterized by a prefixed /sta/. They are derived mainly from verbs and adjectives; a few are derived from nouns.

Underlying Verb		Form X	
ʕimil	*he made*	staʕmal	*he used, utilized*
ġafar	*he pardoned, forgave (a sin)*	staġfar	*he sought forgiveness*
jaawab	*he answered*	stajaab	*he responded (to a request)*
faad	*he, it benefited s.o.*	stafaad	*he benfited*
naṭag	*he pronounced, said s.th.*	stanṭag	*he interrogated*

Underlying Adjective		Form X	
ṣaʕb	*difficult*	staṣʕab	*he found s.th. difficult*
ġani	*rich*	staġna(ʕan)	*he did without*
raxiiṣ	*cheap*	starxaṣ	*he found s.th. cheap*

Underlying Noun		Form X	
ḥagg	*right, one's due*	staḥagg	*he deserved*
winseh	*good time*	staʔnas	*he had a good time*
ḥayaaʔ	*embarrassment*	(ʔi) stḥa	*he was embarrassed*
xabar	*news item*	staxbar	*he asked to be informed*
raaḥah	*rest*	staraaḥ	*he rested*

Most Form X verbs derived from Form I verbs denote the general meaning of seeking, asking, or demanding for oneself what is expressed by the Form I verb: /staġfar/ 'he sought forgiveness,' staʕmal 'he used,' etc. From adjectives Form X verbs express the general meaning of finding or considering s.th. as what is expressed by the underlying adjective: /staṣʕab/ 'he found s.th. difficult,' /starxaṣ/ 'he found s.th. cheap,' etc.

6.3 Quadriliteral Verbs

Quadriliteral verbs, sometimes referred to as quadriradical verbs, have four radicals. They can be simple (sound, weak, or reduplicated[13] from Form I doubled verbs) or derived. The derived ones are formed by prefixing /t-/ to the quadriliteral simple verb. Examples of simple quadriliteral verbs:

$C_1C_2C_3C_4$:

ṣalfaʕ	*he slapped*
gambar	*he sat down*
ġawbar	*he made s.th. dusty*
kawbal	*he piled up s.th.*
xarbaṭ	*he mixed, messed s.th. or s.o. up*
zagraʕ	*he was overjoyed*
falḥas	*he massaged s.o. gently*
šawlaḥ	*he cried loud*
xadras	*he was delirious*
fayṭas	*he was on vacation*
fanṭas	*he had a good time*

$C_1C_2C_3C_3$:

baḥlal	*it became livid*
baxšaš	*he tipped s.o.*
garḏ̣aḏ̣	*it gnawed*
baʕsas	*he exaggerated*
ʕanṭaṭ	*he was overweenning*
garṭaṭ	*he crunched*

$C_1C_2C_3C_2$:

ʕanwan	*he addressed (a letter)*

$C_1C_2C_1C_2$:

rašraš	*he sprayed*
laflaf	*he saved (e.g., money)*
gaṭgaṭ	*he talked a lot*
lamlam	*he gathered*
gaṣgaṣ	*he cut up s.th.*
gargar	*it gurgled*

Examples of derived quadriliteral verbs:

Quadriliteral		Derived Quadriliteral	
ʕanwan	*he addressed (a letter)*	tʕanwan	*it (the letter) was addressed*
laflaf	*he saved (money)*	tlaflaf	*it was saved*
baxšaš	*he tipped*	tbaxšaš	*he was tipped*
kawbal	*he piled up s.th.*	tkawbal	*it was piledup*
rašraš	*he sprayed*	trašraš	*it was sprayed*

There are some derived quadriliterals that have no corresponding quadriliterals:

tšawraʕ	*he walked in the street*
tmaxyal	*he rode a horse*
tʔaymar	*he was bossy*
tkaysal	*he pretended to be lazy*
tġalmaš	*he wrapped, covered himself because of the cold*
tgambaʕ	*he walked arrogantly; he jumped for joy*

Derived quadriliteral verbs that have a corresponding quadriliteral verb, as far as derivation is concerned, are similar in meaning to Form V verbs: both verbs have the prefix /t-/; the structure of a Form V verb is of the pattern $tC_1aC_2C_2aC_3$; that of a derived quadriliteral verb is of the pattern $tC_1aC_2C_3aC_4$. As for meaning, most derived quadriliteral verbs are related to quadriliteral verbs in the same way as Form I verbs are related to Form VIII verbs: most derived quadriliteral and Form VIII verbs denote the passive meaning of transitive simple quadriliteral and Form I verbs, respectively. Examples: /kawbal/ 'he piled up s.th.' and /tkawbal/ 'it was piled up'; /labaj/ 'he hit s.o.' and /ltabaj/ 'he was hit.'

It has already been pointed out in 6.2.4 and 6.2.7 that usually the negative imperfect of Form V and Form VIII verbs denotes a passive potential meaning. The negative imperfect of derived quadriliteral verbs has a similar meaning:

maa yitgarðaðš	*it cannot be gnawed*
maa yitkawbalš	*it cannot be piled up*

Section Seven

7. VERBS--INFLECTION

SA verbs are inflected for aspect (perfect and imperfect), person (first, second, and third), gender (masculine and feminine), number (singular and plural), and mood (indicative, subjunctive, and imperative).[14] A perfect verb is not inflected for mood, i.e., a perfect verb does not express mood. The first person singular form of the verb is not inflected for gender, i.e., there is only one form for the person speaking, regardless of sex. Similarly there is one form for the first person plural. Unlike some other dialects of Arabic, e.g., Lebanese, Jordanian, Egyptian, etc., SA has separate verb forms for the second and third person feminine plural.

7.1 Perfect Tense

The perfect in SA corresponds to the following English tenses: simple past, e.g., he came; present perfect, e.g. he has come; and past perfect, e.g., he had come.

7.1.1 Sound Verbs

The inflections of the perfect Forms, usually known as the inflectional suffixes, are all suffixes. They are the same for all verbs in the language, and are listed in the following chart in the right-hand column. The complete perfect conjugation of /ragad/ 'he slept' is given as a model for all sound verbs. There are some variations in the conjugation of weak verbs, which are given in 7.1.2 below. Note that the /d/ of /ragad/ assimilates to a following /t/: dt →tt, but the d is kept in this transcription in order to preserve the underlying structure of the word.

	Pronoun	Verb	Meaning	Suffix
3rd p.	huw	rágad	*he slept*	Ø
	hum	rágaduw	*they (m.) slept*	-uw
	hiy	rágadat	*she slept*	-at
	hin	rágadayn	*they (f.) slept*	-ayn
2nd p	?ant	ragádt	*you (m.s.) slept*	-t
	?antu	rágadtuw	*you (m.p.) slept*	-tuw
	?anti	rágadtiy	*you (f.s.) slept*	-tiy
	?antayn	rágadtayn	*you (f.p.) slept*	-tayn
1st p.	?ana	ragádt	*I slept*	-t
	ḥna	rágadna	*we slept*	-na

Note the following comments on the above perfect-tense forms:

a. The forms are built on and derived from the 3rd person masculine singular form of the verb, which is referred to as the stem: ragad 'he slept.' This stem is used to refer to the verb as a whole, in the same way as the infinitive is used in English. Thus, when we say the verb ragad, which literally means 'he slept,' we refer to what corresponds to the English infinitive 'to sleep'.

b. There are other alternate forms[15] for hum, ?antu, and ?anti:

ragaduw ~ ragadow

ragadtuw ~ ragadtow

ragadtiy ~ ragadtey

Forms II - X[16]

The conjugation of sound Form II verbs is regular; there are no stem changes, e.g., darras 'to teach' has the following forms with the inflected suffixes in parentheses. Note the stress marks.

dárras	(-θ)
dárrasuw	(-uw)
dárrasat	(-at)
dárrasayn	(-ayn)
dárrast	(-t)
dárrastu	(-tu)
dárrastiy	(-ti)
dárrastayn	(-tayn)
dárrasna	(-na)

Forms III - X are also regular and thus conjugated in the same way as Form II verbs. Sound quadriliteral and derived quadriliteral verbs are regular and thus conjugated with no stem changes.

7.1.2 Weak Verbs[17]

A. Defective

Defective verbs have two stems: one is used before the third person suffixes and the other is used before the other suffixes, e.g., the verb /bana/ 'to build' has the two stems ban - before -a, -uw, -at and banay- before the rest of the suffixes. Below is the full conjugation of the verb /bana/ 'to build'.

Pronoun	Verb	Meaning	Suffix
huw	bana	*he built*	-a
hum	banuw	*they (m.) built*	-uw
hiy	banat	*she built*	-at
hin	banayn	*they (f.) built*	-n
ʔant	banayt	*you (m.s.) built*	-t
ʔantu	banaytuw	*you (m.p.) built*	-tuw
ʔanti	banaytiy	*you (f.s.) built*	-tiy
ʔantayn	banaytayn	*you (f.p.) built*	-tayn
ʔana	banayt	*I built*	-t
ḥna	banayna	*we built*	-na

Defective verbs of Forms II through VIII, Form X and the quadriliterals are conjugated in the same way as /bana/ above. Examples of such verbs are:

Form II

bawwa	*to shine shoes*
ṣalla	*to pray*
ġadda	*to give lunch to s.o.*
ʔadda	*to give*

Form III

ʕaada	*to be at war with s.o.*
naada	*to call s.o.*
ḥaaza	*to tell an anecdote*
baaʔa	*to bleat*

Form IV

ʔaḥša	*to stuff*
ʔamḥa	*to destroy*
ʔamᵭa	*to sign*
ʔaxfa	*to conceal*

Form V

tʕašša	*to dine*
twaṭṭa	*to be lowered*
tgawwa	*to become strong*
tġadda	*to have lunch*

Form VI

tʕaafa	*to recuperate*
traaya	*to dream*

Form VIII

štaka	*to complain*
štara	*to buy*

Form X

staḥa	*to be embarrassed*
staġna(ʕan)	*to do without*

Quadriliterals

gahwa	*to welcome s.o. with coffee*
tgahwa	*he had coffee; he was given coffee*

B. Hollow

Hollow verbs are based on roots whose second radical is /w/ or /y/, e.g., GWL 'to say,' KYL 'to weigh,' etc. In SA there are hollow verbs in Forms I, VIII, and X.

Form I

Like defective verbs, hollow verbs have two perfect tense stems. For one such form of hollow verbs, the two perfect stem patterns are <u>CaaC</u>- for the third person endings and CuC- for the other persons. Below are the full perfect forms of the verb /gaal/ 'to say'

gaal	gaaluw	gaalat	gaalayn	
gult	gultuw	gultiy	gultayn	gulna

Other verbs that conform to this pattern are: /ʕaam/ 'to swim', /baal/ 'to urinate', /ṣaam/ 'to fast', /šaar/ 'to advise', /ṭaaf/ 'to go around', /ðaab/ 'to melt', etc.The other subclass of hollow verbs have the perfect stem patterns CaaC- and CiC- only:

/kaal/ to weigh

kaal	kaaluw	kaalat	kaalayn	
kilt	kiltuw	kiltiy	kiltayn	kilna

Other verbs that belong to this category are: /baan/ 'to appear', /faaš/ 'to spread', /ṭaaʕ/ 'to obey', /saar/ 'to leave', /baað̣/ 'to lay eggs', /xaaf/ 'to be afraid', etc.

Forms VIII and X

Forms VIII and X hollow verbs have the perfect stems CtaaC-/CtaC- and StaCaaC-/StaCaC-, respectively:

Form XIII: /xtaar/ 'to select

xtaar	xtaaruw	xtaarat	xtaarayn	
xtart	xtartuw	xtartiy	xtartayn	xtarna

Form X: /stafaad min/ 'to benefit from'

stafaad	stafaaduw	stafaadat	stafaadayn	
stafadt	stafadtuw	stafadtiy	stafadtayn	stafadna

Note that the /d/ of /stafaad/ assimilates to a following /t/: dt →tt, but the /d/ is kept in this transcription in order to preserve the underlying structure of the word.

7.1.3 Double Verbs

The perfect-tense stems of doubled verbs end with two identical consonants. The stems of these verbs remain unchanged before the third person suffixes; before the other suffixes the diphthong -ay- is added, e.g., /šannayt/ 'I filtered (water)'. In this category there are verbs of Form I, VIII, and X. Below are the perfect-tense forms of /šall/ 'to take away s.th.; to steal':

šall	šalluw	šallat	šallayn	
šallayt	šallaytuw	šallaytiy	šallaytayn	šallayna

Other examples of Form I doubled verbs are /xaṭṭ/ 'to draw a line', /ʕass/ 'to feel s.th.', /mazz/ 'to squeeze', /garr/ 'to confess', etc.

Form VIII

btall	*to wet oneself*
mtadd	*to stretch*
šṭaṭṭ	*to be ripped*
mtazz	*to be squeezed*

Form X

staḥagg	*to deserve*
stamarr	*to continue*
staʕadd	*to be ready*
staʕarr	*to be ashamed of one's family*

7.2 Imperfect Tense

SA imperfect-tense verbs have three moods: indicative, subjunctive, and imperative. The inflectional affixes of the imperfect tense are either prefixes or a combination of prefixes and suffixes. Each imperfect-tense verb is made up of a subject marker and a stem.

7.2.1 Sound Verbs

Below is a model conjugation of the imperfect /ragad/[18] 'to sleep'.

	Verb	Meaning	Affixes
huw	yurgud	*he sleeps*	yu-
hiy	turgud	*she sleeps*	tu-
?ant	turgud	*you (m.s.) sleep*	tu-
?anti	turgudiy	*you (f.s.) sleep*	tu-iy
?ana	?argud	*I sleep*	?a-
hum	yurguduw	*they (m.) sleep*	yu-uw
hin	yurgudayn	*they (f.) sleep*	yu-ayn
?antu	turguduw	*you (m.p.) sleep*	tu-uw
?antayn	turgudayn	*you (f.p.) sleep*	tu-ayn
na	nurgud	*we sleep*	nu-

Note the following comments on the above imperfect-tense forms:

a. The third person masculine prefix is /yu/-; for the second person it is tu-; for the first person singular it is /?a/- and for the first person plural it is /nu-/.

b. The third person feminine singular and the second person masculine singular prefixes are identical, i.e., /tu-/; the second and third person masculine plural suffixes are identical (-uw) are identical and in addition the feminine plural suffixes are also identical (-ayn).

c. The prefixes /yu-/ and /tu-/ have two other corresponding free variants, namely /ya-/ and /ta-/, but the former are more commonly used. The second person feminine singular suffix /-iy/ is in free variation with -ey and similarly /-uw/ with /-ow/ in the second and third person masculine plural forms. /ya-/, /ta-/, /-ey/, and /-ow/ are less commonly used than /yu-/, /tu-/, /-iy/, and /-uw/, respectively.

d. The imperfect tense in SA expresses one or both of the following meanings:

(i) habitual: ?agra ʕarabi yawmiyeh. *I study Arabic daily.*

(ii) general truth value ("generic," "dispositional," etc.):
yigra ʕarabi zaarathiin. *He studies Arabic sometimes.*

Stem Vowels

Both perfect and imperfect verbs have stem vowels. The stem vowel of a triradical verb, whether perfect or imperfect, is the vowel preceding the last radical. In literary Arabic and in most dialects of Arabic (including SA) the stem vowel of the perfect tense of a triradical verb may be /a/, /i/, or /u/ chosen arbitrarily and not conditioned by any phonological environment. The alternation between the stem vowels of the perfect and the imperfect forms of the verb in literary Arabic and in a few dialects is predictable in most cases. The predictability lies in the fact that "the relation between the stem vowel of the perfect and the imperfect is one of inverse height that can be accounted for by means of a rule (Ablaut)."[20] In SA the predictability of the imperfect stem vowel lies in the quality of consonants (i.e., C_2 or C_3) of the perfect tense. There are exceptions, which will be cited and commented on. Note the following:

A. Stem Vowel /u/

The stem vowel of a sound non-derived verb is /u/ if:

(1) C_2 or C_3 is a velarized consonant (/ṣ/, /ṭ/, /ð̣/) and the perfect tense of that verb is not of the /fuʕul/ pattern:

Perfect	Imperfect	Meaning
gabáṣ	yugbuṣ	*to pinch*
ʕaṣab	yuʕṣub	*to bandage*
ragaṣ	yurguṣ	*to dance*
ʕaṣar	yuʕṣur	*to squeeze*
ʕaṭas	yuʕṭus	*to sneeze*
xabaṭ	yuxbuṭ	*to beat*
lagaṭ	yulguṭ	*to raise s.th.*
naṭag	yunṭug	*to say, pronounce*
gabað̣	yugbuð̣	*to arrest, seize*
hað̣am	yuhð̣um	*to digest*
nað̣ar	yunð̣ur	*to observe*

Excluded from this category of verbs are verbs such as /luguṣ/ 'to bite', /ʕuṭuš/ 'to be thirsty', /xuluṣ/ 'to be ready,' etc. because they are of the pattern /fuʕul/ Their imperfect stem vowel is /a/ (see below).

(2) C_2 or C_3 is the voiceless velar stop /k/:

sakat	yuskut	*to be silent*
sakab	yuskub	*to pour*
šakar	yuškur	*to thank*
sakan	yuskun	*to live, dwell*

ḥakam	yuḥkum	*to rule*
ʕakam	yuʕkum	*to swarm, teem with s.th.*
šabak	yušbuk	*to fasten, attach*
ḥabak	yuḥbuk	*to twist, twine*
sabak	yusbuk	*to perfect; to master*

If C_2 is a /k/ followed by the bilabial nasal /m/, then C_1 should be a pharyngeal /ḥ/ or /ʕ/ as in the examples above. Otherwise the stem vowel is /i/, e.g. /dakam/ - /yidkim/ 'to bump into s.th.', /lakam/ - /yilkim/ 'to punch s.o.', etc.

(3) C_2 is /r/ or /l/ and C_1 is a velarized consonant (/ṣ/, /ṭ/, /ð̣/) or a laryngeal (/ḥ-ʕ/, x-ġ/, /h/):

ṣarax	yuṣrux	*to shout*
harab	yuhrub	*to flee*
xaraj	yuxruj	*to go out*
ʕaraj	yuʕruj	*to limp*
faram	yufrum	*to mince*
ð̣arab	yuð̣rub	*to hit*
ṣaraf	yuṣruf	*to spend*
ṣarab	yuṣrub	*to harvest*
ṭalab	yuṭlub	*to request*
ḥalab	yuḥlub	*to milk*
ḥalag	yuḥlug	*to have a haircut*

Excluded from this category of verbs are verbs of the /fuʕul/ pattern, such as /xuluṣ/ 'to be ready', /ṭuluʕ/ 'to sprout, break forth', etc., and verbs of the /fiʕil/ pattern, such as /ʕirif/ 'to know', /ġirig/ 'to drown', /ḥirig/ 'to burn', etc. For the imperfect stem vowel of these verbs see below.

(4) C_3 is a nasal (/m/ or /n/) or the bilabial stop /b/ and C_1 or C_2 is a /k/ sound. Examples:

katam	yuktum	*to keep secret, conceal*
katab	yuktub	*to write*
sakab	yuskub	*to spill*
sakan	yuskun	*to dwell in a place*

There are exceptions to the above-mentioned rules. Those exceptions are due to the exposure of SA speakers to mass media and education. The following exceptions are very commonly used in SA and they actually have the same underlying structure as literary Arabic, except /sarag/ 'to steal'.

gatal	yugtul	*to kill*
sarag	yusrug	*to steal*
šakar	yuškur	*to thank*
ragad	yurgud	*to sleep*
ḥalaf	yiḥlif	*to take an oath*
ḥaram	yiḥrim	*to deprive*

B. Stem Vowel /a/

The imperfect stem vowel of a sound non-derived verb is /a/ if (1) C2 or C3 is a laryngeal sound (/ḥ-ʕ/, (x-ġ/, h-ʔ/) or if (2) the perfect-tense pattern is fuʕul or fiʕil.

Examples of (1):

saḥab	yisḥab	*to drag, pull*
ðabaḥ	yiðbaḥ	*to slaughter*
ṭaḥan	yiṭḥan	*to grind, mill*
laḥas	yilḥas	*to lick*
madaḥ	yimdaḥ	*to praise*
ṣanaʕ	yiṣnaʕ	*to manufacture*
zaraʕ	yizraʕ	*to plant*
laʕan	yilʕan	*to curse, damn*

nasax	yinsax	*to copy*
dabax	yidbax	*to cook*
sabaġ	yisbaġ	*to dye*
dabaġ	yidbaġ	*to tan s.th.*
baġaḍ̱	yibġaḍ̱	*to hate*
gahar	yighar	*to annoy; to subdue*
rahan	yirhan	*to pawn*
fahag	yifhag	*to hiccup*
saʔal	yisʔal	*to ask*

Examples of (2):

ʕuṭuš	yiʕṭaš	*to be thirsty*
xuluṣ	yixlaṣ	*to be ready*
luguṣ	yilgaṣ	*to bite*
ḍ̱uḥuk	yiḍ̱ḥak	*to laugh*
kumul	yikmal	*to be completed*
kubur	yikbar	*to be older*
kuθur	yikθar	*to be abundant*
muṭur	yimṭar	*to be drenched by rain*
xulug	yixlag	*to be created*
liʕib	yilʕab	*to play*
nikiʕ	yinkaʕ	*to fall down (on the ground)*
ʔisir	yiʔsar	*to take captive*
ʕišig	yiʕšag	*to fall in love*
ligif	yilgaf	*to eat a lot*
ribig	yirbag	*to talk a lot*
ḥinig	yiḥnag	*to be mad*
širib	yišrab	*to drink*

Note that some of the verbs of the /fuʕul/ pattern are passive in meaning, e.g., /muṭur/ 'to be drenched by rain', /xulug/ 'to be created', etc. Most of the SA verbs of the pattern /fiʕil/ have their underlying literary Arabic pattern as /faʕila/, the imperfect tense of which is /yafʕalu/. Only one exception was noted, i.e., /nahal/ 'to breath heavily,' the imperfect stem vowel of which is /i/.

C. Stem Vowel /i/

The stem vowel of sound non-derived verbs is /i/ if their structural description does not meet the conditions for either the verb forms in A. or B. above:

tafal	yitfil	*to spit*
galam	yiglim	*to mow*
gafad	yigfid	*to overturn s.th.*
sabar	yisbir	*to prepare s.th.*
našad	yinšid	*to praise*
ġazal	yiġzil	*to be dizzy*
našat	yinšit	*to blow one's nose*
xatan	yixtin	*to circumcise*
ʕaraf	yiʕrif	*to know*
sajad	yisjid	*to bow in worship*
xabaz	yixbix	*to bake bread*
labaj	yilbij	*to hit s.o.*
ʕabad	yiʕbid	*to worship*
samar	yismir	*to have a good time*

Note that the second radical of verbs belonging to this group cannot be a velarized consonant, a laryngeal or a /k/; the third radical can be any of the following consonants /t, d, k, g, n, l, r, s, š, ð, θ, j, z/. No exceptions were recorded in this section.

Glide-Initial Verbs

Glide-initial verbs are verbs whose C_1 is a glide, i.e. a /w-/ or a /y-/. There are only two verbs with initial /y-/ that could be found: /yibis/ 'to be or become dry' and /yiʔis/ 'to give up hope'. Note the following examples:

	Perfect	Imperfect	Meaning
A.	waṣaf	yuuṣuf	*to describe*
	waʕað̣	yuuʕuð̣	*to preach*
	waṣal	yuuṣul	*to arrive*
B-1.	wulid[21]	yuulad	*to give birth; to be born*
	wuriθ	yuuraθ	*to inherit*
	wujib	yuujab	*to be necessary*
	wugiʕ	yuugaʕ	*to take place*
	wuð̣iḥ	yuuð̣aḥ	*to be clear*

B-2.	wujad	yuujad	*to find*
	wugaf	yuugaf	*to come to a stop*
	wujaʕ	yuujaʕ	*to be painful*
B-3.	wiθig	yuuθag	*to trust*
	wirim	yuuram	*to be or become swollen*
B-4.	yibis	yiibas	*to be or become dry*
	yiʔis	yiiʔas	*to give up hope*
C.	wazan	yuuzin	*to weigh*
	wahab	yuuhib	*to grant; to endow*
	waʕad	yuuʕid	*to promise*
	wagad	yuugid	*to ignite, burn*

The imperfect stem vowel of a glide-initial verb is /u/ if C_2 or C_3 is a velarized consonant and the perfect-tense pattern is /faʕal/ as in the examples in A. above. If neither C_2 or C_3 is a velarized consonant and the perfect-tense pattern is /faʕal/, the stem vowel is /i/ as in the examples in C. Elsewhere, the stem vowel is /a/ as in the examples in B-1 through B-4, which have the perfect patterns as /fuʕil/ in B-1, /fuʕal/ in B-2 and /fiʕil/ in B-3 and B-4.

Note that the initial glides /w/ and /y/ in the examples above do not appear in the imperfect forms. Instead, the vowel of the imperfect prefix is lengthened due to a process known as vowel assimilation: /yuwṣuf/ →/yuuṣuf/ 'he describes' and /yiybas/ →/yiibas/ 'to be or become dry'.

The Imperative

The imperative is used in giving commands, i.e., in telling or asking someone or a group of people to do something, e.g., /ʔuktub/ 'write (m.s.)!' and /ʔišrabayn/ 'drink (f.p.)!' etc. All imperatives in SA have four different forms, reflecting difference in gender and number: masculine singular, masculine plural, feminine singular, and feminine plural. Nearly all the imperative forms are formed from the imperfect stems of verbs. The masculine singular form of the imperative is the base of all the other forms which are formed by suffixing /-iy/ (f.s.), /-uw/ (m.p.), and /-ayn/ (f.p.). Below are the forms of the imperative of the verb 'to sleep'. The imperfect stem is /-rgud-/:

ʔurgud	*sleep (m.s.)!*
ʔurgudiy	*sleep (f.s.)!*
ʔurguduw	*sleep (m.p.)!*
ʔurgudayn	*sleep (f.p.)!*

Note that the vowel of the prefix /ʔu/ is the same as that of the imperfect stem vowel. In the speech of some nomadic tribes the prefix /ʔu-/ tends to be dropped: /rgud/, /rgudiy/ (var. /rgudey/), /rguduw/ (var. /rgudow/), and /rgudayn/.

The rules following the examples below pertain to the formation of the masculine singular imperatives of sound and initial-glide verbs.

Imperfect Stem	Imperative	Meaning
-rgu-	ʔurguṣ	*dance (m.s.)!*
-ḍrub-	ʔuḍrub	*hit (m.s.)!*
-srug-	ʔusrug	*steal (m.s.)!*
-zraʕ-	ʔizraʕ	*plant (m.s.)!*
-lgaṣ-	ʔilgaṣ	*bite (m.s.)!*
-glim-	ʔiglim	*mow (m.s.)!*
-tfil-	ʔitfil	*spit (m.s.)!*
-wṣuf-	ʔuuṣuf	*describe (m.s.)!*
-wgaf-	ʔiwgaf/ʔuugaf	*stop (m.s.)!*
-wθag-	ʔiwθag/ʔuuθag	*trust (m.s.)!*
-yʔas-	ʔiyʔas	*give up hope (m.s.)!*
-ʔkul-	kul	*eat (m.s.)!*
-ʔxuð-	xuð	*take (m.s.)!*

The vowel of the imperative prefix is /u/ if the imperfect stem vowel is /u/; otherwise it is /i/, with the exception of hamzated verbs, which drop the imperative prefix and their first radical (the hamza) for their imperative forms.

Forms II-X and Quadriliterals

The imperfect stem vowel of sound verbs of Forms II-IV, VIII, and X is /i/, except in the environment of a velarized sound, in which case it is /u/. That of the other Forms, i.e., V and VI, is /a/. The vowel of the imperfect prefix is /i/, although /a/ is rarely heard. Sound quadriliterals have the stem vowel /i/ after the third radical and derived quadriliterals have the stem vowel /a/ after the third radical. Examples of imperfect-tense verbs with /i/ as a stem vowel:

	Perfect	Imperfect	Meaning
Form II			
	xazzan	y(i)xazzin	*to chew qat*
	naššaṭ	y(i)naššuṭ	*to encourage*
Form III			
	xaalaf	y(i)xaalif	*to violate*
	ʕaayan	y(i)ʕaayin	*to observe*

Form IV

(ʔi)bsar	yibsir	*to see*
ʔaṭlag	yuṭlug	*to set free*

Form VIII

(ʔi)ṣṭabaḥ	yiṣṭabiḥ	*to have breakfast*
(ʔi)ktasar	yiktasir	*to break*

Form X

(ʔi)staxbar	yistaxbir	*to ask to be informed*
(ʔi)stanṭag	yistanṭug	*to interrogate*

Examples of imperfect-tense verbs with /a/ as a stem vowel:

Form V

tbannan	yitbannan	*to eat a lot*
tḥayyal	yitḥayyal	*to elude*

Form VI

tḥaarab	yitḥaarab	*to be at war*
traasal	yitraasal	*to correspond with each other*

Sound quadriliterals have the stem vowel /i/ after the third radical:

gambar	yigambir	*to sit down*
kawbal	yikawbil	*to pile up s.th.*
laflaf	yilaflif	*to save*

Sound derived quadriliterals have the stem vowel /a/ after the third radical:

tmaxyal	yitmaxyal	*to ride a horse*
tšawraʕ	yitšawraʕ	*to walk in the street*
tkawbal	yitkawbal	*to be piled up*

The Imperative

The imperative forms of sound verbs of Forms II, III, V, VI, VIII, X and of quadriliterals are the same as the imperfect stems of those verbs.

Form	Perfect	Imperfect Stem	Imperative (m.s.)
II	xazzan	*to chew qat* -xazzin-	xazzin! *chew qat!*
III	ʕaayan	*to observe* -ʕaayin-	ʕaayin! *observe!*
IV	(ʔi)bsar	*to see* -bsir-	(ʔi)bsir! *see!*
V	tkallam	*to speak* -tkallam-	tkallam! *speak!*
VI	tšaawar	*to consult with s.o.* -tšaawaar!-	tšaawar! *consult with s.o.*
VIII	ṣṭabaḥ	*to have breakfast* -ṣṭabiḥ-	ṣṭabiḥ! *have breakfast!*
X	stanṭag	*to interrogate* -stanṭig-	stanṭig! *interrogate!*
Quad.	lamlam	*to save* -lamlim-	lamlim! *save!*
Der. Quad.	tmaxyal	*to ride a horse* -tmaxyal-	tmaxyal! *ride a horse!*

7.2.2 Weak Verbs[22]

A. Defective

Defective verbs are verbs whose perfect structure is C_1iC_2i/ C_1aC_2a, or C_1aC_2a. Those whose perfect structure is of the pattern C_1iC_2i or both C_1iC_2ai and C_1aC_2a have their imperfect forms on the pattern yiC_1C_2a:

Perfect	Imperfect	Meaning
ligiy/laga	yilga	*to find*
bigiy/baga	yibga	*stay*
nisiy/nasa	yinsa	*forget*
xiriy	yixra	*defecate*
riwiy	yirwa	*quench one's thirst*
ġiliy	yiġla	*be or become more expensive*

The other type of defective verbs whose structure is only of the C_1aC_2a (or sometimes C_1C_2a) pattern have their imperfect forms as yiC_1C_2iy:

Perfect	Imperfect	Meaning
bana	yibniy	*to build*
daʕa	yidʕiy	*to call; to invite*
saga	yisgiy	*to irrigate*
ḥama	yiḥmiy	*to defend*
šaka	yiškiy	*to complain*
ʕaṣa	yiʕṣiy	*to disobey*

The paradigms below give the imperfect forms of both kinds of defective verbs.

Perfect	Imperfect	Meaning
ligiy	yilga	*he finds*
ligyuw	yilgaw	*they (m.) find*
ligyat	tilga	*she finds*
ligyayn	yilgayn	*they (f.) find*
ligiit	tilga	*you (m.s.) find*
ligiituw	tilgaw	*you (m.p.) find*
ligiitiy	tilgay	*you (f.s.) find*
ligiitayn	tilgayn	*you (f.p.) find*
ligiit	ʔalga	*I find*
ligiina	nilga	*we find*
bana	yibniy	*he builds*
banaw	yibnaw	*they (m.) build*
banat	tibniy	*she builds*
banayn	yibnayn	*they (f.) build*
banyt	tibniy	*you (m.s.) build*
banaytuw	tibnaw	*you (m.p.) build*
banaytiy	tibnay	*you (f.s.) build*
banaytayn	tibnayn	*you (f.p.) build*
banayt	ʔabniy	*I build*
banayna	nibniy	*we build*

Note that the (imperfect) third person plural suffixes are identical in both stem types. Similarly the second person plural and the second person feminine singular are also identical. Note the following vowel elisions:

yilga	he finds + -uw	→	yilgaw	*they (m.) find*
yibniy	he builds + -uw	→	yibnaw	*they (m.) build*
tilgay	you (f.s.) find + -ayn	→	tilgayn	*you (f.p.) find*
tibnay	you (f.s.) build + -ayn	→	tibnayn	*you (f.p.) build*

The imperative forms of Form I defective verbs have the prefix /ʔi/:

ʔilga	*find (m.s.)!*	ʔilgaw	*find (m.p.)!*
ʔilgay	*find (f.s.)!*	ʔilgayn	*find (f.p.)!*
ʔibniy	*build (m.s.)!*	ʔibnaw	*build (m.p.)!*
ʔibnay	*build (f.s.)!*	ʔibnayn	*build (f.p.)!*

The imperfect of verbs of Forms II-IV, VIII, and X have the stem vowel /i/:

Form II

xalla	*to leave; to let*	y(i)xalliy	*he leaves; he lets*
ġanna	*to sing*	y(i)ġanniy	*he sings*

Form III

baawa	*to shine shoes*	y(i)baawiy	*he shines shoes*
naada	*to call s.o.*	y(i)naadiy	*he calls s.o.*

Form IV

(ʔa)xfa	*to conceal*	yixfiy	*he conceals*
(ʔa)ḥša	*to stuff s.th.*	yiḥšiy	*he stuffs s.th.*

Form VIII

ltaga	*to meet with s.o.*	yiltagiy	*he meets with s.o.*
btada	*to begin, start*	yibtadiy	*it begins, starts*
(ʔi)tka[23]	*to lean*	yitkiy	*he leans*
(ʔi)šta[24]	*to want*	yištiy	*he wants*

Form X

staʕfa	*to resign*	yistaʕfiy	*he resigns*
staḥa	*to be embarrassed*	yistaḥiy	*he gets embarrassed*

The other two forms, i.e., V and VI have the stem vowel /a/ for their imperfect forms:

Form V

tġadda	*to have lunch*	yitġadda	*he has lunch*
trabba	*to be brought up*	yitrabba	*he is brought up*

Form VI

traaya	*to dream*	yitraaya	*he dreams*
tʕaafa	*to recuperate*	yitʕaafa	*he recuperates*

Note the following:

a. The final vowel of all defective verbs in the imperfect tense is dropped before suffixes.

b. The imperfect stems and the perfect stems of derived defective verbs are identical except for the final vowel.

c. Initial /ʔa-/ (sometimes /ʔi-/) is dropped from Form IV verbs before the derivational prefix /yi-/.

The imperative forms of derived defective verbs have no prefixes except for verbs of Form IV, which usually have the prefix /ʔiy-/.

xalliy!	(Form II)	*let; leave (m.s.)!*
naadiy!	(Form III)	*call (m.s.)!*
ʔixfiy!	(Form IV)	*conceal (m.s.)!*
tġadda!	(Form V)	*have lunch (m.s.)!*
traaya!	(Form VI)	*dream (m.s.)!*
btadiy!	(Form VIII)	*begin (m.s.)!*
staʕfiy!	(Form X)	*resign (m.s.)!*

B. Hollow

Form I

Form I hollow verbs have three imperfect stem patterns: - C_1uuC_3 -, -C_1iiC_3 -, and -C_1aaC_2-:

Pattern I: C1uuC3-: /gaal/ *to say* → /yiguul/ *he says*

ʔaguul	*I say*	niguul	*we say*
yiguul	*he says*	yiguuluw	*they (m.) say*
tiguul	*she says*	yiguulayn	*they (f.) say*
tiguul	*you (m.s.) say*	tiguuluw	*you (m.p.) say*
tiguuliy	*you (f.s.) say*	tiguulayn	*you (f.p.) say*

Other verbs that belong to this category are:

/maat/	*to die*
/ʕaam/	*to swim*
/zaar/	*to visit*
/šaar/	*to consult*
/gaam/	*to rise*
/ðaab/	*to melt*
/faar/	*to boil*
/daam/	*to last*
/ṭaaf/	*to walk around, etc.*

Pattern II: C_1iiC_3-: /kaal/ *to weigh s.th.* → /yikiil/ *he weighs s.th.*

yikiil	*he weighs*	yikiiluw	*they (m.) weigh*
tikiil	*she weighs*	yikiilayn	*they (f.p.) weigh*
tikiil	*you (m.s.) weigh*	tikiiluw	*you (m.p.) weigh*
tikiiliy	*you (f.s.) weigh*	tikiilayn	*you (f.p.) weigh*
?akiil	*I weigh*	nikiil	*we weigh*

Other verbs that belong to this category are:

/ṭaar/	*to fly*
/zaad/	*to increase*
/ṭaa?/	*to obey*
/ʕaaš/	*to live*
/saar/	*to leave*
/baaḍ/	*to lay eggs*
/zaan/	*to weigh*
/faaš/	*to spread (e.g., news, rumors, etc.)*

The verb /jaa?/ 'to come' is usually used with ?imaalah in the third person masculine singular and it is irregular. The perfect-tense forms are:

jee?	*he came*	jaw	*they (m.) came*
jaa?at	*she came*	jaa?ayn	*they (f.) came*
ji?t	*you (m.s.) came*	ji?tuw	*you (m.p.) came*
ji?tiy	*you (f.s.) came*	ji?tayn	*you (f.p.) came*
ji?t	*I came*	ji?na	*we came*

/jet/ or /jit/ 'she came' is less commonly used than /jaa?at/.

The corresponding imperfect forms are regular:

yijiy	*he comes*
yijuw	*they (m.) come*
tijiy	*she comes*
yijayn	*they (f.) come*
tijiy	*you (m.s.) come*
tijuw	*you (m.p.) come*
tijiy	*you (f.s.) come*
tijayn	*you (f.p.) come*
?aji	*I come*
niji	*we come*

Pattern III: -C_1aaC_3-: /xaaf/ *to be afraid* → /yixaaf/ *he is afraid*

yixaaf	*he is afraid*
tixaaf	*she is afraid*
tixaaf	*you (m.s.) are afraid*
tixaafiy	*you (f.s.) are afraid*
?axaaf	*I am afraid*
yixaafuw	*they (m.) are afraid*
yixaafayn	*they (f.) are afraid*
tixaafuw	*you (m.p.) are afraid*
tixaafayn	*you (f.p.) are afraid*
nixaaf	*we are afraid*

Other verbs that belong to this category are: /baan/ 'to appear', /naal/ 'to obtain, get', /baat/ 'to spend the night', etc.

The imperative forms of Form I hollow verbs are the same as their imperfect stems:

zuur	*visit (m.s.)!*	zuuruw	*visit (m.p.)!*
zuuriy	*visit (f.s.)*	zuurayn	*visit (f.p.)!*
kiil	*weigh (m.s.)!*	kiiluw	*weigh (m.p.)!*
kiiliy	*weigh (f.s.)!*	kiilayn	*weigh (f.p.)!*
naal	*obtain (m.s.)!*	naaluw	*obtain (m.p.)!*
naaliy	*obtain (f.s.)!*	naalayn	*obtain (f.p.)!*

For some reason, the masculine singular imperative form of hollow verbs of Pattern I whose first radical is /g/ is on the pattern C_1uC_3 rather than C_1uuC_2. Examples: /gul/ 'say (m.s.)!' and /gum/ 'rise (m.s.)!'. No other verbs could be found.

Derived hollow verbs that occur in SA are those of Forms VIII and X only:[25]

Form VIII

(?i)ḥtaaj	yiḥtaaj	*to need s.th.*
(?i)xtaar	yixtaar	*to choose, select*
(?i)rtaaḥ	yirtaaḥ	*to rest*

Note that the inflectional prefix is usually /yi-/. The imperative form of these verbs is the same as their imperfect stems:

(ʔi)xtaar	*choose (m.s.)!*	(ʔi)xtaaruw	*choose (m.p.)!*
(ʔi)xtaariy	*choose (f.s.)!*	(ʔi)xtaarayn	*choose (f.p.)!*

Form X

Form X hollow verbs have -staC1iiC3- as their imperfect stem pattern. The derivational prefix is usually /yi-/, although /ya-/ is sometimes heard:

yistariiḥ	*he rests*	yistariiḥuw	*they (m.) rest*
tistariiḥ	*she rests*	yistariiḥayn	*they (f.) rest*
tistariiḥ	*you (m.s.) rest*	tistariiḥuw	*you (m.p.) rest*
tistariiḥiy	*you (f.s.) rest*	tistariiḥayn	*you (f.p.) rest*
ʔastariiḥ	*I rest*	nistariiḥ	*we rest*

7.2.3 Doubled Verbs

Form I

Doubled verbs of Form I are of the pattern $C_1aC_2C_2$. They have two imperfect stem vowels: /u/ and /i/. The imperfect stem vowel is /u/ if: (1) C_1 or C_2 is a velarized consonant(/ṣ/, /ṭ/, /ð̣/) or (2) C_2 is a velar stop (k, g). Elsewhere, it is /i/. Below are the imperfect forms of the verbs /ð̣ann/ 'to think' and /šann/ 'to filter'.

yið̣unn	yišinn
tið̣unn	tišinn
tið̣unniy	tišinniy
ʔað̣unn	ʔašinn
yið̣unnuw	yišinnuw
yið̣unnayn	yišinnayn
tið̣unnuw	tišinnuw
tið̣unnayn	tišinnayn
nið̣unn	nišinn

Other verbs that have the same stem vowel as /ðann/ are:

ṭall	yiṭull	*to command a view*
ðarr	yiðurr	*to harm*
ṣarr	yiṣurr	*to creak (door)*
šaṭṭ	yišuṭṭ	*to tear*
maṣṣ	yimuṣṣ	*to suck*
gaṣṣ	yiguṣṣ	*to cut*
xaṭṭ	yixuṭṭ	*to write (a letter)*
ḥakk	yiuḥkk	*to scratch*
dakk	yidukk	*to demolish*
ʕakk	yiʕukk	*to confuse*
dagg	yidugg	*to telephone*
ʕagg	yiʕugg	*to groan, moan*

Other verbs that have the same stem vowels as /šann/ are:

garr	yigirr	*to confess*
gazz	yigizz	*to shear*
mazz	yimizz	*to squeeze*
šall	yišill	*to take, carry away*
sadd	yisidd	*to obstruct*
dass	yidiss	*to insert*
sarr	yisirr	*to please*
ḥall	yiḥill	*to untie*
farr	yifirr	*to flee*
ḥajj	yiḥijj	*to go on pilgrimage*

The imperative forms of doubled verbs of Form I are the same as their imperfect stems:

guṣṣ	*cut (m.s.)!*	guṣṣuw	*cut (m.p.)!*
guṣṣiy	*cut (f.s.)!*	guṣṣayn	*cut (f.p.)!*
girr	*confess (m.s.)!*	girruw	*confess (m.p.)!*
girriy	*confess (f.s.)!*	girrayn	*confess (f.p.)!*

The imperfect stem vowel of doubled verbs of Form VIII is /a/. Examples:

-htamm-	*to be concerned; to be interested*
-ḥtall-	*to occupy*

The imperative forms of these verbs are the same as their perfect stems:

htamm	*be concerned (m.s.)!*

Form X doubled verbs have the imperfect stem vowel /i/. Below are the imperfect forms of the verb /staḥagg/ 'to deserve'.

yistaḥigg	*he deserves*
tistaḥigg	*she deserves*
tistaḥigg	*you (m.s.) deserve*
tistaḥiggiy	*you (f.s.) deserve*
ʔastaḥigg	*I deserve*
yistaḥigguw	*they (m.p.) deserve*
yistaḥiggayn	*they (f.p.) deserve*
tistaḥigguw	*you (m.p.) deserve*
tistaḥiggayn	*you (f.p.) deserve*
nistaḥigg	*we deserve*

The imperative forms of these verbs are the same as their imperfect stems:

staʕidd	*get ready (m.s.)!*
staridd	*get s.th. back (m.s.)!*
stamirr	*go on (doing s.th.)(m.s.)!*

No doubled quadriliterals or derived quadriliterals have been recorded. However, borrowings from literary Arabic and from the speech of Arab immigrants in San'a have been heard on formal occasions, e.g., /šmaʔazz/ (imperfect /yišmaʔizz/) 'to feel, be disgusted,' /ṭmaʔann/ (imperfect /yiṭmaʔinn/) 'to be reassured," etc.

Section Eight

8. The Future

Future time in SA is expressed by prefixing /ša-/ or /ʕa-/ to the imperfect tense of the verb. /ša-/ is usually used in the city of San'a with the first person singular and /ʕa-/ is used with the other persons. In other regions, however, /ša-/ is used with all the persons. When /ša-/ is used, the glottal stop of the imperfect prefix is dropped:

ša + ʔaktub → ša-ktub *I will write.*

A sample conjugation of the imperfect tense with the future particle is given below:

ʕa-yuktub	*he will write*
ʕa-tuktub	*she will write*
ʕa-tuktub	*you (m.s.) will write*
ʕa-tuktubiy	*you (f.s.) will write*
ša-ktub	*I will write*
ʕa-yuktubuw	*they (m.) will write*
ʕa-yuktubayn	*they (f.) will write*
ʕa-tuktubuw	*you (m.p.) will write*
ʕa-tuktubayn	*you (f.p.) will write*
ʕa-nuktub	*we will write*

Section Nine

9. NOUNS -- DERIVATION

The majority of nouns in SA are derived from verbs, adjectives, and other nouns. Examples:

nakaʕ	*to fall down*	→	nukuuʕ	*falling down*
gabaṣ	*to pinch*	→	gabṣ	*pinching*
ʔamiin	*honest*	→	ʔamaaneh	*honesty*
ð̣aʕiif	*weak*	→	ð̣uʕf	*weakness*
rajjaal	*man*	→	rajaaleh	*manhood*

9.1 Verbal Nouns

Verbal nouns are nouns, the great majority of which are derived from verbs, which express or name the underlying notion of the verb, as opposed to concrete nouns, e.g., the verbal noun /swaagah/ 'driving' denotes the act of driving as opposed to /sawwaag/ 'driver', which denotes the person whose job is driving. Verbal nouns may indicate an event, a function, a state, or a quality of the underlying verb, as will be shown below.

9.1.1 Form I

The derivation of verbal nouns from Form I verbs is irregular. There are many patterns of the verbal noun, which might be of use to the student, but it is best to learn the verbal noun along with its root verb. The following are the most common patterns[26] for Form I triradical verbs:

1. faʕl

Verb		Verbal Noun	
xatan	*to circumcise*	xatn	*circumcision*
gabaṣ	*to pinch*	gabṣ	*pinching*
galam	*to mow*	galm	*mowing*
naðag	*to throw s.th.*	naðg	*throwing*
gaðaf	*to throw up*	gaðf	*throwing up*
tafal	*to spit*	tafl	*spitting*
kaðab	*to tell lies*	kaðb	*telling lies*
maat	*to die*	mawt	*death*
xalas	*to undress*	xals	*act of undressing*

/faʕl/ is also a common pattern for triradical doubled verbs:

wann	*to moan*	wann	*moaning*
mazz	*to squeeze*	mazz	*squeezing*
šann	*to filter (water)*	šann	*filtering (water)*
gazz	*to shear*	gazz	*shearing*
ḥaθθ	*to encourage*	haθθ	*encouragement*
šakk	*to doubt*	šakk	*doubt(ing)*

Only a few triradical doubled verbs do not have /faʕl/ as a pattern for their verbal nouns:

xaff	*to be light*	xiffeh	*state of being / becoming light*
sabb	*to call s.o. bad names*	sabuub	*calling s.o.bad names*

2. f(i)ʕaaleh / faʕaaleh

kirih	*to dislike*	karaaheh[27]	*dislike*
zaad	*to increase*	zyaadeh	*increase*
ktab	*to write*	ktaabeh	*writing*
garaʔ	*to read*	graayeh	*reading*
rama	*to shoot, fire*	rimaayeh	*shooting, firing*
šaka	*to complain*	škaayeh	*complaining; complaint*
daras	*to study*	diraaseh	*studying; studies*
diri	*to know*	diraayeh	*knowing*

3. f(u)ʕuul

nakaʕ	*to fall down*	nukuuʕ	*falling down*
wugiʕ	*to happen*	wuguuʕ	*act of happening*
ragad	*to sleep*	ruguud	*act of sleeping*
našat	*to blow one's nose*	nušuut	*act of blowing one's nose*
sakat	*to be silent*	skuut	*silence*
sakan	*to calm down*	skuun	*calm*

4. faʕal

ġirig	*to be angry; to drown*	ġarag	*anger; drowning*
ġuluṭ	*to make a mistake*	ġalaṭ	*act of making a mistake*
ʕuṭuš	*to be thirsty*	ʕaṭaš	*thirst*
šigi	*to toil, labor*	šaga	*toil, labor*
wusiʕ	*to be roomy*	wasaʕ	*state of being roomy*
ḥinig	*to be mad*	ḥanag	*state of being mad*

5. faʕleh

harab	*to flee, escape*	harbeh	*fleeing, escape*
ḥamal	*to carry*	ḥamleh	*carrying*
ragad	*to sleep*	ragdeh	*act of sleeping*
nisi	*to forget*	nasweh	*forgetting*
rama	*to shoot, fire*	ramyeh	*shooting, firing*
ṣadam	*to collide, clash*	ṣadmeh	*collision*
riḥim	*to be merciful*	raḥmeh	*mercy*
ʕaad	*to return*	ʕawdeh	*return(ing)*
riġib	*to desire, wish*	raġbeh	*desire, wish*
falat	*to escape, slip away*	falteh	*escape, slipping away*
nisi	*to forget*	nasweh	*forgetting*
simir	*to enjoy oneself*	samreh	*act of enjoying oneself*

Some of the verbal nouns in this section, e.g., /ḥamleh/, /ragdeh/, /ṣadmeh/, etc., are also instance nouns. See 9.2 below.

6. fuʕl

širib	*to drink*	šurb	*drinking*
ṭuwil	*to become long*	ṭuul	*length*
ðalam	*to oppress*	ðulm	*oppression, injustice*
baġað	*to hate*	buġð	*hatred*
šakar	*to thank*	šukr	*thanking*
ḥakam	*to rule*	ḥukm	*rule, ruling*
ṣanaʕ	*to make, manufacture*	ṣunʕ	*making, manufacturing*
kirih	*to detest, dislike*	kurh	*dislike, distaste*

7. mafʕileh

ʕirif	*to know*	maʕrifeh	*knowledge*
gidir	*to be able*	magdirah	*ability*
gaal	*to say*	maguuleh	*speech, talk*

8. faʕaal

bigi	*to remain, stay*	bagaaʔ	*staying*
ġili	*to become expensive*	ġalaaʔ	*rise in prices*
gaða	*to decree, decide*	gaðaaʔ	*divine decree, destiny*
daam	*to last, continue*	dawaam	*duration*
baan	*to be evident*	bayaan	*state of being evident*
samaḥ	*to permit; to pardon*	samaaḥ	*permission, pardon(ing)*
ʔimin	*to feel safe*	ʔamaan	*safety; security*

Note that /faʕaal/ is a verbal noun pattern for most defective and hollow verbs.

9. fiʕaal

ġaab	*to be absent*	ġiyaab	*absence*
gaam	*to rise*	giyaam	*rising*
bana	*to build*	binaaʔ	*building s.th.*
ligi	*to encounter, find*	ligaaʔ	*encounter*
ṣaaḥ	*to shout, yell*	ṣiyaaḥ	*shouting, yelling*
farr	*to flee*	firaar	*fleeing, escape*

10. faʕuul

sabb	*to call s.o. bad names*	sabuub	*act of calling s.o. bad names*
šamm	*to smell*	šamuum	*act of smelling*
ḍ̱amm	*to gather, collect*	ḍ̱amuum	*gathering, collecting*
ðamm	*to dispraise*	ðamuum	*dispraise, censure*

11. faʕiil

raḥal	*to depart, leave*	raḥiil	*departure*
našad	*to sing*	našiid	*singing*
rabaš	*to mix up s.o. or s.th.*	rabiiš	*act of mixing up s.o. or s.th*
nadaš	*to scatter s.th.*	nadiiš	*scattering*

12. faʕalaan

ṭaar	*to fly*	ṭayaraan	*flights.th.*
faar	*to boil*	fawaraan	*boiling*
θaar	*to revolt, rebel*	θawaraan	*revolt, rebellion*
haaj	*to get agitated*	hayajaan	*agitation*
daar	*to revolve, go around*	dawaraan	*revolving*

9.1.2 Form II

The verbal nouns of most verbs of Form II follow predictable patterns. The patterns are /tafʕiil/ for sound verbs and /tafʕileh/ for defective verbs:

Verb		Verbal Noun	
darras	*to teach*	tadriis	*teaching, instructing*
faššal	*to disappoint*	tafšiil	*disappointing*
xazzan	*to chew qat*	taxziin	*chewing qat*
gattal	*to massacre*	tagtiil	*slaughter, butchery*

jarras	*to insult*	tajriis	*act of insulting*
bakkaʕ	*to tear off*	tabkiiʕ	*tearing off*
rabba	*to bring up*	tarbiyeh	*bringing up*
ḥayya	*to greet s.o.*	taḥiyyeh	*greeting s.o.; a greeting*
gawwa	*to strengthen*	tagwiyeh	*strengthening*

Some Form II verbs have other verbal noun patterns:

ġanna	*to sing*	ġuna	*singing*
ṣalla	*to pray*	ṣalaah	*praying; prayer*
ṭallab	*to beg*	ṭullaab	*begging*
ʕammal	*to have, get s.th. done*	taʕmuul	*having, getting s.th.done*
ṣayyaḥ	*to shout, yell*	ṣiyaaḥ	*shouting, yelling*
gayyal	*to chew qat in a magiil*	giyyaal	*act of chewing qat in a magiil*

9.1.3 Form III

Verbal nouns of Form III verbs have two patterns: /m(u)faaʕaleh/ for sound verbs and /m(u)faaʕaah/ for defective verbs:

xaalaf	*to violate*	muxaalafeh	*violation*
ḥaawal	*to try*	muḥaawaleḥ	*trial, act of trying*
ʕaayan	*to examine*	muʕaayaneh	*act of examining*
gaayas	*to measure*	mugaayaseh	*act of measuring*
ʕaada	*to be at war with s.o.*	mʕaadaah	*state of being at war with s.o.*
ġaawa	*to deceive*	mġaawaah	*deceit, deceiving*

The verbal noun from /saafar/ 'to travel' is /safar/ 'travel(ing)'.

9.1.4 Form IV

Most verbal nouns of Form IV verbs are of the pattern /(i)fʕaal/:

(ʔi)dxal	*to admit, let enter*	(ʔi)dxaal	*inclusion, introduction*
(ʔi)xraj	*to dismiss s.o.*	(ʔi)xraaj	*dismissal*
(ʔi)xlas	*to skin (an animal)*	(ʔi)xlaas	*skinning (an animal)*
(ʔa)ṭlag	*to set free*	(ʔi)ṭlaag	*setting free*
(ʔa)hlak	*to annihilate,destroy*	(ʔi)hlaak	*annihilation*
(ʔa)ʕlan	*to announce*	(ʔi)ʕlaan	*announcement*

The verbal noun associated with /(ʔi)bsar/ 'to see' is /basuur/ 'seeing'.

9.1.5 Form V

Verbal nouns of Form V verbs have two patterns: /t(i)fiʕʕaal/ for sound verbs and /fiʕʕa/ for defective verbs:

tġassal	*to bathe*	tġissaal	*bathing*
tḥayyal	*to employ artful means*	tḥiyyaal	*act of employing artful means*
tbannan	*to stuff oneself with food*	tbinnaan	*act of stuffing oneself with food*
tšaggar	*to peek*	tšiggaar	*peeking*
tʕajjab	*to be amazed*	tʕijjaab	*being amazed; amazement*
tjammal	*to be courteous*	tjimmaal	*state of being courteous*
tʕallam	*to learn*	tʕillaam	*learning*
tġayyar	*to change*	tġiyyaar	*change*
tʕarras	*to get married*	tʕirraas	*getting married*
trabba	*to be brought up*	tribba	*acting of being brought up*

The verbal noun from /twaḍḍaʔ/ 'to perform ablution' is /wuḍuuʔ/ 'ablution'.

9.1.6 Form VI

There is no particular pattern for verbal nouns of Form VI verbs in SA. Most Form VI verbs have the verbal noun patterns of Form III verbs, i.e., /m(u)faaʕaleh/ for sound verbs and /m(u)faaʕaah/ for defective verbs:

tʕaagab	*to be punished*	muʕaagabeh	*punishment*
txaabar	*totelephone each other*	muxaabarah	*telephoning each other; telephone call*
tjaawab	*to respond to each other*	mujaawabeh	*resonding, response*
tšaawar	*to consult with each other*	mšaawarah	*consulting with each other;consultation*
tʕaafa	*to resign*	muʕaafaah	*resignation*
txaawa	*to associate as brothers*	muxaawaah	*act of associating as brothers*

9.1.7 Form VII (See 6.2.6 above.)

9.1.8 Form VIII

Most verbal nouns of Form VIII verbs are of the /(ʔi)ftiʕaal/ pattern:

ltabaj	*to be hit*	ltibaaj	*state of being hit*
jtamaʕ	*to have a meeting*	jtimaaʕ	*meeting; a meeting*
xtaar	*to choose*	xtiyaar	*choice*
htamm	*to be concerned with s.o. or s.th.*	htimaam	*concern*
ḥtafal	*to celebrate*	ḥtifaal	*celebration*
ntabah	*to be cautious*	ntibaah	*caution; attention;*
ʕtaraf	*to confess*	ʕtiraaf	*confession*
ntaḍ̣ar	*to wait for*	ntiḍ̣aar	*waiting*

Some Form VIII verbs have verbal nouns derived from their corresponding Form I verbs:

mtaḥag	*to be ruined*	maḥg	*ruin(ing)*
ntasa	*to be forgotten*	nasweh	*forgetting*
rtabaš	*to be mixed up*	rabšeh	*state of being mixed up*
ḥtarag	*to be burned*	ḥarg	*burning*
ftaṭar	*to be split*	faṭr	*splitting*

A few Form VIII verbs have other verbal noun patterns:

ṣṭabaḥ	*to have breakfast*	ṣabuuḥ	*having breakfast; breakfast*
štaġal	*to work*	šuġl	*work(ing)*
ḥtaaj	*to need*	ḥaajeh	*need(ing)*
ktafa	*to be satisfied*	kifaayeh	*satisfaction*

9.1.9 Form IX (See 6.2.8 above).

9.1.10 Form X

Verbal nouns of Form X have two patterns: /stifʕaal/ for sound and doubled verbs and /stifaaʕah/ for hollow verbs:

1. Sound and doubled: /stifʕaal/

staʕmal	*to use, utilize*	stiʕmaal	*use, utilization*
stanṭag	*to interrogate*	stinṭaag	*interrogation*
staxbar	*to inquire*	stixbaar	*inquiry*
staṣʕab	*to find s.th.difficult*	stiṣʕaab	*finding s.th.difficult*
staḥagg	*to deserve*	stiḥgaag	*worthiness*

2. Hollow: /stifaaʕah/

stagaal	*to resign*	stigaaleh	*resignation*
stajaab	*to respond*	stijaabeh	*response*
stafaad	*to benefit*	stifaadeh	*benefit*
staraaḥ	*to rest, relax*	stiraaḥah	*rest, relaxation*

9.1.11 Quadriliterals

Most verbal nouns of quadriliterals have the pattern $C_1aC_2C_3aaC_4$ or $C_1iC_2C_3aaC_4$:

ḏ̣aʕfar	*to lose*	ḏ̣aʕfaar	*loss*
tarjam	*to translate*	tirjaam	*translation*
gambar	*to sit down*	gimbaar/gambarah	*act of sitting down*
baxšaš	*to tip; to bribe*	bixšaaš	*tipping; bribery*

Other verbs have other patterns, e.g., the verbal noun of /xawraj/ 'to lower the price' is /xuraaj/.

Derived quadriliterals do not have verbal nouns associated with them; usually they have the same pattern as for quadriliterals:

tḏ̣aʕfar → ḏ̣iʕfaar
tbaxšaš → bixšaaš

9.2 Instance Nouns

Instance nouns, also known as nouns of single occurrence, are derived from verbal nouns or other kinds of nouns by suffixing /-a/, sometimes with appropriate stem changes. They are usually of the patterns /faʕleh/ /faʕlah/ and /fiʕleh/ (See 9.4 for the occurrence of /-eh/ and /-ah/.) Instance nouns express the meaning of a single occurrence (or a particular instance) of the underlying word or "spell" of such a state. Examples of instance nouns derived from verbal nouns:

Verb		Verbal Noun		Instance Noun	
liʕib	*to play*	liʕib	*playing*	liʕbeh	*a game*
luguṣ	*to bite*	lagṣ	*biting*	lagṣah	*a reptile bite*
gabaṣ	*to pinch*	gabṣ	*pinching*	gabṣah	*a pinch*
baġað̣	*to hate*	buġð̣	*hatred*	baġð̣ah	*a kind of hatred*
dafaʕ	*to vomit*	dafʕ	*vomiting*	dafʕah	*one act of vomiting*
razaf	*to sing*	razf	*singing*	razfeh	*a song*
xuṭi	*to walk*	xaṭi	*walking*	xaṭyeh	*a footstep*
širib	*to drink*	šurb	*drinking*	šarbeh	*a drink*
laṭam	*to slap*	laṭm	*slapping*	laṭmeh	*a slap*
ḥarag	*to burn*	ḥariig	*burning*	ḥargah	*a fire*
maat	*to die*	mawt	*death*	mawteh	*a certain kind of death*
wirim	*to be swollen*	waram	*swelling*	warmeh	*swollen part*
ġazal	*to be dizzy*	ġazl	*dizziness*	ġazleh	*an epileptic seizure*

Some instance nouns have patterns different from those of the corresponding verbal nouns:

tkallam	*to speak*	kalaam	*talk, speech*	kalmeh	*a word*
štaġal	*to work*	šuġl	*work*	šaġleh	*a piece of work*

Instance nouns, unlike verbal nouns, are inflected for number. Their dual is formed by /θintayn/ 'two (f.)' + the sound feminine plural of the instance noun or by suffixing /-tayn/[28] to the singular with appropriate changes:

liʕbeh	*a game*	θintayn liʕbaat/liʕbatayn	*two games*
lagṣah	*a reptile bite*	θintayn lagṣaat/lagṣatayn	*two reptile bites*
dafʕah	*one act of vomiting*	θintayn dafʕaat/dafʕatayn	*two acts of vomiting*

The plural is formed by suffixing -aat with appropriate changes:

liʕbeh	*a game*	liʕbaat	*games*
xaṭyeh	*a footstep*	xaṭyaat	*footsteps*

Derived verbs (Forms II-X) and quadriliterals do not usually have instance nouns.

9.3 Unit Nouns

Unit nouns indicate an individual unit or an individual item of the underlying noun. They are derived from collective nouns by adding /-eh/ /-ah/ or /-i/, sometimes with appropriate stem changes. Note that most instance nouns are derived from verbal nouns by suffixing /-eh/ /-ah/[29]. Where an instance noun designates a single occurrence of the underlying verbal noun, a unit noun designates an individual unit of the underlying collective noun. Thus the instance noun /lagṣah/ 'reptile bite' is derived from the verbal noun /lagṣ/ 'biting', and the unit noun /firsikeh/ 'a peach' is derived from the collective noun /firsik/ 'peaches'. Almost all kinds of vegetables, fruits, grains, flowers, fruit trees, grasses, etc., are collective nouns. Examples of collective and unit nouns:

A. Almost all inanimate collective nouns form their unit nouns by adding /-eh/ /-ah/:

Collective Noun		Unit Noun	
šijar	*trees*	šijareh	*a tree*
firsik	*peaches*	firsikeh	*a peach*
bayð̣	*eggs*	bayð̣ah	*an egg*
ḥabḥab	*watermelons*	ḥabḥabeh	*a watermelon*
tuffaaḥ	*apples*	tuffaaḥah	*an apple*
burtagaal	*oranges*	burtagaaleh	*an orange*
tamr	*dates*	tamrah	*a date*
buṭaaṭ	*potatoes*	buṭaaṭah	*a potato*
lawz	*almonds*	lawzeh	*an almond*
dajaaj	*chicken; hens*	dajaajeh	*a hen*
nuub	*bees*	nuubeh	*a bee*
sawd	*charcoal*	sawdeh	*a piece of charcoal*

barad	*hail*	baradeh	*a hailstone*
šamʕ	*wax; candles*	šamʕah	*a candle*
gaml	*lice*	gamleh	*a louse*
riiš	*feathers*	riišeh	*a feather*
gawgaʕ	*(fruit) pits*	gawgaʕah	*a (fruit) pit*
ḥabb	*grains (e.g. of wheat)*	ḥabbeh	*a grain*
xar	*feces; excrement*	xaryeh	*a lump of feces*

The only unit nouns which have been noted and which require stem changes are:

ṭamaaṭiis	*tomatoes*	ṭumṭusah	*a tomato*
dubbeh	*zucchini*	dubbaayeh	*a zucchini*

B. The unit nouns of most animate nouns are formed by adding /-i/ to their collective nouns:

gummal	*fleas*	gummali	*a flea*
ġurraab	*ravens*	ġurraabi	*a raven*
šawṣar	*crickets*	šawṣari	*a cricket*
ḥamaam	*pigeons*	ḥamaami	*a pigeon*
ʕaṣfar	*sparrows*	ʕaṣfari	*a sparrow*
ʕakbar	*field mouse*	ʕakbari	*a field mouse*
nummas	*mosquitoes*	nummasi	*a mosquito*
gurrad	*ticks*	gurradi	*a tick*
mawz	*bananas*	mawzi	*a banana*
bisbaas	*hot peppers*	bisbaasi	*a hot pepper*
biibar	*bell peppers*	biibari	*a bell pepper*
ʕaskar	*soldiers*	ʕaskari	*a soldier*
duud	*worms*	duudi	*a worm*

C. A special group of collective nouns called "ethnic collectives" belong to this category:

ʕarab	*Arabs*	ʕarabi	*an Arab*
yahuud	*Jews*	yahuudi	*a Jew*
ʔamrikaan	*Americans*	ʔamrikaani	*an American*
ʔarman	*Armenians*	ʔarmani	*an Armenian*
kurd	*Kurds*	kurdi	*a Kurd*

D. With some grains, such as wheat, rice, barley, etc. the word /ḥabbeh/[30] 'a piece' is used before the collective noun to indicate an individual unit; with other kinds of nouns, words such as /ʕuudi/ 'branch', /ġuṣn/ 'twig', /ḥšarah/ 'small amount', /guḥṭah/ 'handful', /raʔs/ 'head', etc., are used

birr	*wheat*	ḥabbat birr	*a grain of wheat*
šaʕiir	*barley*	ḥabbat šaʕiir	*a grain of barley*
ðirah	*corn*	ḥabbat ðirah	*a grain of corn*
rizz	*rice*	ḥabbat rizz	*a grain of rice*
gušmi	*radishes*	raʔs gušmi	*a radish*
baṣal	*green onions*	buṣli, raʔs baṣal	*an onion*
salaṭah	*lettuce*	raʔs salaṭah	*a head of lettuce*
gaat	*qat*	ʕuudi gaat	*a branch of qat*
ʕadas	*lentils*	guḥṭat ʕadas	*a handful of lentils*
ṭaḥiin	*flour*	ḥšarat ṭaḥiin	*a handful of flour*
ḥilbeh	*fenugreek*	ḥsamat ḥilbeh	*a handful of fenugreek*

Unit nouns are feminine singular and, like instance nouns, have a dual form and a plural form.

Examples of dual forms:

šijaratayn/θintayn šijar	*two trees*
tuffaaḥatayn/θintayn tuffaaḥ	*two apples*
ġurraabayn/ʔiθnayn ġurraab	*two ravens*
ʕaṣfarayn/ʔiθnayn ʕaṣfar	*two sparrows*

Examples of plural forms:

θalaaθah mawz	*three bananas*
xamsah šawṣar	*five crickets*
sittah ḥamaam	*six pigeons*
θalaaθah ṭamaaṭiis	*three tomatoes*

9.4 Feminine Nouns

In this section we are concerned with those feminine nouns that refer to female human beings and some animals, which are formed from their corresponding masculine nouns by suffixing -eh /-ah, sometimes with appropriate stem changes /-eh/ and /-ah/ are used interchangeably unless preceded by any of the pharyngealized consonants (/ṣ/, /ṭ/, /ð̣/ or by the velars /x-ġ/, or the pharyngeals /ḥ-ʕ/, in which case only /-ah/ is used.[31] In those examples where /-eh/ and /-ah/ are used interchangeably /-eh/ is more commonly used.:

ṣaʕbeh	*jenny ass*
waaḥideh	*one (f.)*
wariiθeh	*heiress*
ʕammeh	*paternal aunt*
ḥajjeh	*pilgrim (f.)*
waalideh	*mother*
jaddeh	*grandmother*
ʕaṣfareh	*sparrow (f.)*
ʕasiireh	*difficult (f.)*
ʕaziizeh	*dear (f.)*
ð̣aʕiifeh	*weak (f.)*
ʕaaṭišeh	*thirsty (f.)*
ʕigʕigah	*female frog*
ḥaamileh	*carrying (f.)*
ṭabiineh	*second wife*
ḥareeweh	*bride*
naahiyeh	*beautiful (f.)*
yahuudiyeh	*Jewess*

Examples with /-ah/ ending:

mutġaṣġaṣah	*sickly, depressed (f.)*
mixayyiṭah	*seamstress*
mariið̣ah	*ill (f.)*
mumarrið̣ah	*nurse (f.)*
šayxah	*shaikh (f.)*
ṣaaliḥah	*(fem. name)*
faṣiiḥah	*eloquent (f.)*
šuʕšuuʕah	*elegant (f.)*
šuuʕah	*ugly (f.)*
šaabiʕah	*full, not hungry (f.)*

It should be pointed out that /-eh/ and /-ah/ are also encountered in (1) feminine nouns that do not have corresponding masculine nouns, (2) instance nouns, (3) unit nouns, (4) the third person masculine singular suffixed pronoun, and (5) certain masculine plural nouns. The same rules for the occurrence of /-eh/ and /-eh/ apply here.

Examples of (1):

rugbeh	*neck*
ṭawḥah	*dizziness*
gaḥbeh	*prostitute*
nusxah	*copy*
miizeh	*characteristic*
naafiseh	*midwife*
guṣṣah	*story*
zarnaṭah	*swallowing*
gurḍ̣ah	*borrowing*
madaaʕah	*water pipe*
digneh	*chin*
šiigaareh	*cigarette*
gišleh	*fortress*
šaṭaleh	*fork*
tihaameh	*Tihama*
daymeh	*Yemeni kitchen*
ġudweh	*tomorrow*
nuxreh	*nose*
faaniiliyeh	*sweater*
ḥuzwiyeh	*anecdote*

Examples of (2):

ragdeh	*a nap*
razfeh	*a song*
gabṣah	*a pinch*
šarbeh	*a drink*
liʕbeh	*a game*
lagṣah	*a reptile bite*

Examples of (3):

darajeh	*a step*
baradeh	*hailstone*
ṣaʕbeh	*jenny ass*
balaseh[32]	*fig; prickly pear*
ḥamaameh	*pigeon*
bayḍ̣ah	*an egg*

Examples of (4):

galbeh	*his heart*
liḥyateh	*his beard*
bayteh	*his house*
ṣabuuḥah	*his breakfast*
ṭaagateh	*his window*
juuxah	*his broadcloth*
buṭaaṭah	*his potatoes*
baʕḍ̣ah	*some of it*
rabḥah	*his monkey*
samaaḥah	*his forgiveness*

Examples of (5):

ʔaṣaaṭiyeh:	*p. of* /ʔusṭah/	*craftsman*
ṭaraagaʕah:	*p. of* /ṭurgaʕi/	*thief*
magaadimeh:	*p. of* /magdami/	*head of a troop*
baḥriyeh:	*p. of* /baḥḥaar/	*seaman*

Some feminine nouns are derived from their corresponding masculine nisbah (i.e., "relative") nouns[33] by suffixing /-yeh/ or /-yyeh/. Forms with /-yeh/ are more commonly used.

suʕuudi	→	suʕuudiyeh	*Saudi (f.)*
yamani	→	yemeniyeh	*Yemeni (f.)*
ðamaari	→	ðamaariyeh	*characteristic of Dhamar (f.)*
maṣri	→	maṣriyeh	*Egyptian (f.)*
yahuudi	→	yahuudiyeh	*Jewess*
ṣanʕaani	→	ṣanʕaaniyeh	*characteristic of San'a (f.)*
naahi	→	naahiyeh	*fine, good, nice (person or thing)(f.)*

Some other nouns (i.e., not nisbah nouns) that end with /-i/ form their corresponding feminine nouns by suffixing /-eh/, sometimes with appropriate stem changes. Some of these nouns are unit nouns:

šugri	→	šugareh	*coll.* /šugar/	*young chicken (f.)*
ʕaṣfari	→	ʕaṣfareh	*coll.* /ʕaṣfar/	*sparrow (f.)*
ṣaʕbi	→	ṣaʕbeh	*p.* /ʔaṣʕub/	*jenny ass*
kuskusi	→	kuskusiyeh	*p.* /kasaakis/	*puppy (f.)*
ḥamaami	→	ḥamaameh	*coll.* /ḥamaam/	*pigeon (f.)*

9.5 Participles as Nouns

Active and passive participles will be dealt with under participles and adjectives below (see 11.4 and 11.5).

9.6 Occupational Nouns

Nouns that indicate people who have certain occupations or vocations are called occupational nouns. Most of the corresponding feminine nouns are formed by suffixing /-eh/ or /-ah/,[34] the feminine morpheme. Occupational nouns are of certain patterns, the most frequent of which are the following:

A. faaʕil

Occupational nouns of the /faaʕil/ pattern are derived from Form I verbs:

Verb	Occupational Masc. Noun	Occupational Fem. Noun
katab *to write*	kaatib *clerk (m.)*	kaatibeh *clerk (f.)*
xadam *to serve*	xaadim *servant (m.)*	xaadimeh *servant (f.)*
gaḏ̣a *to decree, decide*	gaaḏ̣i *judge (m.)*	gaaḏ̣iyeh *judge (f.)*
šigi *to toil*	šaagi *laborer (m.)*	*********
gatal *to kill*	gaatil *killer (m.)*	gaatileh *killer (f.)*

B. faʕʕaal

Most occupational nouns of the /faʕʕaal/ pattern are derived from verbs:

Underlying Word	Occupational Masc. Noun	Occupational Fem. Noun
sabak *to perfect; to master*	sabbaak *pipe fitter (m.)*	*********
laḥḥam *to weld*	laḥḥaam *welder (m.)*	*********
gaṣab *to cut meat*	gaṣṣaab *butcher (m.)*	*********
dajal *to deceive*	dajjaal *quack; swindler (m.)*	dajjaaleh *quack (f.)*

xabaz *to bake bread*	xabbaaz *baker (m.)*	xabbaazeh *baker (f.)*
fšar *to brag*	faššaar *braggart (m.)*	faššaarah *braggart (f.)*
kaðab *to tell lies*	kaððaab *liar (m.)*	kaððaabeh *liar (f.)*
baaʕ *to sell*	bayyaaʕ *seller (m.)*	bayyaaʕah *seller (f.)*
ʕamar *to build*	ʕammaar *mason, builder (m.)*	*********
ḥalag *to have a haircut*	ḥallaag *barber (m.)*	*********
najar *to saw wood*	najjaar *carpenter (m.)*	*********
ṭabaʕ *to type*	ṭabbaaʕ *typist (m.)*	ṭabbaaʕah *typist (f.)*
gašam *to harvest vegetables*	gaššaam *green grocer (m.)*	gaššaameh *green grocer(f.)*
saag *to drive*	sawwaag *driver*	*********
zanaṭ *to exaggerate*	zannaaṭ *exaggerator (m.)*	zannaaṭah *exaggerator(f.)*

C. mufaʕʕil/mifaʕʕil

Almost all the masculine occupational nouns of this pattern are derived from Form II verbs:

Verb	Occupational Masc. Noun	Occupational Fem. Noun
ʔaððan *to call to prayer*	muʔaððin *muezzin (m.)*	*********
sabbaḥ *to glorify God*	musabbiḥ *one who glorifies God (m.)*	musabbiḥah *one who glorifies God (f.)*
sajjal *to register*	musajjil *registraar (m.)*	musajjileh *registrar (f.)*
darras *to teach*	mudarris *teacher (m.)*	mudarriseh *teacher (f.)*
kayyas *to massage*	mukayyis *masseur*	mukayyiseh *masseuse*
ṭaaban *to polygamize*	muṭabbin *polygamist*	*********

nuḥaas *copper*	minaḥḥis *copper smith (m.)*	*********
fallag *to cut wood*	mifallig *woodcutter (m.)*	*********
ṭallab *to beg*	muṭallib *beggar (m.)*	muṭallibeh *beggar (f.)*
wassad *to upholster*	miwassid *upholsterer (m.)*	miwassideh *upholsterer (f.)*
ḥawwat *to catch fish*	miḥawwit *fisherman*	*********
sabbar *to cater (food)*	misabbir *(food) caterer(m.)*	misabbireh *(food) caterer(f.)*
xayyaṭ *to sew*	mixayyiṭ *tailor (m.)*	mixayyiṭah *seamstress*
naggal *to make shoes*	minaggil *shoemaker (m.)*	*********

D. mufaʕlil/mifaʕlil

Most occupational nouns of this pattern are derived from quadriliterals:

Underlying Word	Occupational Mas. Noun	Occupational Fem. Noun
handas *to engineer*	muhandis *engineer (m.)*	muhandiseh *engineer (f.)*
tarjam *to translate*	mutarjim *translator (m.)*	mutarjimeh *translator (f.)*
baʕsas *to make trouble*	mibaʕsis *troublemaker (m.)*	mibaʕsiseh *troublemaker (f.)*
bardag *to snuff*	mibardig *snuff manufacturer(m.)*	*********
naxal *to sieve*	minaxwil *sieve maker (m.)*	minaxwileh *sieve maker (f.)*
ḥalaaweh *sweets*	miḥalwi *sweets maker (m.)*	miḥalwiyeh *sweets maker (f.)*
xarwa *to collect feces*	mixarwi *one who collects feces for public baths (m.)*	*********

9.7 Instrumental Nouns

An instrumental noun, or a noun of instrument, indicates the instrument or object with which the act described by the underlying word can be performed. Most instrumental nouns in SA are derived from verbs. The following are the most commonly used patterns.

A. mifʕaal/mufʕaal

Verb		Instrumental Noun	
fataḥ	*to open*	miftaaḥ	*key*
nagar	*to peck*	mingaar	*beak*
wazan	*to weigh*	miizaan	*scales, balance*
nafax	*to blow, puff*	mimfaax	*bellows; air pump*
ḥaraθ	*to plough*	miḥraaθ	*plough*
lagaṭ	*to pick up (with tongs)*	mulgaaṭ	*pair of tongs*

B. mafʕal/mafʕaleh

barad	*to file (metal)*	mabrad	*file, rasp*
ð̣arab	*to hit*	mað̣rab	*(tennis)racket;bat*
fakk	*to unscrew*	mafakk	*screwdriver*
gaṣṣ	*to cut*	magaṣṣ	*scissors*
gaḥaf	*to shovel*	magḥaf	*shovel*
ṭarag	*to hammer*	maṭragah	*hammer*
ʔibsar	*to see*	mabsarah	*eyeglasses*
šann	*to filter (water)*	mišann	*(water) filter*
dagg	*to pound*	madaggah	*pounder, pestle*
kannas	*to sweep*	maknuseh	*broom*
saṭṭar	*to draw lines*	masṭareh	*ruler*
naššaf	*to dry with a towel*	manšafeh	*towel*

C. faʕʕaaleh/faʕʕaalah

masaḥ	*to erase*	massaaḥah	*eraser*
gašaṭ	*to sharpen (a pencil)*	gaššaaṭah	*(pencil) sharpener*
ṭaar	*to fly*	ṭayyaarah	*airplane*
saar	*to leave*	sayyaarah	*car*
θallaj	*to refrigerate*	θallaajeh	*refrigerator*

D. Other Patterns

dismiis	*screwdriver*	kaawiyeh	*an iron*
gaṣʕah	*(tomato, cheese) can*	maknis	*broom*
madaaʕah	*water pipe*	malʕagah	*spoon*

9.8 Locative Nouns

A locative noun, or a noun of place, designates the place where the action designated by the underlying word takes place. The following are the most frequently used locative noun patterns in SA.

A. mafʕaleh/mafʕalah

Underlying Word		Locative Noun	
katab	*to write*	maktabeh	*library*
daras	*to study*	madraseh	*school*
gabar	*to bury*	magbarah	*cemetery*
ḥakam	*to rule*	maḥkameh	*law court*
najar	*to saw wood*	manjarah	*carpenter shop*
(ʔa)zhar	*to blossom*	mazharah	*flower vase*

B. mafʕal/mafʕil

tafal	*to spit*	matfal	*spittoon*
tfarraj	*to look at s.th.*	mafraj	*(overlooking) reception hall*
(ʔa)tka	*to chew qat*	matka	*reception hall*
katab	*to write*	maktab	*office*
ṭuʕum	*to taste*	maṭʕam	*restaurant*
tuḥfeh	*souvenir*	matḥaf	*museum*
daxal	*to enter*	madxal	*entrance*
xaraj	*to exit*	maxraj	*exit*
kaan	*to be*	makaan	*room (in a house)*
xalaʕ	*to extract, pull*	maxlaʕ	*public bath dressing room*
ġaṭas	*to sink*	maġṭas	*plunge bath*
rakaz	*to settle*	markiz	*center*
ṭaar	*to fly*	maṭaar	*airport*
sajad	*to kneel*	masjid	*mosque*

C. mifʕaaleh

xabaz	*to bake*	mixbaazeh	*bakery*
gahweh	*coffee*	mighaayeh	*coffee house*
samak	*fish*	mismaakeh	*fish market*
ʕaṭṭaar	*spice vendor*	miʕṭaarah	*spice shop*
ʕaṣar	*to press, squeeze*	miʕṣaarah	*press, squeezer*
najar	*to saw wood*	minjaarah	*carpenter shop*

9.9 Diminutive Nouns

Diminutive nouns, usually known as diminutives, are derived mainly from nouns and adjectives used as nouns. Diminutives indicate a small or insignificant variety of that which is designated by the underlying word. They may also indicate affection or endearment. The most commonly used diminutive patterns in SA are two:

1. fuʕayyil:

   /zuġayyir/ 'tiny' from /ṣaġiir/ or /zġiir/ 'small'

   /ḥubayyib/ 'little darling' from /ḥabiib/ 'sweetheart'

   /guṣayyir/ 'very short' from /gaṣiir/ 'short'

2. fuʕfuli:

   /gurguši/ 'little hood worn by children' from /garguuš/ 'headgear worn by women'

   /zugzugi/ 'little path, lane' from /zugaag/ 'lane, alley'

A few diminutives are derived from personal names.:

Personal Name	Diminutive	
mḥammad	mḥammadi	*Muhammad*
ʔaḥmad	ḥumaadi	*Ahmad*
ʕabdalla	ʕubduli	*Abdalla*
saalim	swaylim	*Salim*
ṣaaliḥ	ṣwayliḥ	*Salih*

9.10 Foreign Nouns

SA has some foreign vocabulary, mainly English, Turkish, and Persian. One of the main reasons for this linguistic influence is the presence of foreign communities in Yemen. The turks were in Yemen for a long time. In addition to borrowings from English, Turkish, and Persian, there are a few borrowings from French and Hindi-Urdu, most of which are present in other dialects of Arabic. Only a few of those borrowings remain unmodified; most of them have undergone phonological, morphological, and semantic changes. In phonology the following modification or sound changes have been observed. The examples given are from English.

A. Diphthongs and Vowels

kuut	*coat*
frayzar	*freezer*
ʔaaydiin	*iodine*
ʔaryil	*aerial*
kayk	*cake*
makrafoon	*microphone*
mawtar	*car; motor*
waayir	*wire*
friim	*frame*
dabal	*double*
keeymara	*camera*
kartoon	*carton*
moodeel	*model*
santraal	*central*
biikab	*pickup*
loori	*lorry*
burayk	*brake*
liistah	*list*

B. Consonants

Consonants that do not exist in SA are replaced by consonants that share similar articulation features, e.g., point, manner, etc. Other consonant replacements occur:

banšar	*flat tire (cf. puncture)*
ṣandal	*sandals*
lambah	*lamp*
blaakaat	*(spark) plugs*
helekabtar	*helicopter*
gaaz	*(kerosine) gas*

C. Omission

Sometimes a whole syllable, especially the first syllable, in a word, is omitted. Consonant and vowel omission also occur:

kandeyšin	*air conditioning*
blaak	*spark plug*
saykal	*motorcycle*
kabat	*cupboard*
laysan	*license*
ʔitriik	*flash light*

In morphology, most borrowed verbs are those of Form II and they are wholly Arabized:

dabbal	*(from double) to double s.th.*
fannaš	*(from finish) to finish, come to an end*

Examples of other verbs:

šaat	*(from shoot) to shoot (e.g., in soccer)*
banšar	*(from puncture) to become punctured; to fail, not to pass (e.g., an examination)*

For the plural form of borrowed nouns either a sound feminine plural pattern or a broken plural pattern is used:

makrafoon	*microphone*	*p.* makrafoonaat
blaak	*spark plug*	*p.* blaakaat
kabat	*cupboard*	*p.* kabataat
kuut	*coat*	*p.* ʔakwaat
laysan	*license*	*p.* layaasin
bodi	*body (of a car)*	*p.* bawaadi
taaniki	*(water) tank*	*p.* tawaanik
kabtin	*captain*	*p.* kabaatinah

Below are some of the commonest borrowed nouns:

English

baaṣ	*bus*
buskoot	*biscuits*
blanti	*penalty (in soccer)*
bamp	*pump*

buuti	*boots*
taksi	*taxi*
silindar	*cylinder*
sways	*car key (cf. switch)*
siinama	*cinema*
šoort	*shorts*
friim	*frame*
fyuuz	*fuse*
karbaytar	*carburetor*
kamb	*camp*
kiliš	*(car) clutch*
kayk	*cake*
kliinix	*Kleenex*
kiiluw	*kilogram*
moodeel	*model*
makiinyeh	*machine*
waayir	*wire*
naayloon	*nylon*
kitli	*(tea) kettle*
glaaṣ	*glass*

Turkish

(ʔu)sṭa	*craftsman*
baaruut	*gunpowder*
baxṣam	*bread sticks*
burġi	*screw*
buuri	*(car) horn*
tanakeh	*tin container*
juux	*broadcloth*
balas	*prickly pears*
sumki	*bayonet*
ṭaabuur	*battalion*
fuuṭah	*man's skirt*
gunṭurah	*shoes*
guuzi	*lamb*
yurt	*yogurt*
baṭṭaaniyeh	*blanket*
booyaji	*shoe shiner*

booyah	*shoe polish*
ṭubši	*gunner*
daftar	*notebook*
šamṭa	*suitcase, bag*

Persian

bugšeh	*bundle of clothes*
baxšiiš	*tip; bribe*
birwaaz	*picture frame*
bas	*enough*
bistaan	*orchard*
bayrag	*flag*
titin	*tobacco*
jumrug	*customs, duty*
guuṭi	*can (e.g., of tomatoes)*
xaašuugah	*spoon*
daayeh	*midwife; servant*
darzi	*tailor*
zanjiil	*chain*
sanbuuk	*small boat*
meez	*table*
namuuneh	*sample*
niišaan	*medal*
buġmeh	*gulp of water*

French

stišwaar	*hair dryer*
ʔaṣanṣeer	*elevator*
baaruukeh	*wig*
balṭah	*overcoat*
baanyo	*bathtub*
bantaloon	*trousers*
dušš	*bath, shower*
ṣaaloon	*living room*
kulaanyah	*cologne*
šambuu	*shampoo*
wunayt	*small pickup*

Section Ten

10. NOUNS – INFLECTION

10.1 Gender

Nouns in SA have gender, either masculine or feminine, and a few nouns have both genders. Nouns, including personal names, that refer to males are masculine, and those referring to females are feminine. Thus, /yaḥya/ 'Yahia', /ʔaḥmad/ 'Ahmad', /ʕali/ 'Ali' and /ʔaḷḷaah/ 'God' are masculine, while /xadiijeh/, /faaṭimeh/ 'Fatima', and /tagiyyeh/ 'Tagiya' are feminine. This distinction is grammatically important, since the choice of pronoun depends on the gender of the noun or person involved, and it is the function of noun gender that governs the gender inflection of verbs and adjectives. The following nouns and proper names are feminine in SA:

A. Almost all nouns with the ending -ah/-eh[35] or /-aah/ are feminine. Those nouns do not have corresponding masculine forms.:

ṭabiineh	*second wife*
mabsarah	*eyeglasses*
bugšeh	*small money unit*
ʕaareh	*borrowing*
janbiyeh	*dagger*
madaaʕah	*water pipe*
nuxreh	*nose*
masbaḥah	*rosary beads*
ṭaagah	*window*
gubbeh	*dome*
ṣalaah	*prayer*
šaah	*nanny goat*

These nouns include foreign nouns:

tišwaar	*hair dryer (French)*
ʔaṣanṣeer	*elevator (French)*
kulaanyah	*cologne (French)*
šiigaareh	*cigarette (English)*
lambah	*lamp (English)*
keeymarah	*camera (English)*
makiinyeh	*machine (English)*

fuuṭah	*man's skirt (Turkish)*
gunṭurah	*shoes (Turkish)*
booyah	*shoe polish (Turkish)*
tanakeh	*tin container (Turkish)*

daayeh	*midwife (Persian)*
xaašuugah	*spoon (Persian)*
namuuneh	*sample (Persian)*

It should be pointed out that a few nouns ending in -ah/-eh are masculine. Some of them are human plural nouns. Examples:

xaliifeh	*Caliph*
ʔaṣaaṭiyeh	*craftsmen* (p. of /ʔuṣṭa/)
šaybeh	*old man*
malaaʔikeh	*angels* (p. of /malaak/)
taraagaʕah	*mountaineers* (p. of /tirgaaʕi/)
jabaliyeh	*mountaineers* (p. of /jabali/)

Among the feminine nouns that belong here are those that are derived from their corresponding masculine nouns.[36]

dimm	*cat (m.)*	dimmeh	*cat (f.)*
rabḥ	*monkey (m.)*	rabḥah	*monkey (f.)*
ḥareew	*bridegroom*	ḥareeweh	*bride*
mukayyis	*masseur*	mukayyiseh	*masseuse*
kalb	*dog*	kalbeh	*bitch*
misabbir	*(food) caterer (m.)*	misabbireh	*(food) caterer (f.)*
kuskusi	*puppy (m.)*	kuskusiyeh	*puppy (f.)*

Instance nouns [37] are derived from verbal nouns or other kinds of nouns by suffixing -eh/-ah and are feminine in gender:

Verbal Noun		Instance Noun	
gabṣ	*pinching*	gabṣah	*a pinch*
ġazl	*dizziness*	ġazleh	*an epileptic seizure*
razf	*singing*	razfeh	*a song*
laṭm	*slapping*	laṭmeh	*a slap*

Unit nouns[38] end with the suffix -eh/-ah and are all feminine singular. Most collective nouns[39], from which unit nouns are derived, are masculine singular, though the English translation may be plural, e.g., /ḥabḥab/ 'watermelons':

Collective Noun		Unit Noun	
firsik	*peaches*	firsikeh	*a peach*
sawd	*charcoal*	sawdeh	*a piece of charcoal*
ʕaṣfar	*sparrows*	ʕaṣfari	*a sparrow*
bisbaas	*hot peppers*	bisbaasi	*a hot pepper*
gušmi	*radishes*	raʔs gušmi	*a radish*

B. Some nouns do not have the feminine ending -eh/-ah, but they are feminine by usage. These nouns include:

1. Double parts of the body:

yad	*hand*
ʕayn	*eye*
rijl	*foot; leg*
ʔiðn	*ear*
faxð	*thigh*
saag	*leg*
ʔuṣbuʕ	*finger*
baṭn	*belly*

2. Names of cities, towns, and countries:

ṣanʕa	*San'a*
ʔal-ḥudaydah	*Hudaida*
ʔabu ḍ̄abi	*Abu Dhabi*
bayruut	*Beirut*
ʔal-yaman	*Yemen*
gaṭar	*Qatar*
ʔamriika	*America*
ʕumaan	*Oman*

3. Nouns which denote females. Such nouns have corresponding masculine nouns of different stems:

Masculine		Feminine	
ʔab	*father*	ʔumm	*mother*
ʔax	*brother*	ʔuxt	*sister*
ʔibn	*son*	bint	*daughter*
rajjaal	*man*	mareh	*woman*
šaybeh	*old man*	ʕajuuz(eh)	*old woman*

4. Females of most animals:

Masculine		Feminine	
ḥimaar	*donkey*	bahiimeh	*donkey*
diik	*rooster*	dajaajeh	*hen*
θawr	*bull*	bagarah	*cow*
ḥuṣaan	*horse*	faras	*mare*
jamal	*camel*	naagah	*camel*
tays	*ram*	miʕzeh	*sheep*
ṭaliy	*billy goat*	šaah	*nanny goat*

Note that /ðakar/ 'male' and /ʔunθa/ 'female' can be used for either a male or a female human being or an animal:

ðakar al-mareh huw ar-rajjaal	*The male of woman is man.*
ʔad-dajaajeh ʔunθa d-diik	*The hen is the female of a rooster.*

5. A few common words, including many foreign nouns:

sikkiin	*knife*
šams	*sun*
saykal	*motorcycle*
naar	*fire*
riiḥ	*wind*
gamar	*moon*
ʔarḍ	*land, earth*
biir	*well*
muus	*razor blade*
helekbatar	*heliocopter*
laysan	*license*
blaak	*spark plug*

10.2 Number

Nouns in SA have three numbers: singular, dual, and plural.

10.2.1 Singular

Singular nouns include both count and mass nouns. Count nouns designate countable entities and mass nouns indicate uncountable nouns. Singular nouns occur in a variety of patterns and it is difficult to predict the plural of a noun from the singular pattern except in a few cases,[40] which will be pointed out below. Examples of count and mass nouns:

Count		Mass	
masjid	*mosque*	laḥm	*meat*
šaybeh	*old man*	mee?	*water*
ʕajuuz(eh)	*old woman*	xubz	*bread*
ḥuuti	*a fish*	ḥuut	*fish*
ḥareew	*bridegroom*	ðahab	*gold*
madaaʕah	*water pipe*	mraysi	*sugar*

10.2.2 Dual

In English, nouns are either singular or plural; in SA they are singular, dual or plural. In general the dual is formed by either: /ʔiθnayn/ 'two (m.)', /θintayn/ 'two (f.)' + the plural of that noun or: by adding the suffix /-ayn/ to a masculine noun or /-tayn/ to a feminine noun ending with -eh/-ah. The former construction, i.e., ʔiθnayn/θintayn + the plural is more commonly used:

Singular		Dual	
ʕayn	*eye*	θintayn ʕuyuun/ʕaynayn	*two eyes*
ʔuṣbuʕ	*finger*	θintayn ʔaṣaabiʕ/ ʔuṣbuʕayn	*two fingers*
bugšeh	*parcel,bundle*	θintayn bugaš/bugšatayn	*two parcels*
bayt	*house*	ʔiθnayn biyuut/baytayn	*two houses*
mustašfa	*hospital*	ʔiθnayn mustašfayaat/mustašfayayn	*two hospitals*
mareh	*woman*	θintayn nisee?/maratayn	*two women*
masjid	*mosque*	ʔiθnayn masaajid/masjidayn	*two mosques*
ṣanʕaani	*one from San'a*	iθnayn ṣanaaʕinah/ṣanʕaaniyyayn	*two from San'a*

If the dual indicates two people or two things from a country then its formation is usually /ʔiθnayn/ or /θintayn/ + from the country:

yamani	*Yemeni*	→	ʔiθnayn min al-yaman	*two from Yemen*
suʕuudi	*Saudi*	→	ʔiθnayn min as-suʕuudiyah	*two from Saudi Arabia*
ʔamriikiyehh	*American* (f)	→	θintayn min ʔamriika	*two from America*

The dual of nouns that indicate weight, measurement, and money is made by suffixing -ayn/-tayn only:

kiiluw	*kilogram*	→	kiiluwayn	*two kilograms*
raṭl	*pound*	→	raṭlayn	*two pounds*
mitr	*meter*	→	mitrayn	*two meters*
miil	*mile*	→	miilayn	*two miles*
ðraaʕ	*cubit*	→	ðraaʕayn	*two cubits*
ryaal	*riyal*	→	ryaalayn	*two riyals*
duulaar	*dollar*	→	duulaarayn	*two dollars*
diinaar	*dinar*	→	diinaarayn	*two dinars*

Note that if /ðraaʕ/ means 'arm,' the dual is usually /ʔinayn ðraaʕaat/ and if it is a unit of measure 'cubit', the dual is usually /ðraaʕayn/. Similarly /bugšeḥ/ → /bugšatayn/ if it indicates a unit of money,and /θintayn bugaš/ if it indicates 'parcel, bundle'. Some words that indicate amounts or unspecified weights form their dual by suffixing -ayn/-tayn, e.g., /šaġθeh/ 'handful' → /šaġθatayn/ and /waṣlah/ 'piece of meat' → /waṣlatayn/.

A. Masculine Nouns

The dual of nisbah nouns and other nouns ending in /-i/ takes /-yy-/ or /-y-/ before /-ayn/ is added:

ṣanʕaani	*from San'a*	→	ṣanʕaaniyyayn/anʕaaniyayn	*two from San'a*
ḥudaydi	*from Hudaida*	→	ḥudaydiyyayn/ḥudaydiyayn	*two from Hudaida*
ġani	*rich man*	→	ġaniyyayn/ġaniyayn	*two rich men*

Nonhuman masculine nouns ending in /-aaʔ/ form their dual either by adding /-ayn/ or by reducing /-aaʔ/ to /-a/ and adding /-yayn/:

ʕašaaʔ	*dinner*	→	ʕašaaʔayn/ʕašayayn	*two dinners*
ġadaaʔ	*lunch*	→	ġadaaʔayn/ġadayayn	*two lunches*

Human nouns ending in -eh/-ah form their dual by dropping -eh/-ah and adding -atayn:

šaybeh	*old man*	→	šaybatayn	*two old men*
xaliifeh	*Caliph*	→	xaliifatayn	*two Caliphs*
nazġah	*liar*	→	nazġatayn	*two liars*

If the masculine noun ends in /-u/ or /-w/ it drops /-u/ or /-w/ and adds /-wayn/:

ʕadu(w)	*enemy*	→	ʕaduwayn	*two enemies*
ʕuḏ̣u	*member*	→	ʕuḏ̣wayn	*two members*
ʔabu	*father*	→	abwayn	*two fathers*

B. Feminine Nouns

Feminine nouns that do not end with -eh/-ah form their dual by adding /-ayn/:

faras	*mare*	→	farasayn	*two mares*
sikkiin	*knife*	→	sikkiinayn	*two knives*
saykal	*motorcycle*	→	saykalayn	*two motorcycles*
naar	*fire*	→	naarayn	*two fires*
rijl	*foot; leg*	→	rijlayn	*two feet; two legs*

If they end with -eh/-ah, their dual is formed by dropping -eh/-ah and adding /-atayn/; if they end with /-h/, they drop /-h/ before /-tayn/ is added:

ḥareeweh	*bride*	→	ḥareewatayn	*two brides*
ṭabiineh	*second wife*	→	ṭabiinatayn	*two second wives*
madraseh	*school*	→	madrasatayn	*two schools*
nuxreh	*nose*	→	nuxratayn	*two noses*
ṣalaah	*prayer*	→	ṣalaatayn	*two prayers*
šaah	*nanny goat*	→	šaatayn	*two nanny goats*

10.2.3 Plural

There are two kinds of plurals of nouns in SA: sound plurals and broken plurals. Sound plurals are of two kinds: sound masculine and sound feminine plurals.

10.2.3.1 Sound Plurals

A. Sound Masculine

Most sound masculine plural nouns refer to male human beings or a group in which there is at least one male. Sound masculine plurals are formed by suffixing /-iin/ to the singular noun, sometimes with appropriate stem changes. Sound masculine plural nouns are of a variety of patterns among which the following are the most frequent:

1. Nouns of Participle Origin

   Active and passive participles, derivation and meaning, are discussed in 11.4. The following are only examples:

Singular	Plural	
mṭallib	mṭallibiin	*beggar*
muslim	muslimiin	*Moslem*
muʔmin	muʔminiin	*believer*
ṣaaʔim	ṣaaʔimiin	*one who feasts*
mṭabbin	mṭabbiniin	*polygamist*

2. Nisbah Nouns[40]

   All nisbah nouns end with -i or -iy, which is rarely heard. The plural of these nouns takes /-y/ or /-yy-/ before /-iin/ is added. /-yy/ is less commonly used; /-y-/ is adopted throughout.

Singular	Plural	
yamani	yamaniyiin	*from Yemen*
ʕumaani	ʕumaaniyiin	*Omani*
ṣanʕaani	ṣuʕaaniyiin	*from San'a*
suʕuudi	suʕuudiyiin	*Saudi*
ðamaari	ðamaariyiin	*from Dhamar*
gaṭari	gaṭariyiin	*from Qatar*
kuwayti	kuwaytiyiin	*Kuwaiti*

3. Occupational Nouns[41]

mibtariʕ	mibtariʕiin	*dancer*
jazzaar	jazzaariin	*butcher*
mudallik	mudallikiin	*masseur*
gaššaam	gaššaamiin	*greengrocer*
ʕammaar	ʕammaariin	*builder*
musabbir	musabbiriin	*(food) caterer*
mudarris	mudarrisiin	*teacher*

4. Diminutive Nouns[42]

Almost all sound masculine diminutive nouns are of adjective origin and of the /fuʕayyil/ pattern. They take the /-iin/ suffix for their plural forms:

zuġayyir	zuġayyiriin	*tiny*
ḥubayyib	ḥubayyibiin	*sweetheart*
ruxayyiṣ	ruxayyiṣiin	*very cheap*

B. Sound Feminine

Sound feminine plural nouns are formed by adding /-aat/ to the singular; if the singular ends in -eh/-ah, -eh/-ah is omitted before adding /-aat/. It is used for the following classes of nouns:

1. Those referring to female human beings:

yamaniyeh	yamaniyaat	*Yemeni*
musabbireh	musabbiraat	*(food)caterer*
mudallikeh	mudallikaat	*masseuse*
daktoorah	daktooraat	*doctor*
ʔamriikiyeh	ʔamriikiyaat	*American*
mudiireh	mudiraat	*director*

A few nouns that belong to this category are irregular, e.g.:

ʔuxt	xawaat	*sister*
bint	banaat	*girl; daughter*
keelu	keelaat	*kilogram*

2. Most feminine singular nouns ending in -eh/-ah:

luġah	luġaat	*language*
saaʕah	saaʕaat	*hour; clock*
baṭṭaaniyeh	baṭṭaaniyaat	*blanket*
sayyaarah	sayyaaraat	*car*

Included here are the following classes of nouns: unit, instance, verbal, and nouns of participle origin:

firsikeh	*a peach*	firsikaat	*individual peaches*
bayḏ̣ah	*an egg*	bayḏ̣aat	*individual eggs*
bagarah	*a cow*	bagaraat	*individual cows*
buṭaaṭah	*a potato*	buṭaaṭaat	*individual potatoes*
gabṣah	*a pinch*	gabṣaat	*pinches*
wagfeh	*posture*	wagfaat	*postures*
muxaabarah	*telephone conversation*	muxaabaraat	*telephone conversations*
stigaaleh	*resignation*	stigaalaat	*resignations*

The feminine nouns /madraseh/ 'school', /layleh/ 'night', and /madiineh/ 'city' take broken plural forms (see 10.2.3.2). The plural of /saneh/ 'year' is the irregular /sanawaat/.

3. Some masculine nouns including nouns of foreign origin.

maṭaar	maṭaaraat	*airport*
ṭalab	ṭalabaat	*application*
jawaaz	jawaazaat	*passport*
baaṣ	baaṣaat	*bus*
kabat	kabataat	*cupboard*
galaṣ	galaṣaat	*glass*
kandeešin	kandeešinaat	*air conditioning unit*
ʔaryil	ʔaryilaat	*aerial*

10.2.3.2 Broken Plurals

Broken plurals are formed from the singular by changing the internal structure of the word, not by adding suffixes as in the case of sound plurals. There are a number of pluralizing patterns, a few of which can be predicted from the singular pattern, but in most cases it is very difficult if not impossible to deduce the plural pattern from the singular. For this reason, the plurals of nouns should be learned individually as they are encountered. The following are the most common broken plural patterns of nouns of triradical roots:

1. ʔafʕaal

The great majority of nouns with this plural pattern have singular patterns as /faʕl/, /fuʕl/, /faʕal/. Some singular forms have weak middle radicals or final (identical) doubled consonants.

Singular	Plural	
baab	ʔabwaab	*door*
xaal	ʔaxwaal	*maternal uncle*
biir	ʔaabaar	*well*
diik	ʔadyaak	*rooster*
diin	ʔadyaan	*religion*
kuut	ʔakwaat	*coat*
yawm	ʔayyaam	*day*
muus	ʔamwaas	*razor blade*

Singular	Plural	
jadd	ʔajdaad	*grandfather*
sinn	ʔasnaan	*tooth*
ʔab	ʔaabaaʔ	*father*
gurṭ	ʔagraaṭ	*earring*
ḥawð̣	ʔaḥwaað̣	*trough*
gawl	ʔagwaal	*saying*
yawm	ʔayyaam	*day*
ʔiðn	ʔaaðaan	*ear*

2. fuʕuul

Most nouns of this plural pattern have a singular pattern as /faʕl/.

raʔs	ruʔuus	*head*
ʔaṣl	ʔuṣuul	*origin*
ḥarb	ḥuruub	*war*
jayš	juyuuš	*army*
mahr	muhuur	*dower*
sagf	suguuf	*ceiling*
farð̣	furuuð̣	*religious duty*
faṣl	fuṣuul	*season*

baṭn	buṭuun	*belly*
farg	furuug	*difference*
bayt	buyuut	*house*
ʕayn	ʕuyuun	*eye*
galb	guluub	*heart*
jayb	juyuub	*pocket*
malik	muluuk	*king*
šaahid	šuhuud	*witness*
šarṭ	šuruuṭ	*stipulation, condition*
tays	tuyuus	*billy goat*
dars	duruus	*lesson*
hindi	hunuud	*Indian*

3. faʕaalil

An alternative pattern is /faʕaaʔil/. Most singulars of this plural pattern are (1) feminine nouns with the feminine ending -eh/-ah[43] and are characterized by the long vowel /-ii-/ between the second and the third radicals or by the long vowel /-aa-/ between the first and the second radicals and (2) quadriliterals. Examples:

gabiili[44]	gabaayil	*mountaineer*
jariideh	jaraaʔid	*newspaper*
dagiigah	dagaaʔig	*minute*
kaniiseh	kanaaʔis	*church*
faakihah	fawaakih	*fruit*
bayrag	bayaarig	*flag*
bašmag	bašaamig	*sandals*
darzan	daraazin	*dozen*
sunbuk	sanaabik	*sailboat*
farmaleh	faraamil	*brake*
ḥadiigah	ḥadaaʔig	*garden*
ṭabiineh	ṭabaaʔin	*second wife*
naṣiiḥah	naṣaaʔiḥ	*advice*
raaʔiḥah	rawaaʔiḥ	*scent*
ʕajuuz(eh)	ʕajaaʔiz	*old lady*
šiigaareh	šagaayir	*cigarette*
gunṭurah	ganaaṭir	*shoes*
gumgumi	gamaagim	*motor oil can*
mušguri	mašaagir	*flowers worn in the hair*
daaʔirah	dawaaʔir	*department*

4. faʕaaliil

A. This has the rare variant pattern /fiʕaaliil/. Some nouns of this pattern have the singular /fiʕlaan/ or /fuʕlaan/.

bustaan	bisaatiin	*orchard*
diinaar	danaaniir	*dinar*
diiwaan	dawaawiin	*living room*
dukkaan	dakaakiin	*shop*
duulaab	diwaaliib	*wardrobe*
finjaan	fanaajiin	*cup*
fustaan	fasaatiin	*dress*
sirwaal	saraawiil	*baggy pants*

B. Some others have the singular pattern /faʕliil/ or /fiʕliil/.

dahliiz	dahaaliiz	*corridor*
sikkiin	sakaakiin	*knife*
gandiil	ganaadiil	*light bulb*
barmiil	baraamiil	*barrel*

C. Some others have various singular patterns:

ḥaanuut	ḥawaaniit	*shop*
ṣanduug	ṣanaadiig	*box*
garguuš	garaagiiš	*scarf*
faanuus	fawaaniis	*lantern*
šayṭaan	šayaaṭiin	*devil*
tannuur	tanaaniir	*bread baking oven*
gaanuun	gawaaniin	*law*
gaaruurah	gawaariir	*bottle*
faatuurah	fawaatiir	*invoice*
sulṭaan	salaaṭiin	*Sultan*

Note that most of the nouns belonging to this plural pattern have quadriliteral roots.

5. mafaaʕil

No variants of this pattern have been recorded. Most singular nouns of this plural pattern have patterns as maffal/maffil and maffaleh/maffalah.

matfal	mataafil	*spittoon*
mawtar	mawaatir	*car*
maʕgam	maʕaagim	*threshold*
maktab	makaatib	*office*
maṭraf	maṭaarif	*ladle*
maġṭas	maġaaṭis	*plunge bath*
mafraj	mafaarij	*reception room*
mašfar	mašaafir	*lip*
mawlid	mawaalid	*birthday*
mawgif	mawaagif	*parking place*
madraseh	madaaris	*school*
madaaʕah	madaayiʕ	*water pipe*
mazharah	mazaahir	*vase*
mabsarah	mabaasir	*eyeglasses*
maʔdubeh	maʔaadib	*banquet*
mablaġ	mabaaliġ	*sum of money*
mabna	mabaani	*building*
matka	mataaki	*cushion, pad*
matḥaf	mataaḥif	*museum*
madxal	madaaxil	*entrance*

Note that almost all the nouns above are either instrumental[45] or locative nouns.[46]

6. fiʕlaan

This has the variant pattern /fuʕlaan/. The singular patterns of the nouns of this plural pattern are various:

xuzgi	xizgaan	*hole*
ʕuudi	ʕiidaan	*stick*
duudi	diidaan	*worm*
ḥanaš	ḥinšaan	*snake*
daraj	dirjaan	*stairway*
ðubbi	ðubbaan	*fly*
ʔaʕwar	ʕiwraan	*one-eyed person*
agð̣aʕ	guð̣ʕaan	*bald*
ṭaaseh	ṭiisaan	*drum*

faʔr	fiiraan	*mouse*
faas	fiisaan	*adz*
gaaʕ	giiʕaan	*quarter (of a city)*
ṭaagah	ṭiigaan	*window*
balad	buldaan	*country*
ʔaʕjam	ʕijmaan	*dumb*
ʔaʕma	ʕimyaan	*blind person*
ġazaal	ġizlaan	*deer*
waadi	widyaan	*valley*

7. fuʕal

No variants of this pattern have been recorded. Most singular nouns of this plural pattern are of the pattern /fuʕleh ~ fuʕlah/:

ʔusrah	ʔusar	*family*
bugšeh	bugaš	*parcel*
dawleh	duwal	*government*
fuuṭah	fuwaṭ	*towel*
gubbeh	gubab	*dome*
šuggah	šugag	*apartment*
munḥah	munaḥ	*grant*
sunneh	sunan	*Sunna*

8. fiʕal

Most nouns of this pattern have the singular pattern as /fiʕleh ~ fiʕlah/ or /faʕleh ~ faʕlah/.

jirbeh	jirab	*land*
ʔibreh	ʔibar	*needle*
mihneh	mihan	*profession*
biimeh	biyam	*warranty*
daymeh	diyam	*Yemeni kithchen*
gaṣʕah	giṣaʕ	*small can*
silʕah	silaʕ	*commodity*

9. mafaaʕiil

No variants of this pattern have been recorded. Most singular nouns of this plural pattern have patterns as /mafʕuul/ or /mifʕaal/.

majnuun	majaaniin	*crazy person*
mandiil	manaadiil	*handkerchief*
mawð̣uuʕ	mawaað̣iiʕ	*subject*
mawʕid	mawaaʕiid	*appointment*
miizaan	mawaaziin	*scales*
maydaan	mayaadiin	*field*
maktuub	makaatiib	*letter*
maṣruuf	maṣaariif	*expense*
maṭluub	maṭaaliib	*requirement*
miftaaḥ	mafaatiiḥ	*key*
mixzaan	maxaaziin	*store room*
mismaar	masaamiir	*nail*

10. fuʕl

Most singular nouns of this plural pattern are adjectives of color and defect of the pattern /ʔafʕal/.

ʔadran	durn	*deaf*
ʔaltag	lutg	*stammerer*
ʔaʕraj	ʕurj	*lame*
ʔaṣnaj	ṣunj	*dumb*
ʔaswad	suud	*black*
ʔaṣfar	ṣufr	*yellow*
ʔaxð̣ar	xuð̣r	*green*
ʔazrag	zurg	*blue*
ʔaḥmar	ḥumr	*red*
ʔabyað̣	biið̣	*white*
daar	duur	*house*
faarisiy	furs	*Iranian*
turkiy	turk	*Turk*
kurdiy	kurd	*Kurd*

11. fuʕalaaʔ

Almost all singular nouns of this plural pattern have the pattern /faʕiil/ and they are human nouns. Most of them indicate titles of professionals:

raʔiis	ruʔasaaʔ	*president; head of state*
ḥakiim	ḥukamaaʔ	*doctor; wise person*
ʔamiir	ʔumaraaʔ	*prince; title of princes of a ruling house*
fagiih	fugahaaʔ	*jurisprudent; learned person*
kafiil	kufalaaʔ	*guarantor; sponsor*
šariif	šurafaaʔ	*honest, respectable person; sherif (title)*
kariim	kuramaaʔ	*generous person*
fagiir	fugaraaʔ	*poor person*
ġariim	ġuramaaʔ	*litigant; creditor*
safiir	sufaraaʔ	*ambassador*
šariik	šurakaaʔ	*partner*

12. fuʕuul

Most nouns of this plural pattern have a singular pattern as /faʕl/.

bank	bunuuk	*bank*
ṣaff	ṣufuuf	*class(room)*
raʔs	ruʔuus	*head*
najm	nujuum	*star*
ṣadr	ṣuduur	*bosom*
bayt	buyuut	*house*
xaṭṭ	xuṭuuṭ	*letter*
ḍ̄ayf	ḍ̄uyuuf	*guest*
hindi	hunuud	*Indian*
baṭn	buṭuun	*belly*
malik	muluuk	*king*
dars	duruus	*lesson*

13. fiʕaal

This plural pattern has the variants /fʕaal/ or /fuʕaal/. Most adjectives of the /faʕiil/ pattern have this plural pattern.

kabiir	kibaar ~ kubaar	*big; old (age)*
ṣaġiir	ṣiġaar ~ ṣuġaar ~ zuġaar	*small; young (age)*
gaṣiir	giṣaar ~ guṣaar	*short*
rajjaal	rijaal	*man*
daluw	dlaaw	*bucket*
jamal	jimaal	*camel*
jabal	jibaal	*mountain*
rabḥ	rubaaḥ	*monkey*
gaḥbeh	giḥaab	*prostitute*
mareh	nisaaʔ	*woman*
ʔunθa	ʔinaaθ	*female*

14. fawaaʕil

Most singular nouns of this plural pattern are (1) feminine nouns with the feminine ending -eh/-ah and are characterized by the long vowel /-aa-/ between the first and the second radicals, and (2) nouns with three consonants and a long vowel after the first consonant:

šaariʕ	šawaariʕ	*street*
jaamiʕ	jawaamiʕ	*mosque*
šaarib	šawaarib	*moustache*
ʕaaʔileh	ʕawaayil	*family*
gaafileh	gawaafil	*caravan*
jaanib	jawaanib	*side*
ṭaabig	ṭawaabig	*floor, flat*
dawsari	dawaasir	*belonging to the Dosari tribe*
dawmari	dawaamir	*belonging to the Domari tribe*
ʕansi	ʕanaawis	*belonging to the Ansi tribe*
saʕwani	saʕaawin	*belonging to the village of Saʔwan*

15. fuʕʕaal

This pattern has the variant pattern of /fiʕʕaal/. Almost all nouns of this plural pattern are occupational nouns,[47] and their singular forms are of the /faaʕil/ pattern.

ḥaakim	ḥukkaam	*ruler*
ḥaaris	ḥurraas	*guard*
ḥajj	ḥijjaaj	*pilgrim*
jaahil	jihhaal	*child*
kaatib	kuttaab	*clerk*
saakin	sukkaan	*inhabitant*
taajir	tujjaar	*merchant*
ṭaalib	ṭullaab	*student*
kaafir	kuffaar	*heathen*
zaaʔir	zuwwaar	*visitor*

16. faʕaali

No variants of this pattern have been recorded. Some singular nouns of this plural pattern are of the pattern /fuʕli ~ fiʕli/.

kursi	karaasi	*chair*
buuri	bawaari	*trumpet*
kitli	kataali	*tea kettle*
baliyyeh	balaawi	*misfortune*
daahiyeh	dawaahi	*calamity*
janbiyeh	janaabi	*dagger*
ḥuzwiyeh	ḥazaawi	*anecdote*
saahi	sawaahi	*absent minded*

17. ʔafʕul

No variants of this pattern have been recorded. Some singular nouns of this plural pattern have the patterns /faʕl/ or /fiʕl/.

nafs	ʔanfus	*soul*
saṭḥ	ʔasṭuḥ	*surface*
rijl	ʔarjul	*foot*
šaṭr	ʔasṭur	*part, portion*
šahr	ʔašhur	*month*
ʕimaameh	ʔaʕmum	*turban*

18. ʔafʕileh

This pattern has the variant pattern of /ʔafʕilah/.[48] Most singular nouns of this plural pattern have the pattern /fiʕaal/.

silaaḥ	ʔasliḥah	*weapon*
dawaaʔ	ʔadwiyeh	*medicine*
niðaam	ʔanðimeh	*order*
karš	ʔakriš eh	*belly*
jibaaʔ	ʔajbiyeh	*ceiling, roof*
ʕamuud	ʔaʕmideh	*pillar*

19. ʔafaaʕil

The following plural patterns (19-35) are of limited membership; only a few examples have been recorded.

ʔajnabi	ʔajaanib	*foreigner*
ʔuṣbuʕ	ʔaṣaabiʕ	*finger*
gariib	ʔagaarib	*relative*
ʔarð̣	ʔaraað̣i	*land*

20. fiʕaal

baḥr	biḥaar	*sea*
balad	bilaad	*country*
gafaṣ	gifaaṣ	*package*
gahwah	ghaaw	*coffee*

21. faʕiil/fiʕiil

ḥimaar	ḥamiir	*jackass*
mareh	ḥariim	*woman*
tanakeh	tiniik	*tin container*
šamṭa	šimiiṭ	*suitcase*
ʕabd	ʕabiid	*slave*
jamneh	jimiin	*coffee pot*

22. faʕaalileh/faʕaliilah

ṣaydali	ṣayaadileh	*pharmacist*
daktoor	dakaatirah	*doctor*

23. ʔafʕilaaʔ

ṭabiib	ʔaṭibbaaʔ	*medical doctor*
nabi	ʔanbiyaaʔ	*prophet*

24. fuʕaah

gaaḍ̱i	guḍ̱aah	*judge*
šaagi	šugaah	*laborer*

25. fuʕʕal

ṣummaaṭah	ṣummaṭ	*men's headgear*
šamiiz	šummaz	*shirt*

Section Eleven

11. NOUN MODIFIERS

11.1 Construct Phrases[49]

A noun construct is a construction composed of two noun phrases syntactically bound together. The first element consists of a noun which must always be indefinite in form. The entire construction is definite or indefinite in accordance with the second element, which can be a single noun or a noun phrase:

gaṣʕat ṭamaaṭiis	*a can of tomatoes or a tomato can*
gaṣʕat a-ṭamaaṭiis	*the can of tomatoes or the tomato can*
gaṣʕat ṭamaaṭiis kabiirah	*a large tomato can*
gaṣʕat ṭamaaṭiis ar-rajjaal	*the man's can of tomatoes or the man's tomato can, the tomato can of the man*

The second noun may be another noun construct or a series of constructs:

bayt ʔimaam al-jaamiʕ	*the house of the Imam of the mosque*
bayt ʔimaam jaamiʕ aš-šuhadaaʔ	*the house of the Imam of the Mosque of Martyrs*

What determines definiteness or indefiniteness in a noun construct is the second element. If the second element is definite, the first one is "treated as definite";[50] if it is indefinite, the first one is indefinite also:

maktabat jaamiʕ kabiirah	*a big mosque library*
maktabat al-jaamiʕ al-kabiirah	*the big mosque library*

If both elements of a noun construct have the same gender, structural ambiguity results:

ḥammaam al-maydaan al-kabiir	*the bath of the big square,the big bath of the square*
ʔumm ḥareeweh ḥaaliyeh	*the mother of a beautiful bride,the beautiful mother of a bride*

This type of structural ambiguity is usually resolved by the use of /ḥagg/ 'belonging to, characteristic of':

ʔal-ḥammaam ḥagg al-maydaan al-kabiir	*the bath of the big square*
ʔal-ḥammaam al-kabiir ḥagg al-maydaan	*the big bath of the square*

Noun constructs are classified as "verb-derived" (i.e., the underlying structure contains a verb), or, simply, "derived" and "ordinary" (i.e., all others). In the following analysis the meanings of ordinary and derived noun constructs are defined in terms of their underlying structures:

11.1.1 Ordinary Noun Constructs

1. Possession
   a. alienable

garguuš al-bint	*the girl's scarf*

Here /al-bint/ 'the girl' is a concrete noun semantically capable of owning /garguuš/ 'scarf.' The whole phrase is related to /ʔal-garguuš ḥagg al-bint/ 'the scarf belongs to, is for the girl.' Other examples:

galam al-walad	*the boy's pen(cil)*
zalaṭ aš-šaagi	*the laborer's money*
gunṭurat ʔibni	*my son's shoes*
ʕuṣyet šaybeh	*an old man's cane*
bilzigi l-ḥareeweh	*the bride's bracelet*

   b. inalienable

wašš al-jaahil	*the child's face*
ðanab al-kalb	*the dog's tail*
raʔs al-ḥanaš	*the head of the snake*
janaaḥ al-ḥamaami	*the pigeon's wing*
riiš ad-diik	*the rooster's feathers*

2. Naming

madiinat ṣanʕa	*the city of San'a*
xaliij ʕadan	*the Gulf of Aden*
bani ḥšayš	*the sons of (i.e., family of) Hushaysh*
jabal ʕaybaan	*Mount Ayban*
waaḥat al-buraymi	*the Buraimi Oasis*

The first noun is usually a deletable geographical noun, and the second is a proper noun. /madiinat ṣanʕa/ is derived from /al-madiineh ʔusumha ṣanʕa/ 'the name of the city is San'a'.

3. Container — Contents

finjaan bunn	*here: a cup of coffee, not a coffee cup*
kitli šaahi	*here: a kettle of tea, not a tea kettle*
gaṣʕat ṭamaaṭiis	*here: a can of tomatoes, not a tomato can*
gumgumi saliiṭ	*here: a can of motor oil, not a motor oil can*
galaṣ meeʔ	*here: a glass of water, not a water glass*

The first noun is a noun denoting some kind of receptacle, and the second is a concrete noun of material. /finjaan bunn/ is derived from /finjaan min al-bunn/.

4. Composition

xaatim ðahab	*a gold ring*
bilzigi fiḍḍah	*a silver bracelet*
šamiiz ṣuuf	*a wool shirt*
bašmag blaastiik	*(a pair of) plastic slippers*
kursi jild	*a leather chair*

The first noun is a concrete noun, and the second is a noun of material /xaatim ðahab/ is derived from: /ʔal-xaatim min ðahab/ 'the ring is made of gold.'

5. Qualification

ʔayyaam(aat) al-bard	*the days of the cold, cold days*
ʔayyaam(aat) al-ḥama	*the days of hot weather, hot days*
kalaam aṣ-ṣudg	*the words of truth, truthful words*

This type of construct reflects a relationship wherein the second noun describes the first. The second noun is an abstract noun with a non-specified (generic) determiner. The construct formation of N[51] + N can be paraphrased by N + adjective.

6. Limitation

kitli šaahi	*a tea kettle*
madrasat banaat	*a girls' school*
šajarat firsik	*a peach tree*
gafaṣ šagaayir	*a cigarette package*
maaʕ baḥr	*water of a sea, sea water*

The second noun limits or restricts the first one. The formation of N + N can be paraphrased by N is for N or is of the class (or characteristic) of N.

11.1.2 Verb-Derived Noun Constructs

Verb-derived noun constructs have as their first element a verbal noun, an active or a passive participle[52] or a locative noun, and as their second element the agent or the goal of the action. They show the following major grammatical relationships:

1. Intransitive Verb and Subject

$\text{Verb}_{\text{intra}}$ — Subj.

kuθrat an-naas *the great number of people*	→	ʔan-naas yukθuruw *People increase.*
ziyaadat al-maʕaaš *the increase in salary*	→	ʔal-maʕaaš yaziid. *The salary increases.*
ṭuul al-wagt *the whole time*	→	ʔal-wagt yaṭuul. *Time lingers (long).*
gillat al-gaat *the scarcity of qat*	→	ʔal-gaat yigill. *Qat becomes scarce.*

2. Transitive Verb and Object

tadriib al-junuud	*the training of soldiers*
tarbiyat al-jihhaal	*the bringing up of children*
taxziin al-gaat	*the chewing of qat*
(ʔi)stinṭaag al-muttaham	*the interrogation of the accused*
tiniḥḥa š-šugaah	*the termination of workmen*

Constructs that belong to this category might be ambiguous: if /tadriib al-junuud/ is related to /x yudarrib al-junuud/ 'x trains the soldiers,' then the grammatical relationship is Vtra obj.; but if it is related to /ʔal-junuud yudarribuw X/, then the construction is related to V_{intra} —subj.

3. Subject and Object

a. sub. – obj.

saarig as-saaʕah *the watch thief*	→	ʔas-saarig yisrig as-saaʕah. *The thief steals the watch.*
sawwaag as-sayyaarah *the car driver*	→	ʔas-sawwaag yisuug as-sayyaarah. *The driver drives the car.*
mursil ar-risaaleh *the letter sender*	→	ʔal-mursil yirsil ar-risaaleh. *The sender sends the letter.*

b. obj. subj.

muwaððaf al-ḥukuumeh *the government employee*	→	ʔal-ḥukuumeh tuwaððif al-muwaððaf. *The government employs the employee.*
mabʕuuθ al-wizaarah *the delegate of the ministry*	→	ʔal-wizaarah tabʕaθ al-mabʕuuθ. *The ministry sends the delegate.*

4. Noun (loc.) – Subj.

matka r-rijaal *the place where men sit (lit., "lean") and chew qat*	→	ʔar-rijaal yitkuw fi l-matka. *The men sit (lit. "lean") and chew qat in the matka.*
magyal an-nisaaʔ *the place where women hold a siesta and chew qat*	→	ʔan-nisaaʔ yigayyilayn fi l-magyal. *The women hold a siesta and chew qat in the magyal.*
majlis aš-šaʕb *the people's council (of state)*	→	ʔaš-šaʕb yijlisuw fi l-majlis. *The people sit in the council room.*
madrasat al-ʔaytaam *the school for orphans*	→	ʔal-ʔaytaam yudrusuw fi l-madraseh. *The orphans study at the school.*

The first noun, N, is a locative noun, which is derived from the underlying intransitive verb:

matka	*(lit. "a place for relaxation and chewing qat"):* /tka/ *to chew qat*
magyal	*(lit. "a place where women hold a siesta and chew qat"):* /gayyal/ *to hold a siesta?*
majlis	*(lit. "a place for sitting"):* /jalas/ *to sit*
madraseh	*(lit., "a place for studying"):* /daras/ *to study*

5. Noun (loc.) — Obj.

ṭaffaayat šiigaareh *an ash tray*	→	maḥall yiṭaffuw fiih aš-šagaayir. *a place where they put out cigarettes*
maʕraḍ malaabis *a display (lit., "an exhibit") of clothes*	→	maḥall yiʕriḍuw fiih al-malaabis *a place where they display clothes*
maṣnaʕ blaastiik *the plastics factory*	→	maḥall yiṣnaʕuw fiih al-blaastiik *a place where they make plastics*
maṣnaʕ ganaaṭir *a shoe factory*	→	maḥall yiṣnaʕuw fii ganaaṭir *a place where they make shoes*

11.2 Elative Constructs

An elative construct is one in which the first element is an elative adjective.[53] This form, derived from the corresponding (positive) adjective, is termed in Arabic grammar an elative adjective. It is an adjective of rating, i.e., 'the best one,' 'the worst one,' 'the most beautiful one,' etc.

ʔaḥsan rajjaal	*the best man*
ʔaḥsan ar-rijaal	*the best (of the) men*

An elative may be used in construct with either an indefinite singular or plural noun, or a definite plural noun:

ʔaḥsan rajjaal	*the best man*
ʔaḥsan rijaal	*the best men*
ʔaḥsan ar-rijaal	*the best (of the) men*

It is to be noted that an elative used in construct with an indefinite noun is rendered in English as if it were definite as in the first phrase above. /ʔaḥsan rajjaal/ 'the best man' has the same meaning as that expressed by the attributive construction:

ʔar-rijaal al-ʔaḥsan	*the best men*

The last phrase in the examples above is ambiguous with respect to the number of things being described. It means either 'the best one of the men' (partitive) or 'the best who are men'.

The gender and number of an elative construct depend upon its referent, regardless of the following term:

haaða ʔaḥsan ar-rijaal	*This is the best man.*
haaðawlaaʔ ʔaḥsan ar-rijaal	*These are the best men.*

But if the following term is indefinite, gender and number concord depends upon that of the following term:

haaðih ʔaḥla bint	*This is the most beautiful girl.*
haaðawlaaʔ ʔaḥla bintayn	*These are the (two) most beautiful girls (f. dual).*
haaðawlaaʔ ʔaḥla banaat.	*These are the most beautiful girls (f.p.).*

11.3 The Determiner System

11.3.1 The Article Prefix

a. Proper Nouns

Proper nouns in SA include the names of people, places, books, films, newspapers, etc. Proper nouns have a particular syntactic role in SA and literary Arabic. They do not need any marking for definiteness, for they are definite by virtue of being proper nouns. There are two subclasses of proper nouns--one that takes the article prefix /ʔal-/ and another that does not. Whether proper nouns appear with or without the article prefix is a matter of lexical etymology, and a realization of two different states of definiteness. It is interesting to note that the article prefix which appears with some proper nouns is comparable to the /the/ which forms a part of such English phrases as The Rockies, The Mississippi, The Sudan, etc.[54]

/ʔal-/ has shapes depending upon the environment in which it is used: in an initial position it is /ʔal-/; in a post-consonantal position the glottal stop of /ʔal-/ is dropped, e.g., in /min al-yaman/ 'from Yemen', /tayyik al-mareh/ 'that woman', etc. In a post vocalic position /ʔa/ is dropped from /ʔal-/, e.g., /haaða l-kitaab/ 'this book'.
Before nouns or adjectives beginning with /t, θ, ð, r, z, s, š, ṣ, ṭ, ð̣, l, n, the /l-/ is assimilated:

ʔaš-šams	*the sun*
ʔað-ðahab	*the gold*
ʔaθ-θaluuθ	*Tuesday*
ʔaṣ-ṣulṭaan	*the Sultan*
ʔad-dimm	*the cat*
ʔaṭ-ṭamaaṭiis	*the tomatoes*

11.3.2 Quantifiers

11.3.2.1 Numerals

11.3.2.1.1 Cardinals

Cardinals in SA constitute a subclass of nouns and modify only count nouns. They are divided into the following categories:

a. Cardinals1

/waaḥid/ 'one' and /ʔiθnayn/ have the feminine forms /waaḥideh/ and /θintayn/. They obligatorily follow the noun they modify and show full agreement with it:

rajjaal waaḥid	*one man (m.s.)*
rajjaalayn iθnayn	*two men (m. dual)*
bint waaḥideh	*one girl (f.s.)*
bintayn θintayn	*two girls (f.dual)*
ʔar-rajjaal al-waaḥid	*the one man*
ʔar-rajjaalayn al-iθnayn	*the two men*
ʔal-bint al-waaḥideh	*the one girl*
ʔal-bintayn aθ-θintayn	*the two girls*

It was mentioned in 10.2.2 that /ʔθinayn rijaal/ 'two men' and /θintayn banaat/ 'two girls' are more commonly used than /rajjaalayn iθnayn/ and /bintayn θintayn/.Similarly /ʔar-rijaal al-iθnayn/ 'the two men' and /ʔal-banaant aθ-θintayn/ 'the two girls' are more commonly used than /ʔar-rajjaalayn al-iθnayn/ and /ʔal-bintayn aθ-θintayn/. /waaḥid/ and /ʔiθnayn/ are used in counting and in an answer to the question, how many?:

kam waaḥid tištiy?	*How many (ones) do you want?*
waaḥid ʔaw iθnayn.	*One or two.*

/waaḥid/ and /ʔiθnayn/ are used in conjunction with a noun for emphasis, as in /rajjaal waaḥid/ 'one man' and /nisaaʔ θintayn/ 'two women.' The form /ʔaḥad/ is used in a question or a negative statement meaning 'anybody, somebody' as in /šii bih ʔaḥad haana?/ 'Is there anybody here?' /laa·maa bih ʔaḥad haana/ 'No, there isn't anybody here.'

b. Cardinals2

The Cardinals 3-10 have two forms: one used independently (i.e., not followed by a noun), such as in counting, and a tied form used with a noun:

Independent Form

θalaaθeh	*three*
ʔarbaʕah	*four*
xamseh	*five*
sitteh	*six*
sabʕah	*seven*
θamaaniyeh	*eight*
tisʕah	*nine*
ʕašarah	*ten*

Tied Form

If the numeral is used with a following noun, that noun is plural[55]; the cardinal used has the following forms:

θalaaθ/θalaaθeh	*three*
ʔarbaʕ/ʔarbaʕah	*four*
xams/xamseh	*five*
sitt/sitteh	*six*
sabʕ/sabʕah	*seven*
θamaan/θamaaniyeh	*eight*
tisʕ/tisʕah	*nine*
ʕašar/ʕašarah	*ten*

The long vowel /-aa-/ in /θalaaθ/ is often shortened to /-a-/ in normal speech; final /-θ/ is usually assimilated to a following dental, and final /-tt/ of /sitt/ 'six' is assimilated to a following /t/ and /d/. The transcription in this instance shows the word intact, without assimilation.

θalaθ[56]/θalaaθeh	ʔawlaad	*three boys*
θalaθ[57]/θalaaθeh	dakaatirah	*three doctors*
θalaθ[58]/θalaaθeh	ṭamaaṭiis	*three tomatoes*
θalaθ[59]/θalaaθeh	ṭiigaan	*three windows*

The cardinals 3-10 which belong to this category are in a construct form with the noun they precede, but unlike noun constructs such numeral nouns may be definitized by the prefixation of the article /ʔal-/ and can be modified by a demonstrative pronoun, pre-posed or post-posed to the whole phrase:

sitteh ʔawlaad	*six boys*
ʔas-sitteh ʔawlaad	*the six boys*
ʔal-ʔawlaad as-sitteh	*the six boys*
haaðawla s-sitteh ʔawlaad	*these six boys*
ʔas-sitteh ʔawlaad haaðawla	*these six boys*

Most of the days of the week are derived from cardinals 1-5:

ʔas-sabt	*Saturday*
ʔal-ʔaḥad	*Sunday*
ʔal-ʔiθnayn	*Monday*
ʔaθ-θaluuθ	*Tuesday*
ʔar-rabuuʕ	*Wednesday*
ʔal-xamiis	*Thursday*
ʔal-jumʕah	*Friday*

Telling time makes use of cardinals 1-12; the cardinals used are usually the forms without -eh/-ah, except for /waaḥideh/ 'one'. There are two grammatical constructions in SA for the English construction: "It's . . . o'clock":

ʔas-saaʕah waaḥideh.	saaʕat waaḥideh	*It's one o'clock.*
ʔas-saaʕah θintayn.	saaʕat θintayn	*It's two o'clock.*
ʔas-saaʕah xams.	saaʕat xams	*It's five o'clock.*
ʔas-saaʕah θamaan.	saaʕat θamaan	*It's eight o'clock.*
ʔas-saaʕah ḥdaʕš(ar).	saaʕat ḥdaʕš(ar)	*It's eleven o'clock.*
ʔas-saaʕah θnaʕš(ar).	saaʕat θnaʕš(ar)	*It's twelve o'clock.*

Until some time ago the first construction, i.e., /ʔas-saaʕah . . ./ was more commonly used, but nowadays most anʕaanis use the other construction, especially the younger generation.

c. Cardinals3

The cardinal 11-19 have two forms, an independent form and a tied form:

ḥdaʕš/ḥdaʕšar	*eleven*
θnaʕš/θnaʕšar	*twelve*
θalaṭṭaʕš/alaṭṭaʕšar	*thirteen*
ʔarbaʕṭaʕš/ʔarbaʕṭašar	*fourteen*
xamasṭaʕš/xamisṭaʕšar	*fifteen*
siṭṭaʕš/siṭṭaʕšar	*sixteen*
sabaʕṭaʕš/sabaʕṭaʕšar	*seventeen*
θamanṭaʕš/θamanṭaʕšar	*eighteen*
tisaʕṭaʕš/tisaʕṭaʕšar	*nineteen*

The tied form is usually the form with the ending /-ar/, although the independent form is also used.

The noun counted is singular in form and it is only the numeral that takes the article prefix:

ḥdaʕšar bayt	*eleven houses*
θnaʕšar madraseh	*twelve schools*
siṭṭaʕšar ṭaliy	*sixteen lambs*
ʔal-i-ḥdaʕšar bayt	*the eleven houses*
ʔat-tisaʕṭaʕšar ryaal	*the nineteen riyaals*

d. Cardinals4

With 20, 30, 40 through 90, the noun counted is singular in form as it is after cardinals3. These cardinals3 are invariable and can take the article prefix:

ʕišriin rajjaal	*twenty men*
θalaaθiin baṭṭaaniyeh	*thirty blankets*
ʔarbaʕiin šijareh	*forty trees*
xamsiin šaagi	*fifty workmen*
sittiin ryaal	*sixty riyals*
sabʕiin nafs	*seventy souls*
θamaaniin sayyaarah	*eighty cars*
tisʕiin ṭayr	*ninety birds*
ʔal-ʕišriin rajjaal	*the twenty men*
ʔal-xamsiin ryaal	*the fifty riyals*

Compound numerals from 21 through 99 (except for Cardinals4) are expressed by using the units digit first followed by the tens digit with the conjunction wa[60] 'and' in between:

xamseh wa ʕišriin	*twenty-five*
waaḥid wa xamsiin	*fifty-one*
ʔiθnayn wa tisʕiin	*ninety-two*
θamaaniyeh wa sittiin	*sixty-eight*

The noun modified always follows the whole numeral in SA and is singular:

sitteh wa xamsiin ryaal	*fifty-six riyals*

e. Cardinals5
This category comprises the hundreds 100, 200, 300 through 900. The word for 100 is /miʔah/ (var. miyah) and the dual is /miʔatayn/ (var. miyatayn). The cardinal is invariable (the construct form of /miʔah/ or /miyah/ is /miʔat/ or /miyat/) and it can take the article prefix; the noun modified is singular:

miʔat bayt	*100 houses*
miʔatayn ʕaskariy	*200 soldiers*
θalaθmiʔat šurṭiy	*300 policemen*
ʔarbaʕmiʔat rajjaal	*400 men*
xamasmiʔat madraseh	*500 schools*
sittmiʔat kitaab	*600 books*
sabaʕmiʔat duulaar	*700 dollars*
θamaanmiʔat jaamiʕ	*800 mosques*
tisaʕmiʔat raṭl	*900 pounds*
ʔal-miʔat naagah	*the 100 camels (f.)*
ʔas-sittmiʔat gaaruurah	*the 600 bottles*

Compound numerals from 101 through 199 (except for Cardinals5 are expressed by pre-posing these cardinals followed by wa 'and' to compound numerals from 21 through 99 as was pointed out in Cardinals4:

tisaʕmiyeh wa xamseh wa tisʕiin	*995*

f. Cardinals6

These are the thousands and the millions. /ʔalf/ '1,000' has a dual form /ʔalfayn/ '2,000' and the plural /ʔaalaaf/ 'thousands' which is only used independently; /ʔalf/ is used instead. The thousands from 1000 through 10,000 are given below.

ʔalf	*1,000*
ʔalfayn	*2,000*
θalaaθeh ʔalf	*3,000*
ʔarbaʕah ʔalf	*4,000*
xamseh ʔalf	*5,000*
sitteh ʔalf	*6,000*
sabʕah ʔalf	*7,000*
θamaaniyeh ʔalf	*8,000*
tisʕah ʔalf	*9,000*
ʕašarah ʔalf	*10,000*

Thousands 11,000 through 100,000 are expressed by using the numeral from 11-1,000 plus /ʔalf/ '1,000'.:

ḥdaʕšar ʔalf	*11,000*
sitteh wa xamsiin ʔalf	*56,000*

The word for 1,000,000 is /malyoon/ and its dual form /malyoonayn/ '2,000,000'. Like /ʔaalaaf/ 'thousands' /malaayiin/ 'millions' is only used independently as in /malaayiin min an-naas/ 'millions of people'.:

θalaθmiyat malyoon	*300,000,000*
xamasmiyat malyoon	*500,000,000*

The noun after the thousands and the millions is singular:

miyat ʔalf šajareh	*100,000 trees*
malyoonayn ryaal	*2,000,000 riyals*

Compound numerals in which all or some of the cardinals described above are used are expressed according to the following order:

millions + thousands + hundreds + units
tens
units + tens

Each major component except the first one takes the conjunction /wa/ 'and'.:

xamasmiyat malyoon wa θalaθmiyat ʔalf wa miyatayn wa xamseh	*500,300,205*
xamasmiyat malyoon wa θalaθmiyat ʔalf wa miyatayn wa siaṭṭʕš	*500,300,216*
xamasmiyat malyoon wa θalaθmiyat ʔalf wa miyatayn wa sitteh wa sabʕiin	*500,300,276*

In expressing numbers ending in one or two, the units digit, i.e., one or two, is not normally used but the noun modified is repeated:

miyat ryaal wa ryaal	*101 riyals*
ʔalf layleh wa layleh	*1001 nights*
xamasmiyat duulaar wa duulaarayn	*502 dollars*

11.3.2.1.2 Ordinals

Ordinals are derived from cardinals according to the following formula: $C_1aaC_2iC_3$. In some cases the derivation is irregular.

Cardinal	Ordinal (m.)	Ordinal (f.)
waaḥid	ʔawwal	ʔuula
ʔiθnayn	θaaniy	θaaniyeh
θalaaθeh	θaaliθ	θaaliθeh
ʔarbaʕah	raabiʕ	raabiʕah
xamseh	xaamis	xaamiseh
sitteh	saadis	saadiseh
sabʕah	saabiʕ	saabiʕah
θamaaniyeh	θaamin	θaamineh
tisʕah	taasiʕ	taasiʕah
ʕašarah	ʕaašir	ʕaaširah

Ordinals up to the tenth may be post-posed. From the eleventh upward they are obligatorily post-posed; larger ordinals than the hundreds are rarely used in SA. When ordinals are post-posed, they are used attributively as adjectives, and with adjectival inflection. Ordinals are divided into the following subclasses:

a. Ordinals1
The ordinals /ʔawwal/ 'first' and /ʔaaxir/ 'last' stand in construct with a definite or an indefinite singular or plural noun according to the following rules:

(i) If the meaning is 'the first or last n', then n is singular, indefinite and invariable for gender:

ʔawwal madaaʕah	*the first waterpipe*
ʔawwal jaamiʕ	*the first mosque*
ʔaaxir ḥaanuut	*the last shop*
ʔaaxir saneh	*the last year*

(ii) If the meaning is 'the first or last part of n', then n is inanimate, singular, and definite:

ʔawwal as-saneh	*the first part of the year*
ʔawwal aṣ-ṣayf	*the first part of the summer*
ʔaaxir aṭ-ṭariig	*the last part of the road*
ʔaaxir ʔaš-šaariʕ	*the last part of the street*

(iii) The plurals of /ʔawwal/, /ʔawaaʔil/, and /ʔaaxir/, /ʔawaaxir/, may be pre-posed to inanimate, singular, definite nouns that indicate a 'period of time'. The meaning is 'the first, or last, part of n'.

ʔawaaʔil aṣ-ṣayf	*the first part of the summer*
ʔawaaʔil as-saneh	*the first part of the year*
ʔawaaʔil aš-šahr	*the first part of the month*
ʔawaaxir ar-rabiiʕ	*the last part of the spring*

(iv) The plurals, i.e., /ʔawaaʔil/ and /ʔawaaxir/ have the meaning of 'the first, the last,' if they precede a plural animate noun:

ʔawaaʔil aṭ-ṭullaab	*the first students*
ʔawaaxir al-ʕanaawis	*the last (of the) Ansis*

b. Ordinals2

For ordinals /θaaniy/ – /ʕaašir/ 'second-tenth', the form of the ordinal is uninflected if the noun following is singular and indefinite; the entire construction is definite in meaning:

xaamis yawm	*the fifth day*
xaamis madraseh	*the fifth school*

If, however, the ordinal follows the noun, the entire construction is indefinite and agrees with the noun it modifies in gender:

yawm xaamis	*a fifth day*
madraseh xaamiseh	*a fifth school*

If, however, the ordinal follows the noun, the entire construction is indefinite and agrees with the noun it modifies in gender:

yawm xaamis	*a fifth day*
madraseh xaamiseh	*a fifth school*

The members of these ordinals do not stand in construct with indefinite plural nouns. If the noun they stand in construct with is definite plural, then they are inflected for gender; the construct then has a positive meaning:

xaamis al-jihhaal	*the fifth (one) of the children*
xaamisat al-banaat	*the fifth (one) of the girls*

c. Ordinals3

This class includes ordinals from the eleventh upward. These ordinals are subdivided into the following subclasses:

(i) /ʔal-ḥdaʕš(ar)/ 'the eleventh' through /ʔat-tisaʕṭaʕš/ 'the nineteenth' and /ʔal-ʕišriin/ 'the twentieth', /ʔaθ-θalaaθiin/ 'the thirtieth', /ʔal-ʔarbaʕiin/ 'the fortieth' . . . etc. These ordinals do not show cardinal-ordinal distinction in form but they do in word-order: they obligatorily follow the noun-head. They do not show gender concord:

ʔal-madraseh ʔal-ḥdaʕš	*the eleventh school*
ʔal-walad ʔal-ḥdaʕš	*the eleventh boy*
ʔal-maktabeh ʔal-ʕišriin	*the twentieth library*
ʔaš-šaariʕ al-xamsiin	*the fiftieth street*

(ii) Compound cardinals from the twenty-first through the ninety-ninth are expressed by the ordinals from 1-9 followed by the definite ordinals of the tens digit with the conjunction /wa/ 'and' in between:

ʔal-madraseh ʔal-xamiseh wa ʔal-ʕišriin	*the 25th school*
ʔar-rajjaal at-taasiʕ wa ʔat-tisʕiin	*the 99th man*

11.3.2.2 Non-Numerals

11.3.2.2.1 Partitives

Partitives include nouns designating indefinite amounts and quantities. They do not show any concord with the nouns they modify, but are related to them in a partitive relationship:

ʔaġlab	*most of*
ʔakθar	*most of*
muʕḍ̣am	*majority, most of*
galiil min	*a few of, a little of*
kaθiir min	*a lot of*
ʔal-kaθiir min	*a whole lot of*

They modify a definite plural count noun, or a definite collective or a mass noun. Any of the following may be specified or non--specified in meaning:

ʔaġlab ar-rijaal	*most (of the) men*
ʔakθar al-firsik	*most (of the) peaches*
muʕḍ̣am al-meeʔ	*most of the water*

Each one of the partitives on the left can be pre-posed to any of the nouns on the right: /ʔar-rijaal/ '(the) men' (pl., count), /ʔal-firsik/ '(the) peaches' (coll.), and /ʔal-meeʔ/ '(the) water' (mass). This usage is also extended to nouns indicating size, e.g., /baḥr min al-ʕilm/ 'depth of knowledge', /gaṭrah min al-meeʔ/ 'a drop of water', etc.

/ʔaġlabiyyah/ and /ʔakθariyyah/ 'most, majority' belong to this category of partitives, but they tend to modify a human noun:

ʔaġlabiyyat al-muṭabbiniin	*most (of the) polygamists*
ʔakθariyyat al-miwassidiin	*most (of the) upholsterers*

/baʕð̣/ 'some' modifies either a plural count or a definite non-count noun. In either case, the noun modified may be translated as definite or indefinite:

baʕð̣ ar-rijaal	*some (of the) men*
baʕð̣ rijaal	*some men*
baʕð̣ al-mee?	*some of the water*
baʕð̣ aṭ-ṭamaaṭiis	*some (of the) tomatoes*

11.3.2.2.2 Fractions

Cardinals from 3-5 have fractions derived from them; the pattern is /fuʕl/ or /fuʕul/ The environment for the occurrence of /fuʕl/ or /fuʕul/ could not be defined. Thus, /nuṣṣ/ 'half', /θuluθ/[61] 'one-third', /rubʕ/[62] 'one-fourth', etc.

Cardinal		Fraction	
ʔiθnayn	*two*	nuṣṣ	*half*
θalaaθeh	*three*	θulθ/θiliθ	*one-third*
ʔarbaʕah	*four*	rubʕ/rubiʕ	*one-fourth*
xamseh	*five*	xums/xumus	*one-fifth*
sitteh	*six*	suds/sudus	*one-sixth*
sabʕah	*seven*	subʕ/subuʕ	*one-seventh*
θamaaniyeh	*eight*	θumn/θumun	*one-eighth*
tisʕah	*nine*	tusʕ/tusuʕ	*one-ninth*
ʕašarah	*ten*	ʕušur/ʕušir	*one-tenth*

The fractions /nuṣṣ/ 'half', /θulθ/ 'one-third', /rubʕ/ 'one-fourth', and /xums/ 'one fifth' can be made dual and plural. The plural pattern is /ʔafʕaal/:

nuṣṣ	*half*	→	ʔiθnayn anṣaaṣ/nuṣṣayn	*two-halves*
θulθ	*one-third*	→	ʔiθnayn ʔaθlaaθ/θulθayn	*two-thirds*
rubʕ	*one-quarter*	→	ʔiθnayn arbaaʕ/rubʕayn	*two-fourths*
xums	*one-fifth*	→	ʔiθnayn axmaas/xumsayn	*two-fifths*
suds	*one-sixth*	→	θalaaθat asdaas	*three-sixths*
subʕ	*one-seventh*	→	ʔarbaʕat asbaaʕ	*four-sevenths*

Higher fractions are usually expressed periphrastically with the cardinal numerals and the use of the preposition min 'from':

xamseh min siṭṭaʕš	*five-sixteenths*
xamasṭaʕš min miyeh	*fifteen-hundredths*
sitteh min tisʕah wa sabʕiin	*six seventy-ninths*

11.3.3 Intensifiers

Intensifying quantifiers include /kull/ 'all, whole; every', /jamiiʕ/, /ʕumuum/ 'all, whole, entire', and /nafs/ 'same (very), -self'.

The meaning of /kull/ varies, depending upon whether the following noun is definite or indefinite, singular or plural:

kull dimm	*each (every) cat*
kull ad-dimam	*all (the) cats*
kull madiineh	*each (every) city*
kull al-madiineh	*the whole city*

The total intensifiers /jamiiʕ/ and /ʕumuum/ 'all, whole, entire' modify count and non-count nouns:

jamiiʕ aš-šugaah	*all (of the) workmen*
jamiiʕ an-naas	*all (of the) people*
ʕumuum ad-dawaaʔir	*all (of the) departments*
ʕumuum aṭ-ṭalabah	*all (of the) students*

/nafs/ 'same, -self' is used with a definite common noun, and is ambiguous:

nafs ar-rajjaal	*the same man or the man himself*
nafs an-niseeʔ	*the same women or the women themselves*
nafs al-gaat	*the same qat or the qat itself*

11.3.4 Demonstratives[63]

In addition to the article prefix, another part of the determiner system of SA occurs in pre-modification position. It is the demonstrative pronoun. Members of this limited set of pronouns precede only specified definite nouns, and must agree with the nouns they precede in gender and number:

haaða l-mafraj	*this reception hall (m.s.)*
(cf: haaða mafraj)	*(This is a reception hall.)*
haaði ṭ-ṭaagah	*this window (f.s.)*
haaðawla l-mafrajayn	*these two reception halls (m. dual)*
haaðawla ṭ-ṭaagatayn	*these two windows (f. dual)*
haaðawla l-ʔawlaad	*these boys (m.p.)*
haaðawla aṭ-ṭiigaan	*these windows (f.p.)*

In /haaða walad/ 'this is a boy' the demonstrative /haaða/ 'this' occurs as an independent noun head of the noun phrase which is the entire subject of the sentence. On the other hand, to add emphasis to the semantic force of the demonstrative pronoun, it may follow the noun it modifies with the semantic restrictions on its concord as mentioned above:

ʔal-walad haaða	*this boy*
ʔal-waladayn haaðawla	*these two boys*

A demonstrative pronoun as a nominal modifier never precedes a noun construct. It modifies either N1 or N2. If it modifies N1, it must follow the entire construct:

gurṭ al-ḥareeweh haaða — *this earring of the bride*

If it modifies N2, it may precede or follow it:

gurṭ haaðih al-ḥareeweh	gurṭ al-ḥareeweh haaðih	*the earring of this bride*

Of these two choices the former is the usual order in SA. If the two elements of the construct agree in gender and number, ambiguity results:

θaman al-gaat haaða	*the price of this qat* *this price of the qat*
maktabat al-jaamiʕah haaðih	*the library of this university* *this library of the university*

But /θaman haaða l-gaat/ and /maktabat haaðih al-jaamiʕah/ only mean 'the price of this qat' and 'the library of this university', respectively. The other demonstratives are:

ðayyik/haaḍaak	*that (m.s.)*	tayyik/haaðikka	*that (f.s.)*
haaðawla	*these (m. or f.p.)*	haaðawlaak	*those (m. or f.p.)*

Other alternate forms of the demonstratives are given in 12.3 below.

11.4 Participles

A participle is a verbal adjective depicting its referent as being in a state as a necessary consequence of the event, process or activity designated by the underlying verb. For the purposes of this part of the study we are interested in participles as post-nominal modifiers.

11.4.1 Active Participle

11.4.1.1 Derivation

Form I

Sound: faaʕil

Verb		AP	
labaj	*to hit s.o.*	laabij	*having hit s.o.*
liʕib	*to play*	laaʕib	*having played*
ʕaraf	*to know*	ʕaarif	*knowing, having known*
xatan	*to circumcise*	xaatin	*having circumcised*
ragad	*to sleep*	raagid	*sleeping*
tafal	*to spit*	taafil	*having spat*
wuṣul	*to arrive*	waaṣil	*arriving; having arrived*
gabaṣ	*to pinch*	gaabiṣ	*having pinched*

Defective: faaʕiy

daʕa	*to call, to invite*	daʕiy	*calling, inviting or having called; having invited*
ʕaṣa	*to disobey*	ʕaaṣiy	*disobeying; having disobeyed*
xuṭiy	*to walk*	xaaṭiy	*walking; having walked*
ḥama	*to defend*	ḥaamiy	*defending; having defended*

Hollow: faayiʕ

One of the two patterns, /faaʔiʕ/ and /faayiʕ/, the former is more commonly used.

gaal	*to say*	gaayil	*having said*
xaaf	*to be afraid*	xaayif	*afraid*
saar	*to go; to leave*	saayir	*going; leaving or having gone; having left*
kaal	*to weigh*	kaayil	*having weighed*
ʕaam	*to swim*	ʕaayim	*swimming; floating;having swum*
ṭaaʕ	*to obey*	ṭaayiʕ	*obeying, having obeyed*

The active participle of /jaaʔ/ 'to come' is /jaay/ 'coming; having come' which is a borrowing from other Arabic dialects; most SanʕSaanis use /gaadim/ instead. The active participle of /maat/ 'to die' is the irregular /mayyit/ 'dead; having died'.

Doubled:

šann	*to filter*	šaanin	*having filtered*
ð̣arr	*to harm*	ð̣aarir	*having harmed*
gaṣṣ	*to cut*	gaaṣiṣ	*having cut*
ʕagg	*to groan, moan*	ʕaagig	*having groaned*
mazz	*to squeeze*	maaziz	*having squeezed*
ḥajj	*to go on pilgrimage*	ḥaajij	*having performed pilgrimage*
garr	*to confess*	gaarir	*having confessed*

Hamzated:

ʔakal	*to eat*	ʔaakil	*having eaten*
ʔaxað	*to take*	ʔaaxið	*having taken*

Form II

Sound: m(i)faʕʕil

xazzan	*to chew qat*	mxazzin	*having chewed qat*
fallag	*to cut wood*	mfallig	*cutting wood; having cut wood*
ṭallab	*to beg*	mṭallib	*begging; having begged*
ṭawwaf	*to take s.o. around*	mṭawwif	*taking s.o. around; having taken s.o. around*
xayyam	*to camp*	mxayyim	*camping; having camped*
sannab	*to stand up*	msannib	*standing up; having stood up*

Defective: m(i)faaʕiy

ṣalla	*to pray*	mṣalliy	*having prayed*
ḥayya	*to greet*	mḥayyiy	*having greeted*
xalla	*to leave*	mxalliy	*having left*
bawwa	*to shine shoes*	mbawwiy	*having shined shoes*

Form III

Sound: m(u)faaʕil

ʕaayan	*to observe*	mʕaayin	*observing; having observed*
samaḥ	*to forgive s.o.*	msaamiḥ	*having forgiven*
baarak	*to bless*	mbaarik	*having blessed*
saafar	*to travel*	msaafir	*traveling; having traveled*
gaayas	*to measure*	mgaayis	*having measured*
laaʕab	*to engage s.o. in playing*	mlaaʕib	*having engaged s.o. in playing*

Defective: m(u)faaʕiy

naada	*to call s.o.*	mnaadiy	*having called s.o.*
ḥaaza	*to tell an anecdote*	mḥaaziy	*having told an anecdote*
ʕaada	*to be at war with s.o.*	mʕaadiy	*being at war with s.o.;having been at war with s.o.*

Form IV

Sound: mifʕil/mufʕil

(ʔa)bsar	*to see*	mibsir	*seeing; having seen*
(ʔa)rbaš	*to confuse s.o.*	mirbiš	*confusing; having confused s.o.*
(ʔa)xlas	*to skin an animal*	mixlis	*having skinned an animal*
(ʔa)ṭlag	*to set free*	muṭlig	*having set free*

Defective: mifʕiy/mufʕiy

(ʔa)mḥa	*to destroy*	mimḥiy	*having destroyed*
(ʔa)mḏ̣a	*to sign*	mumḏ̣iy	*having signed*
(ʔa)ʕṭa	*to give*	muʕṭiy	*giving; having given*

Form V

Sound: mitfaʕʕil/mutafaʕʕil

tbannan	*to stuff oneself with food*	mitbannin	*having stuffed oneself with food*
tġassal	*to bathe*	mitġassil	*having bathed*
twaḍḍaʔ	*to perform ablution before prayer*	mitwaḍḍiʔ	*having performed ablution before prayer*
tšaggar	*to peek*	mitšaggir	*having peeked*
tġayyar	*to change*	mitġayyir	*changing, changeable; having changed*
tjammal	*to be thankful*	mitjammil	*being thankful; having been thankful*
θθamman	*to be priced*	miθθammin	*having been priced*

Defective: mitfaaʕiy/mutafaaʕiy

tġadda	*to have lunch*	mitġaddiy	*having had lunch*
twaṭṭa	*to be lowered*	mitwaṭṭity	*having been lowered*
tḥadda	*to defy*	mitḥaddiy	*defying*

Form VI

Sound: mitfaaʕil/mutafaaʕil

tgaabal	*to meet s.o.*	mitgaabil	*having met s.o.*
tšaawar	*to consult (deliberate) with s.o.*	mitšaawir	*having consulted with s.o.*
tḥaarab	*to be at war with s.o.*	mitḥaarib	*being at war; having been at war with s.o.*
tmayraḍ	*to pretend to be sick*	mitmayriḍ	*pretending to be sick; having pretended to be sick*
tgaaʕad	*to retire*	mitgaaʕid	*retired*

Defective: mitfaaʕiy/mutafaaʕiy

tʕaafa	*to recuperate*	mitʕaafiy	*having recuperated*
traaya	*to dream*	mitraayiy	*having dreamed*

Form VIII

Sound: miftaʕil

ltabaj	*to be hit*	miltabij	*having been hit*
ḥtafal	*to celebrate*	miḥtafil	*celebrating*
xtalaf	*to be different*	mixtalif	*different*
mtaḥag	*to be ruined*	mimtaḥig	*having been ruined*
ftaṭar	*to be split*	miftaṭir	*having been split*
stamaʕ	*to listen*	mistamiʕ	*listening; having listened*

Defective: miftaʕiy/muftaʕiy

šta[64]	*to want, desire*	mištiy	*desiring, having desired*
štara	*to buy*	mištariy	*having bought*
(ʔi)štka	*to complain*	mištakiy	*complaining; having complained*

Hollow: miftaal/muftaal

rtaaḥ	*to rest*	mirtaaḥ	*comfortable*
ḥtaaj	*to need*	miḥtaaj	*in need of*
xtaar	*to choose*	mixtaar	*having chosen*

Doubled: miftall/muftall

htamm	*to become concerned*	muhtamm	*concerned*
btall	*to become wet*	mubtall	*wet; having become wet*

Form X

Sound: mustafʕil/mistafʕil

staʕmal	*to use*	mustaʕmil	*having used*
staġfar	*to seek forgiveness*	mustaġfir	*seeking forgiveness; having sought forgiveness*
stanṭag	*to interrogate*	mustanṭig	*having interrogated*

Defective: mustafʕiy/mistafʕiy

staġna	*to do without*	mustaġniy	*doing without; having done without*
(ʔi)stḥa	*to be embarrassed*	mustaḥyiy	*embarrassed*
staʕfa	*to resign*	mustaʕfiy	*having resigned*

Hollow: mustafiil/mistafiil

stajaab	*to respond (to a request)*	mustajiib	*responding*
stafaad	*to benefit*	mustafiid	*benefiting; having benefited*
staraaḥ	*to rest, be comfortable*	mustariiḥ	*restful; comfortable*

Doubled: mustafiʕʕ/mistafiʕʕ

Quadriliterals
Sound: mufaʕlil

gambar	*to sit down*	mugambir	*sitting down*
xadras	*to be delirious*	muxadris	*delirious*
zagraʕ	*to be overjoyed*	muzagriʕ	*overjoyed*
fanṭas	*to have a good time*	mufanṭis	*having a good time*

Reduplicated

baxšaš	*to tip s.o.*	mubaxšiš	*tipping; having tipped s.o.*
gaṭgaṭ	*to talk a lot*	mugaṭgiṭ	*talkative; having talked a lot*

Derived Quadriliterals: mutafaʕlil/mitfaʕlil

tġalmaš	*to cover oneself*
mutaġalmiš	*wrapped; having wrapped oneself*
tkawbal	*to be piled up*
mutakawbil	*piled up*
tgarḏ̣aḏ̣	*to be gnawed*
mutagarḏ̣iḏ̣	*gnawed*

11.4.1.2 Meanings of Active Participles

Most active participles in SA have two dimensions of meaning: grammatical and aspectual.

a. Grammatical

ṭayr muġanniy	*a singing bird; a song bird*
wagt mutaġayyir	*a changing, changeable time*
huw mibsir al-gamar.	*He is looking at, has looked at, the moon.*

b. Aspectual

The aspect implied by a participle seems to be in many cases an individual characteristic of the participle itself, i.e., it is lexically conditioned. As will be pointed out below, there are many cases where the participle and the underlying verb do not match. Some participles seem to have a much more aspectual meaning than others, i.e., native speakers of SA often assign more specific aspectual meanings to a participle in very common use than to a less common one, e.g., in /ʔar-rajjaal al-mirbiš/ the active participle, /al-mirbiš/, which is not so commonly used, has the following aspectual meanings: 'the man who is confusing (s.o.)(now); the man who confuses (iterative); the man that has confused (perfective).' In /ʔar-rajjaal ar-raagid/, on the other hand, the active participle, /ʔar-raagid/, which has a higher frequency of occurrence than /ʔal-mirbiš/ means only 'the man who is sleeping (now).

If the underlying verb is an imperfect tense, then the active participle expresses the following aspects:

(i) Concurrent (in progress)

ʔal-maaʔ al-jaariy	*the running water*
ʔal-jihhaal ar-raagidiin	*the children (who are) sleeping*
ʔas-saaʔir fi ṭ-ṭariig	*(the one) walking in the street*
ʔal-faʔr al-mutagambiʕ	*the mouse (that is) jumping out of joy*
walad msannib	*a boy (who is) standing up*

(ii) Iterative (customary, habitual)

ṭayr muġanniy	*a song bird (lit., "a singing bird")*
ʔaḷḷaah al-muʕṭiy	*God is the giving (one), God is the giver*
šaahid ṣaadig	*a truthful witness*

(iii) Dispositional (tending, having the ability, capacity to act)

wagt mitġayyir	*a changeable, changing time*
maṭar mustamirr	*continuous, uninterrupted rain*
ṣuwar mutaḥarrikah	*moveable, moving pictures*

(iv) Future

ʔaz-zaaʔir al-gaadim ġudweh	*the visitor arriving (who is going to arrive) tommorrow*

If the underlying verb is a perfect tense, the corresponding active participle depicts:

(i) Completed Action

ʔal-gaššaam ar-raafiʕ siʕr aṭ-ṭamaaṭiis	*the greengrocer who (has) raised*
	the price of tomatoes
ʔal-muwaḍḍaf al-mustagiil	*the employee who (has) resigned*
ʔal-wašš al-mḥammir	*the face that (has) turned red*
ʔal-walad al-laabij ʔaxuuh	*the boy who (has) hit his brother*

(ii) Resultant Condition

The active participles belonging here convey an aspect not conveyed by either the perfect or the imperfect tense of the corresponding verb. Examples: /msannib/ 'standing up, afoot' from /sannab/ 'he stood up' and /ysannib/ 'he stands up; he stands up regularly,' /mgambir/ 'sitting, seated' from /gambar/ 'he sat up, down' and /ygambir/ 'he sits down, or up (regularly),' /raagid/ 'sleeping, asleep' from /ragad/ 'he slept' and /yurgud/ 'he goes to sleep, sleeps (regularly).

If the underlying verb is either a perfect or an imperfect tense, the corresponding active participle expresses either a progressive or a perfective aspect. Examples:

guḍaah ʕaadiliin	*judges who are just; judges who have been just*
ʔal-mareh al-xaaṭiyeh	*the woman (who is) walking; the woman who has walked*

It was mentioned in 11.4 that a participle is a verbal adjective. Like verbs, an active participle may take a direct object (i.e., a noun, a pronoun, or a suffixed pronoun):

mahdi msabbir al-ʔakl.	*Mahdi is preparing, has prepared the food.*
mahdi msabbir haaðawla.	*Mahdi is preparing, has prepared these.*
mahdi msabbirih.	*Mahdi is preparing, has prepared it.*
mahdi msabbir-lana l-ʔakl.	*Mahdi is preparing, has prepared the food for us.*

Like adjectives, an active participle follows the noun it modifies and agrees with it in gender, number,[65] and definiteness, and is negated by /maaš/:

rajjaal mṣalliy fi l-jaamiʕ	*a man who has prayed in the mosque*
mareh mṣalliyeh fi l-jaamiʕ	*a woman who has prayed in the mosque*
ʔar-rijaal al-muṣalliin fi l-jaamiʕ	*the men who have prayed inthe mosque*
ʔan-nisaaʔ al-muṣalliyaat fi l-jaamiʕ	*the women who have prayed in the mosque*
ʔal-muwaɖɖafayn al-mustagiiliin	*the two employers who have resigned*
ʔal-bintayn al-ḥaaliyaat	*the two beautiful girls*
gaaɖiy maaš ʕaadil	*an unjust judge*
dawaam maaš mutaġayyir	*an unchanging, unchangeable work schedule*

11.4.2 Passive Participles

11.4.2.1 Derivation

Passive participles are derived only from transitive verbs. All unaugmented triradical verbs form their passive participles according to the pattern /mafʕuul/.[66] Examples:

malbuuj	*hit*
malʕuub	*played*
maʕruuf	*known*
maxtuun	*circumcised*
magbuuṣ	*pinched*
madʕiy	*invited*
maʔkuul	*eaten*
marmiy	*thrown away*
mašluul	*stolen, taken away*
mašnuun	*filtered*
magṣuuṣ	*cut, cut up*
mawṣuul	*connected*
mamnuuʕ	*forbidden*
mawzuun	*weighed*

From augmented verbs, the passive participle is formed by the prefixation of /m-/ (or /mu-/ before a consonant cluster) before the first radical of the stem with /a/ as a stem vowel[67] (the vowel preceding the last radical). From quadriliterals, the pattern is /mfaʕlal/.:

mfallag	*cut; split*
mxalla	*left, deserted*
mfayyaš	*revealed*
mxaalaf	*violated*
mbaarak	*blessed*
mnaada	*called; invited*
muḥtall	*occupied*
muntaxab	*selected, elected*
mustaʕmal	*used*
mustaḥabb	*liked, desired*
mġawbar	*made dusty*
mbaxšaš	*tipped; bribed*
mrašraš	*sprayed*
mkawbal	*piled up*

Passive participles derived from transitive verbs that take prepositional objects always have pronouns suffixed to the prepositions. The suffixed pronouns have as their antecedents the noun-head of the construction. The participle does not show agreement with the subject; it remains in the base form (i.e., m.s.):

rajjaal maḥkuum ʕalayh	*a convicted man*
mareh maḥkuum ʕalayha	*a convicted woman*
gaðiyyah masmuuʕ ʕanha	*a known case*
gaðaaya masmuuʕ ʕanhum	*known cases*

11.4.2.2 Meanings of Passive Participles

Every passive participle has two dimensions of meaning: grammatical and aspectual:

a. Grammatical

A passive participle depicts its referent as the goal of the action:

sayyaarah maksuurah	*a broken car*
baab mġallag	*a closed door*
gaat mabyuuʕ	*qat that has been sold*
gumgumi saliiṭ maftuuḥ	*an open motor oil can*

b. Aspectual

(i) Perfective

madaaʕah maksuurah	*a broken waterpipe*
maaʔ mašnuun	*filtered water*
guuzi maṭbuux	*cooked lamb*

The referent is the goal of the action. It is depicted as "having been V-ed."

(ii) Perfective or Progressive

ʔaṭ-ṭamaaṭiis al-mabyuuʕ	*the tomatoes sold (now or regularly)*
ʔas-sayyaaraat al-mustawradeh min ʔamriika	*the cars imported (now or regularly) from America*
ʔal-maxa l-masmuuʕ ʕanha	*Mocha that has been (or is being) heard about*
ʔal-wiḥdah l-mabḥuuθ fiiha	*the union that has been (or is being) discussed*

The referent is depicted as being "capable of being V-ed" or "tending to be V-ed."

11.5 Adjectives

11.5.1 Derivation

11.5.1.1 Positive Adjectives

Most positive adjectives in SA have verbs as their underlying forms and are of the /faʕiil/ pattern:

ṭawiil	*tall; long*	→	ṭuwul	*to grow, turn tall*
gaṣiir	*short*	→	guṣur	*to turn short*
ġaliiḏ̣	*fat*	→	ġuluḏ̣	*to grow fat*
gadiim	*old, ancient*	→	gidim	*to become old*
fagiir	*poor*	→	figir	*to become poor*
raxiiṣ	*inexpensive*	→	ruxuṣ	*to become inexpensive*
kabiir	*big, large*	→	kubur	*to grow big, large*
naḏ̣iif	*clean*	→	nuḏ̣uf	*to turn clean*

One or two positive adjectives of this pattern are derived from nouns:

ʕajiib	*strange*	→	ʕujub	*strangeness*
kariim	*generous*	→	karam	*generosity*

A few positive adjectives are of the /fayyil/ pattern. Most of them are derived from Form I hollow verbs; one or two are derived from nouns:

ṭayyib	*good, fine*	→	ṭaab	*to be good, fine*
hayyin	*easy*	→	haan	*to be easy*
bayyin	*clear*	→	baan	*to be clear*
mayyit	*dead*	→	maat	*to die*
ðayyig	*narrow*	→	ðaag	*to become narrow*
gayyim	*valuable*	→	giimeh	*value*
xayyir	*charitable;*	→	xayr	*benevolence; wealth*

Those of the /faʕiy/ pattern have verbal nouns as their underlying forms. Examples:

ġaniy	*rich*	→	ġina	*richness*
ðakiy	*clever*	→	ðakaaʔ	*cleverness*
gawiy	*strong*	→	guwwah	*strength*
ġabiy	*stupid*	→	ġabaaʔ	*stupidity*

A few positive adjectives are of the /faaʕiy/ pattern and almost all of them are derived from defective verbs. Examples:

ḥaaliy	*sweet; beautiful*	→	ḥily	*to become sweet*
baaliy	*worn out*	→	biliy	*to wear out*
haadiy	*quiet*	→	hidiy	*to become quiet*
ḥaamiy	*hot*	→	ḥimiy	*to become hot*
šaagiy	*miserable*	→	šigiy	*to be miserable*

/naahiy/ 'nice, good; beautiful' is not derived from the verb /naha/ 'to forbid, prohibit' but it has something to do with the literary Arabic abstract noun /nuhan/ 'intelligence, understanding' or the noun /nuhyah/ 'mind, intellect'.

There are other adjectives that are derived from other forms of verbs:

jadiid	*new*	jaddad	*to renew*
muhimm	*important*	htamm	*to be concerned*
majnuun	*crazy*	njann	*to become crazy*

There are adjectives of other patterns:

wasix	*dirty*	→	wasax	*dirt*
murr	*bitter*	→	maraarah	*bitterness*
ḥaadd	*sharp*	→	ḥadd	*edge (e.g. of a knife)*
ksil	*lazy*	→	kasal	*laziness*
dagiig	*thin*	→	diggah	*thinness*
šuuʕ	*ugly*	→		*no underlying form*

11.5.1.2 /faaʕil/ Adjectives

/faaʕil/ adjectives, as their name indicates, are of the /faaʕil/ pattern. Almost all of them are derived from Form I verbs, e.g., /ġirig/ 'to get mad, angry' has the /faaʕil/ adjective /ġaarig/ which describes someone, a male, as being in, or undergoing, a state of anger. It is interesting to point out that literary Arabic and other Arabic dialects, such as Levantine, Gulf, and Egyptian have /faʕlaan/ adjectives, e.g., /taʕbaan/ 'tired', /ʕaṭšaan/ 'thirsty', /farḥaan/ 'happy', etc. instead of /taaʕib/, /ʕaaṭiš/, /faariḥ/, etc. in SA.

The most commonly used /faaʕil/ adjectives in SA are the following:

jaawiʕ	*hungry*	→	juwiʕ	*to be hungry*
šabiʕ	*full (of food)*	→	šibiʕ	*to be full of food*
faariḥ	*happy*	→	firiḥ	*to be happy*
xaarib	*out of order*	→	xirib	*to be out of order*
ġaarig	*mad*	→	ġirig	*to become angry*
baarid[68]	*cold*	→	birid	*to get cold*
naaʕis	*sleepy (person)*	→	niʕis	*to be sleepy*
ʕaarig	*sweaty*	→	ʕirig	*to be sweaty*
ʕaaṭiš	*thirsty*	→	ʕuṭuš	*to be thirsty*
taaʕib	*tired*	→	tiʕib	*to be tired*

ðaamiy	*very thirsty*	→	ðimiy	*to be very thirsty*
ḥaamiy	*hot, running a temperature*	→	ḥimiy	*to be hot*
raawiy	*sated with water*	→	riwiy	*to drink ones fill*
ḥaaliy	*sweet; beautiful*	→	ḥiliy	*to become sweet*
baaliy	*worn out*	→	biliy	*to wear out*
haadiy	*quiet*	→	hidiy	*to become quiet*
šaagiy	*miserable*	→	šigiy	*to become miserable*

11.5.1.3 Nisba Adjectives

Nisba adjectives, sometimes known as relative adjectives, indicate something characteristic of, or having to do with what the underlying word designates. Most nisba adjectives are derived from nouns, a few from adjectives, and a small number from prepositions. They are formed by suffixing /-iy/ to the word, sometimes with appropriate stem changes.

The following are examples of nisba adjectives that require no stem changes:

ʔal-yaman	*Yemen*	→	yamaniy	*Yemeni*
ʕadan	*Aden*	→	ʕadaniy	*from Aden*
ðamaar	*Dhamar*	→	ðamaariy	*from Dhamar*
ʔaryaan	*Aryan*	→	ʔaryaaniy	*from Aryaan*
ʕumaan	*Oman*	→	ʕumaaniy	*from Oman*
ʔal-maḥwiit	*Al-Mahwit*	→	maḥwiitiy	*from Al-Mahwit*
ðahab	*gold*	→	ðahabiy	*gold, golden*
šarg	*east*	→	šargiy	*eastern*
xaliij	*gulf*	→	xaliijiy	*gulf (adj.)*
markiz	*center*	→	markiziy	*central*
ʕagl	*mind*	→	ʕagliy	*mental*
ʔaṣl	*origin*	→	ʔaṣliy	*original; genuine*
baḥr	*sea*	→	baḥriy	*naval*
šahr	*month*	→	šahriy	*monthly*

Some nouns with the -eh/-ah ending lose this ending when /-iy/ is added:

zaydiyeh	*Zaidia*	→	zaydiy	*from Zaidia*
ʔal-manṣuuriyeh	*Al-Mansuria*	→	manṣuuriy	*from Al-Mansuria*
ʔaš-šaarigah	*Sharja*	→	šaarigiy	*from Sharja*
ḥagiigah	*fact*	→	ḥagiigiy	*factual*
suuriyah	*Syria*	→	suuriy	*from Syria*
ʔaṭ-ṭawiileh	*Al-Tawila*	→	ṭawiiliy	*from Al-Tawila*
ḥaddah	*Hadda*	→	ḥaddiy	*from Hadda*
ʔal-baṣrah	*Basra*	→	baṣriy	*from Basra*
barbarah	*Barbara*	→	barbariy	*from Barbara*
ʔal-ḥaymeh	*Haima*	→	ḥaymiy	*from Haima*

One or two nisba adjectives are derived from particles:

fawg	*above; over*	→	fawgaaniy	*located above or higher*
tiḥt	*below; under*	→	tiḥtaaniy	*located below or lower*

A group of nisba adjectives are derived from verbal nouns of color; they indicate the basic meaning of "characteristic of" or "leaning to or toward" what the underlying verbal noun designates. Most of the English adjective equivalents end with /-ish/:

xuḏ̣rah	*greenness*	→	xuḏ̣raaniy	*greenish*
ḥumrah	*redness*	→	ḥumraaniy	*reddish*
sawaad	*blackness*	→	suudaaniy	*blackish*
samaar	*brownness (of skin)*	→	sumraaniy	*brownish (skin)*
ṣafaar	*yellowness*	→	ṣufraaniy	*yellowish*
zurgah	*blueness*	→	zurgaaniy	*bluish*

The nisbah adjective from /bayaaḏ̣/ 'whiteness' is /bayḏ̣aaniy/ 'whitish'.

Some nisbah adjectives are derived from ethnic collectives:[69]

yahuud	*Jews*	→	yahuudiy	*Jewish*
baduw	*Bedouins*	→	badawiy	*Bedouin (adj.)*
kurd	*Kurds*	→	kurdiy	*Kurdish*
ʔarman	*Armenians*	→	ʔarmaniy	*Armenian (adj.)*

Some nisbah adjectives require stem or other changes:

ḥaḍramawt	*Hadhramaut*	→	ḥaḍramiy	*of Hadhramaut*
ṣanʕa(aʔ)	*San'a*	→	ṣanʕaaniy	*of San'a*
ʔal-bayḍaaʔ	*Al-Baida*	→	bayḍaaniy	*of Al-Baida*
ʔabu ḍabiy	*Abu Dhabi*	→	ḍibyaaniy	*Abu Dhabian*
dubayy	*Dubai*	→	min dubayy	*from Dubai*

Human nisba adjectives that indicate inhabitants (of a place) can also be formed by /ṣaaḥib/ 'owner, proprietor' + the name of the place:

ðamaar	*Dhamar*	→	ṣaaḥib ðamaar	*one from Dhamar*
ṣanʕa(aʔ)	*San'a*	→	ṣaaḥib ṣanʕa	*one from San'a*
ʔibb	*Ibb*	→	ṣaaḥib ibb	*one from Ibb*

But /ðamaariy/, /ṣanʕaaniy/ and /ʔibbiy/ are more commonly used than the other forms.

11.5.1.4 Elative Adjectives

Depending upon their root structure, elative adjectives are divided into the following:

A. Sound Roots
   Elatives with sound roots are formed on the pattern /ʔafʕal/ from the corresponding positive adjectives:

Positive		Elative	
ġaliiḍ	*fat*	ʔaġlaḍ	*fatter*
wasix	*dirty*	ʔawsax	*dirtier*
ḥawiiṣ	*narrow*	ʔaḥwaṣ	*narrower*
yaabis	*dry*	ʔaybas	*drier*
ðaahin	*smart*	ʔaðhan	*smarter*
zġiir	*small; little*	ʔazġar	*smaller*
ʕaagil	*rational; sane*	ʔaʕgal	*more rational*
gadiim	*ancient, old*	ʔagdam	*older*
gaṣiir	*short*	ʔagṣar	*shorter*
ṭawiil	*tall; long*	ʔaṭwal	*taller; longer*
ʕaaṭiš	*thirsty*	ʔaʕṭaš	*thirstier*
jaawiʕ	*hungry*	ʔajwaʕ	*hungrier*

B. Weak-Middle Roots

In these elatives the ʕ is either a /y/ or a /w/, depending on the roots of the underlying word:

zaayid	*excessive*	→	ʔazyad	*more (excessive)*
ḏ̣ayyig	*narrow*	→	ʔaḏ̣yag	*narrower*
ṭayyib	*good; delicious*	→	ʔaṭyab	*better; more delicious*
hayyin	*easy*	→	ʔahwan	*easier*
xaayif	*afraid*	→	ʔaxwaf	*more afraid*
šuuʕ	*ugly*	→	ʔašwaʕ	*uglier*

C. Weak-Last Roots

The underlying adjectives in this section end in /-iy/. The elatives, derived from such adjectives, are of the /ʔafʕa/ pattern.

ġaaliy	*expensive*	→	ʔaġla	*more expensive*
raawiy	*sated with water*	→	ʔarwa	*more sated with water*
gawiy	*strong*	→	ʔagwa	*stronger*
ġaniy	*rich*	→	ʔaġna	*richer*
šagiy	*mischievous*	→	ʔašga	*more mischievous*
haadiy	*quiet, tranquil*	→	ʔahda	*quieter*
naahiy	*good, nice*	→	ʔanha[70]	*more beautiful*
ḥaaliy	*sweet; beautiful*	→	ʔaḥla	*sweeter; nicer*
baaliy	*worn out*	→	ʔabla	*more worn out*
ḏ̣aamiy	*very thirsty*	→	ʔaḏ̣ma	*thirstier*
ʕaaliy	*high*	→	ʔaʕla	*higher*
ġabiy	*stupid*	→	ʔaġba	*more stupid*
ḥaamiy	*hot; running a temperature*	→	ʔaḥma	*hotter*
ṣaaḥiy	*conscious*	→	ʔaṣḥa	*more conscious*

D. Double Roots

In these elatives the second and third roots are identical. They are derived from positive adjectives in which the second and third roots are also identical. The pattern is /ʔafaʕʕ/.

xasiis	*low, mean*	→	ʔaxass	*lower, meaner*
jadiid	*new*	→	ʔajadd/ʔajdad	*newer*
xafiif	*light*	→	ʔaxaff	*lighter*
ʕaziiz	*dear*	→	ʔaʕazz	*dearer*
majnuun	*crazy, mad*	→	ʔajann	*crazier, madder*
ḥaadd	*sharp (knife)*	→	ʔaḥadd	*sharper (knife)*
galiil	*few; little*	→	ʔagall	*fewer; less*
murr	*bitter*	→	ʔamarr	*more bitter*
ḥaarr	*hot*	→	ʔaḥarr	*hotter*
dagiig	*thin; skinny*	→	ʔadagg	*thinner; skinnier*
muhimm	*important*	→	ʔahamm	*more important*

A few adjectives do not have any of the elative patterns above. The elative of such adjectives is expressed by post-posing /ʔakθar/ 'more', the elative of /kaθiir/ 'much, a lot' or by pre-posing /ʔakθar/ to the verbal noun derived from the adjective. The former is more commonly used:

ḍ̱aruuriy	*necessary*	ḍ̱aruuriy ʔakθar ʔakθar ḍ̱aruurah	*more necessary*
muxtalif	*different*	muxtalif ʔakθar ʔakθar xtilaaf	*more different*
ḥumraaniy	*reddish*	ḥumraaniy ʔakθar ʔakθar ḥumrah	*more reddish*
ṣufraaniy	*yellowish*	ṣufraaniy ʔakθar ʔakθar ṣufrah	*more yellowish*
bayḍ̱aawiy	*whitish*	bayḍ̱aawiy ʔakθar ʔakθar bayaaḍ̱	*more whitish*

11.5.2 Inflection

11.5.2.1 Gender

Adjectives have two genders: masculine and feminine. They differ from nouns in that nouns are either masculine or feminine; adjectives have two forms, a masculine form and a feminine form, depending upon the gender of the noun they modify. The feminine singular form of the adjective is formed from the masculine singular form by suffixing /-eh/-ah/, sometimes with appropriate stem changes as described below.

1. Adjectives of the patterns /faʕiil/ (or /fʕiil/), /mafʕuul/, or other adjectives that end with either a single consonant preceded by a long vowel or a double consonant preceded by a short or a long vowel require no stem change when -eh/-ah is added:

matruus	→	matruuseh	*full (f.)*
majnuun	→	majnuuneh	*crazy (f.)*
maðbuuḥ	→	maðbuḥah	*slaughtered (f.)*
ġaliiḍ	→	ġaliiḍah	*fat (f.)*
ḥawiiṣ	→	ḥawiiṣah	*narrow (f.)*
zġiir	→	zġiireh	*small; little (f.)*
fagiir	→	fagiireh	*poor (f.)*
xasiis	→	xasiiseh	*low, mean (f.)*
dagiig	→	dagiigah	*thin; skinny (f.)*
jaawiʕ	→	jaawiʕah	*hungry (f.)*
faariḥ	→	faariaḥah	*happy (f.)*
ġaarig	→	ġaarigah	*mad (f.)*
naaḥiy	→	naaḥiyeh	*good, nice (f.)*
naaʕis	→	naaʕiseh	*sleepy (f.)*
šuuʕ	→	šuuʕah	*ugly (f.)*
zaayid	→	zaayideh	*excessive (f.)*
murr	→	murrah	*bitter (f.)*
ḥaadd	→	ḥaaddeh	*sharp (knife)*
ḥaarr	→	ḥaarrah	*hot (f.)*

2. Feminine nisba adjectives are formed from their corresponding masculine forms by either adding -eh/-ah or by changing the suffix /-iy/ into /-iyyeh/. The former pattern is more commonly used.

ṣanʕaaniy	→	ṣanʕaaniyeh/ṣanʕaaniyyeh	*from San'a (f.)*
yamaniy	→	yamaniyeh/yamaniyyeh	*Yemeni (f.)*
ðamaariy	→	ðamaariyeh/ðamaariyyeh	*from Dhamar (f.)*

ʔaryaaniy	→	ʔaryaaniyeh/ʔaryaaniyyeh	*from Aryan (f.)*
suuriy	→	suuriyeh/suuriyyeh	*Syrian (f.)*
bayḏ̣aaniy	→	bayḏ̣aaniyeh/bayḏ̣aaniyyeh	*from Al-Buida (f.)*
yahuudiy	→	yahuudiyeh/yahuudiyyeh	*Jewish (f.)*
badawiy	→	badawiyeh/badawiyyeh	*Bedouin (f.)*
suudaaniy	→	suudaaniyeh/suudaaniyyeh	*blackish (f.)*
ḥumraaniy	→	ḥumraaniyeh/ḥumraaniyyeh	*reddish (f.)*
sumraaniy	→	sumraaniyeh/sumraaniyyeh	*dark-skinned (f.)*

3. Feminine adjectives of color and defect are formed from their corresponding masculine forms according to the pattern /faʕlaaʔ/ or /faʕlee'/ (with imaalah), sometimes shortened to /faʕle'/. If such an adjective is not followed by pause, then only the /faʕlaaʔ/ form is used, e.g., /bayḏ̣aaʔ al-wašš/ 'white-faced' and /haaðih bayḏ̣aaʔ/bayḏ̣ee'/bayḏ̣eʔ 'this (f.) is white'.

Examples:

ʔagṭaʕ	→	gaṭʕaaʔ	*one-handed*
ʔaḥmar	→	ḥamraaʔ	*red*
ʔaxḏ̣ar	→	xaḏ̣raaʔ	*green*
ʔabyaḏ̣	→	bayḏ̣aaʔ	*white*
ʔazrag	→	zargaaʔ	*blue*
ʔaṣfar	→	ṣafraaʔ	*yellow*
ʔasmar	→	samraaʔ	*dark-skinned*
ʔaswad	→	sawdaaʔ	*black*
ʔaʕraj	→	ʕarjaaʔ	*limping, lame*
ʔaʕwar	→	ʕawraaʔ	*one-eyed*
ʔaġbar	→	ġabraaʔ	*chestnut (color)*
ʔaʕma	→	ʕamyaaʔ	*blind*
ʔašwal	→	šawlaaʔ	*left-handed*
ʔasnaj	→	sanjaaʔ	*deaf*
ʔaltag	→	latgaaʔ	*stammering*
ʔaʕwaj	→	ʕawjaaʔ	*crooked*
ʔadran	→	darnaaʔ	*dumb*
ʔaxlaʕ	→	xalʕaaʔ	*careless, irresponsible*
ʔašlag	→	šalgaaʔ	*cross-legged*
ʔaḥwal	→	ḥawlaaʔ	*cross-eyed*
ʔahbal	→	hablaaʔ	*weak-minded*
ʔaʕjam	→	ʕajmaaʔ	*mute*

11.5.2.2 Number

Adjectives, like nouns, have dual and plural forms. In SA the dual of the adjective is very rarely used, e.g., /ʔiθnayn buyuut kibaar/ 'two big houses' instead of /ʔiθnayn buyuut kabiirayn/.[71] Most plural forms are sound masculine forms or broken plural forms; sound feminine forms are not commonly used with nonhuman nouns. A nonhuman noun is modified by either a plural or a singular adjective; the singular adjective is more commonly used:

buyuut kabiireh/kibaar	*big houses*
šawaariʕ ṭawiileh/ṭuwaal	*long streets*
banaat ḥaaliyaat	*beautiful girls*
rijaal naahiyiin	*good men*

The adjectives in this section include those of the patterns /faʕiil/, /fayyil/, /faʕiy/, /faaʕiy/, /fuʕʕ/, /faaʕʕ/, nisba adjectives, and adjectives of participle patterns. Some nisba adjectives and all adjectives of color and defect have broken plural forms.

ḍaʕiif	→	ḍiʕaaf	*weak*
ṭawiil	→	ṭuwaal	*long; tall*
gaṣiir	→	giṣaar	*short*
ḥawiiṣ	→	ḥiwaaṣ	*narrow*
wasix	→	wisaax	*dirty*
haadiy	→	haadiyiin	*quiet, tranquil*
ḥaamiy	→	ḥaamiyiin	*hot*
ḥaadd	→	ḥaaddiin	*sharp (knife)*
ġaaliy	→	ġaaliyiin	*expensive*
xaaṭiy	→	xaaṭiyiin	*walking*
baagiy	→	baagiyiin/ bawaagiy	*remaining; remainder*
murr	→	murriin	*bitter*
ṣanʕaaniy	→	ṣanʕaaniyiin/ṣanaaʕinah	*of San'a*
ʕumaaniy	→	ʕumaaniyiin	*Omani*

Major Broken Plural Patterns

1. f(i)ʕaal

jadiid	→	jidaad	*new*
zġiir	→	zġaar	*small; little*
θagiil	→	θigaal	*heavy*
gaṣiir	→	giṣaar	*short*
dagiig	→	digaag	*thin*

kabiir	→	kibaar	*big; old*
ġaliiḍ	→	ġilaaḍ	*fat*
naḍiif	→	niḍaaf	*clean*
galiil	→	gilaal	*little; few*

2. fuʕl
   Most adjectives of defect and color have this broken plural pattern. The masculine singular form is of the pattern /ʔafʕal/. For forms with a medial -y- the plural pattern is /fiil/, and for forms with a medial -w- the plural pattern is /fuul/. Examples:

ʔaḥmar	→	ḥumr	*red*
ʔazrag	→	zurg	*blue*
ʔabyaḍ	→	biiḍ	*white*
ʔaṣfar	→	ṣufr	*yellow*
ʔasmar	→	sumr	*dark-skinned*
ʔaswad	→	suud	*black*
ʔaxḍar	→	xuḍr	*green*
ʔaṣnaj	→	ṣunj	*deaf*
ʔaltag	→	lutg	*stammering*
ʔadran	→	durn	*dumb*
ʔašlag	→	šulg	*cross-legged*
ʔaḥwal	→	ḥuul	*cross-eyed*
ʔahbal	→	hubl	*weak-minded*
ʔaxlaʕ	→	xulʕ	*careless, irresponsible*
ʔaʕwar	→	ʕuur	*one-eyed*
ʔaʕma	→	ʕumy	*blind*

3. mafaaʕiil
Most of these adjectives are passive participles of Form I verbs. The singular is of the pattern /mafʕuul/:

majnuun	→	majaaniin	*crazy, mad*
madluuz	→	madaaliiz	*dim-witted*
marbuuš	→	maraabiiš	*mixed up*
mazkuum	→	mazaakiim	*having a cold*
madkuum	→	madaakiim	*bumped into*

4. faʕliyeh
Most of these are nisba adjectives derived from common nouns. Quadriliterals have the plural pattern /fawʕaliyeh/:

baḥriy	→	baḥriyeh	*naval*
jiwwiy	→	jawwiyeh	*air (adj.)*
barriy	→	barriyeh	*ground (adj.)*
dawmariy	→	dawmariyeh	*from Dawmar*

5. faʕaawil/fawaaʕil

ʕansiy	→	ʕanaawis	*of the Ansi tribe*
saʕwaniy	→	saʕaawin	*of Saʔwan*
dawsariy	→	dawaasir	*of the Dawsari tribe*

6. faʕaalileh

sanḥaaniy	→	sanaaḥineh	*from Sanhan*
hamdaaniy	→	hamaadineh	*from Hamdan*
ġaḏ̣raaniy	→	ġaḏ̣aarineh	*from Gadran*

7. fuʕalaaʔ

xabiir	→	xubaraaʔ	*experienced*
faġiir	→	fuġaraaʔ	*poor*
ḥakiim	→	ḥukamaaʔ	*wise*
baṣiir	→	buṣaraaʔ	*knowledgeable; not blind*

Section Twelve

12. PRONOUNS

12.1 Independent Pronouns

Independent pronouns are free forms. They are inflected for gender and number. In SA there are ten such pronouns, the most characteristic forms of which are the following:

1st person s.:	ʔana
1st person p.:	ḥna
2nd person m.s.:	ʔant
2nd person m.p.:	ʔantu
2nd person f.s.:	ʔantiy
2nd person f.p.:	ʔantayn
3rd person m.s.:	huw
3rd person m.p.:	hum
3rd person f.s.:	hiy
3rd person f.p.:	hin

The following are the less common variants of some independent pronouns:

Personal Pronoun	Variants
huw	huu, huuh, huwwa
hum	humma
hiy	hii, hiih, hiya
ʔant	ʔanta
ʔantu	ʔantum
ʔantiy	ʔanti
ʔana	ʔane
ḥna	ḥne

Unlike other dialects of Arabic, e.g., Lebanese, Syrian, Jordanian, and Egyptian which use one form of the independent pronouns for both the masculine and the feminine 3rd person plural and Gulf Arabic in which the use of the one form is optional, SA always uses the two independent forms, i.e., /hum/ (m.), /hin/ (f.), /ʔantu/ (m.), and /ʔantayn/ (f.). There are no dual forms of personal pronouns in SA; the plural forms are used instead.

12.1.1 /gad/ + Independent Pronoun

The particle /gad/ may precede an independent pronoun, sometimes with appropriate changes, for emphasis:

gad huw	*he is*
gad hiy	*she is*
gad hum	*they (m.) are*
gad hin	*they (f.) are*
gadak, gadant	*you (m.s.) are*
gad ʔantu, gadantu	*you (m.p.) are*
gad ʔantayn, gadantayn	*you (f.p.) are*
gad ʔanti, gadanti	*you (f.s.) are*
gadaani	*I am*
gadiḥna	*we are*
gad hum ṭayyibiin.	*They (m.) are good.*
gad huw daariy.	*He knows.*
gadaana ʕaaṭiš.	*I am thirsty.*

12.1.2 /maa gad/ + Independent Pron. +/-š/

An independent pronoun, with appropriate changes, may occupy a position between /maa gad/ and the negative particle /-š/. Examples:

maa gadanaaš taaʕib.	*I am not yet tired.*
maa gadantš baaliġ.	*You (m.s.) are not an adult.*
maa gadanaaš muhandis.	*I am not yet an engineer.*

Note the following changes in the independent pronoun:

1. If it ends with a vowel, the vowel is lengthened:

ʔantu	→	maa gadantuuš	*you (m.p.) are not yet*
ʔanti	→	maa gadantiiš	*you (f.s.) are not yet*
ʔana	→	maa gadanaaš	*I am not yet*
ḥna	→	maa gadiḥnaaš	*we are not yet*

(Note the helping vowel -i- in /maa gadiḥnaaš/).

2. If it ends with a diphthong, the diphthong changes into a long vowel as in 1. above. The reason for this change is that those independent pronouns that end with a diphthong have optional forms ending with a vowel: /huw ~ hu/ and /hiy ~ hi/. The /h/ of /huw/ and /hiy/ is optionally elided. Examples:

maa gaduuš	~	maa gadhuuš	*he is not yet*
maagadiiš	~	maa gadhiiš	*she is not yet*

3. Only the diphthong -ay- in /ʔantayn/ you (f.p.) is reduced to the short vowel -a-:

ʔantayn → maa gadantanš *you (f.p.) are not yet*

4. /hum/ they (m.) undergoes only an optional elision of the /h/.

hum → maa gadumš ~ maa gadhumš *they (m.) are not yet*

5. /ʔant/ you (m.s.) does not change:

ʔant → maa gadantš *you (m.s.) are not yet*

It should be pointed out that forms without the /h/ are more commonly used, e.g., /maa gaduuš/ 'he is not yet', is more commonly used than /maa gadhuuš/.

The independent pronoun is used as:

1. The subject or predicate of an equational sentence (see 14.1):

/huw min ṣanʕa/	*He is from San'a.*
/ʔantayn naahiyaat/	*You (f.p.) are good.*

2. The subject of a verbal sentence (see 14.3) is used for emphasis: /huw yištiy yixazzin/ 'He wants to chew qat.' /hiy ṣṭabaḥat/ 'She had breakfast'. /hin saarayn al-madraseh/ 'They (f.) went to school.'

12.2 Suffixed Pronouns

Pronouns may be suffixed to verbs, nouns, active participles, and particles. When suffixed to verbs, they function as the objects of those verbs, and when suffixed to nouns, they usually indicate possession. For active participles see C below, and for particles see 13. PARTICLES below.

A. Suffixed to verbs

The following table shows the personal pronouns and the corresponding verb suffixed forms:

Personal Pronoun	Verb Suffixed Pronoun	
huw	-ih	*he*
hum	-hum	*they (m.)*
hiy	-ha	*she (f.)*
hin	-hin	*they (f.)*
ʔant	-ak	*you (m.s.)*
ʔantu	-kum	*you (m.p.)*
ʔantiy	-iš	*you (f.s.)*
ʔantayn	-kin	*you (f.p.)*
ʔana	-niy	*I*
ḥna	-na	*we*

Example:

ʔabsar	*to see*
ʔabsarih	*he saw him*
ʔabsarhum	*he saw them (m.)*
ʔabsarha	*he saw her*
ʔabsarhin	*he saw them (f.)*
ʔabsarak	*he saw you (m.s.)*
ʔabsarkum	*he saw you (m.p.)*
ʔabsariš	*he saw you (f.s.)*
ʔabsarkin	*he saw you (f.p.)*
ʔabsarni	*he saw me*
ʔabsarna	*he saw us*

When suffixed to verbs, these bound forms require certain changes in the verbs:

1. V Diphthong → VV

Any form of the verb that ends with a short vowel or a diphthong changes its short vowel or diphthong into a long vowel before a suffixed pronoun is added. This process necessitates the elision of i in /-ih/ and /-isʔ/:

ligiy	*he found*	→	ligiih	*he found it*
yilga	*he finds*	→	yilgaah	*he finds it*
ʔilga	*find!*	→	ʔilgaah	*find (m.s.) it!*
ʔadda	*he gave*	→	ʔaddaahum	*he gave them*
ʔaddayna	*we gave*	→	ʔaddaynaakum	*we gave you (m.p.)*
ʔadduw	*they (m.) gave*	→	ʔadduuha	*they (m.) gave her*
ʔadduw	*give (m.p.)!*	→	ʔadduuna	*give (m.p.) us!*

Note that if the negative particles /-š/ is added to the forms above, the same change in 1. above takes place except for the forms that end with /-vvh/:

ligiy	*he found*	→	maa ligiiš	*he did not find*
yilga	*he finds*	→	maa yilgaaš	*he does not find*
ʔilga	*find (m.s.)*	→	maa tilgaaš	*do not find (m.s.)*
ʔadda	*he gave*	→	maa ʔaddaaš	*he did not give*
ʔaddayna	*we gave*	→	maa ʔaddaynaaš	*we did not give*
yidduw	*they (m.) give*	→	maa yidduuš	*they (m.) do not give*

Forms that end with /-vvh/ undergo the following change if /-šš/ is added: the long vowel is shortened and the /h/ assimilates on to the following /-š/, i.e.

2. -vvh + -š → -všš

Examples:

ligiih	*he found it*	→	maa *ligiihš	→	maa ligišš	*he did not find it (m.s.).*
yilgaah	*he finds it*	→	maa *yilgaahš	→	maa yilgašš	*he does not fine it (m.s.).*
ʔilgaah	*find (m.s.) it*	→	maa *tilgaahš	→	maa tilgašš	*you (m.s.) do not find it (m.s.)*
ligyuuh	*they (m.) found it*	→	maa *ligyuuhš	→	maa ligyušš	*they (m.) did not find it (m.s.)*

Otherwise:

ligiiha	*he found it (f.s.)*	→	maa ligiihaaš	*he did not find it (f.s.)*
ʔaddaynaahum	*we gave them (m.)*	→	maa ʔaddaynaahumš	*we did not give them (m.)*

Compare the following:

/maa ligiiš/	*he did not find*	and	/maa ligišš/	*he did not find it (m.s.)*
/maa daʕaynaaš/	*we did not invite*	and	/maa daʕaynašš/	*we did not invite him*
ma tibnuuš	*do not build (m.p.)!*	and	/maa tibnušš/	*do not build (m.p.) it (m.s.)!*

3.

-ayn -tayn	→	-ann-	or	-ayn -tayn	→ →	-ann- -tann-

Verb forms that end with /-ayn/, the third person feminine plural subject marker, or /-tayn/, the second person feminine plural subject marker, change /-ayn/ or /-tayn/ into /-ann/ before a suffixed pronoun is added:

garrayn they (f.) taught

→ garrannih	*they (f.) taught him*
→ garrannaha	*they (f.) taught her*
→ garrannahum	*they (f.) taught them (m.)*
→ garrannak	*they (f.) taught you (m.s.)*
→ garrannakum	*they (f.) taught you (m.p.)*
→ garrannani	*they (f.) taught me*
→ garrannana	*they (f.) taught us*

/garranni/ 'they (f.) taught me' and /garranna/ 'they (f.) taught us' are alternate (but less commonly used) forms for /garrannani/ and /garrannana/ respectively.

If the forms above are negated, then rules 1. and 2. above apply.:

garrannih	*they (f.) taught him*	→ →	maa *garannihš maagarranniš̌š	*they(f.) did not teach him*
garrannaha	*they (f.) taught her*	→	maa garrannahaaš	*they (.f.) did not teach her*
garrannak	*they (f.) taught you (m.s.)*	→	maa garrannakš	*they (f.) did not teach you (m.s.)*
garrannahum	*they (f.) taught them (m.)*	→	maa garrannahumš	*they (f.) did not teach them (m.)*
garranni	*they (f.) taught me*	→	maa garranniišš	*they (f.) did not teach me*
garrayn	*they (f.) taught*	→	maa garrannišš	*they (f.) did not teach you (f.s.)*
garrannana	*they (f.) taught us*	→	maa garrannanaaš	*they(f.) did not teach us*

Other examples:

ligiitannih	*you (f.p.) found him*	→	maa *ligiitannihš	*you (f.p.) did*
		→	maa ligiitannišš	*not find him*
ʔilgannih	*find (f.p.) him!*	→	maa *tilgannihš	*do not find*
		→	maa tilgannišš	*(f.p.) him!*

Note that maa/garrannišš/ *they (f.) did not teach him* or *they (f.) did not teach you (f.s.)* is ambiguous.

The rules above also apply to verbs that take the indirect pronominal suffix /l-/ 'to'.:

gaalatlih	*she told him*	→	maa gaalatlišš	*she did not tell him*
gaaluulih	*they (m.) told him*	→	maa gaaluulišš	*they (m.) did not tell him*
*gaalanlih		→	gaalallih	*they (f.) told him (assimilation)*
gaalallih	*they (f.) told him*	→	maa gaalallišš	*they (f.) did not tell him*
*gultlih		→	gultalih	*I told him (epenthesis)*
gultalih	*I told him*	→	maa gultališš	*I did not tell him*
gultiilih	*you (f.s.) told him*	→	maa gultiilišš	*you (f.s.) did not tell him*
*gaallih		→	gallih	*he told him(vowel shortening)*
gallih	*he told him*	→	maa gallišš	*he did not tell him*
gallaha	*he told her*	→	maa gallahaaš	*he did not tell her*

4. -vh + l- → -vll-

Like rule 2. above (-vvh +š → -všš), where /-h/ assimilates on to the following /š/, /-h/ assimilates on to a following /l-/. Examples:

*gultihlak	→	gultillak	*I said it (m.) to you*
(gult + lak	→	gultalak	*I said to you)*
*gultihlaha	→	gultillaha	*I said it (m.) to her*
*gultihlakum	→	gultillakum	*I said it (m.) to you (m.p.)*
*ʔaddaytihlakin	→	ʔaddaytillakin	*I gave it (m.) to you(f.p.)*
*ʔaddaynaahlahin	→	ʔaddaynaallahin	*we gave it (m.) to them(f.)*

5. -t + -h- → -th- ~ -t-

This rule applies to verb forms that end with the subject markers /-t/ or /-at/ and have the pronominal suffixes /-ha/, /-hin/ and /-hum/. In such a case two alternate forms occur: forms with the /-h-/ or forms in which the /-h-/ is elided. Forms with the /-h-/ are more common. Examples:

ʔaddayt + ha	→	ʔaddaytha	~	ʔaddayta	*I gave her*
ligiit + hin	→	ligiithin	~	ligiitin	*I found them (f.)*
ramayt + hum	→	ramaythum	~	ramaytum	*I shot them (m.)*
daʕat + hin	→	daʕathin	~	daʕatin	*she invited them (f.)*
ʕallamat + ha	→	ʕallamatha	~	ʕallamata	*she taught her*

B. Suffixed to Nouns

As mentioned above, suffixed pronouns indicate possession when added to nouns. However, in SA possession is more commonly expressed by the use of /ḥagg/ belonging to'. Thus, /haaða l-gaat ḥaggi/ 'this qat is mine' is more commonly used than /haaða gaati/ 'this is my qat'. The following are the personal pronouns and the corresponding noun suffixed forms:

Personal Pronoun	Noun Suffixed Pronoun	
huw	-ih	*he*
hum	-hum	*they (m.)*
hiy	-ha	*she*
hin	-hin	*they (f.)*
ʔant	-ak	*you (m.s.)*
ʔantu	-kum	*you (m.p.)*
ʔantiy	-iš	*you (f.s.)*
ʔantayn	-kin	*you (f.p.)*
ʔana	-iy	*I*
ḥna	-na	*we*

The noun suffixed forms above are suffixed to nouns that end with /-vc/ only, e.g., /waladiy/ my son', /waladhum/ 'their (m.) son', /waladiš/ 'your (f.s.) son', etc.

Note that when the pronominal suffixes /-hum/, /-ha/, and /-hin/ are suffixed to nouns ending with the uvulars /x-ġ/ or the pharyngeals /ḥ-ʕ/ preceded by a vowel, progressive assimilation takes place.:

x + h	as in /juxhum/	→	[juuxxum]	*their (m.) broadcloth*
	as in /juxhin/	→	[juuxxin]	*their (f.) broadcloth*
ġ + h	as in /sibaaġha/	→	[sibaaġġæ]	*her fingernail polish*
ḥ + h	as in /ṣabuuḥhum/	→	[ṣabuuuḥḥum]	*their (m.) breakfast*
ʕ + h	as in /juuʕha/	→	[juuʕʕa]	*her hunger*
	as in /juuʕhum/	→	[juuʕʕum]	*their (m.) hunger*

If a uvular or a pharyngeal forms a consonant cluster with a preceding consonant, then the change in 2. below takes place, i.e., the helping vowel /-a-/ is used:

garʕ	+ -kum	→	garʕakum	*your (m.p.) pumpkin seeds*
	+ -hin	→	garʕahin	*their (f.) pumpkin seeds*
	+ -na	→	garʕana	*our pumpkin seeds*
	+ -hum	→	garʕahum/garʕuhum	*their (m.) pumpkin seeds*

Other forms of nouns require appropriate changes in the suffixed pronouns. The major changes are:

1. Masculine Nouns Ending With /-v/

   A masculine noun ending with -a, takes the suffixes /-aah/, /-aahum,/ /-aaha/, /-aahin/, /-aak/, /-aakum/, /-aaš/, /-aakin/, /-aana/, and /-aaya/ for /ʔana/ 'I'. Examples:

mustašfa	hospital	→	mustašfaaya	*my hospital*
			mustašfaahum	*their (m.) hospital*
			mustašfaak	*your (m.s.) hospital*
			mustašfaaha	*her hospital*
			mustašfaana	*our hospital*

Masculine nouns that end with /-aaʔ/, e.g., /ġadaaʔ/ lunch' are usually said with imaalah and long vowel /-aa-/ is shortened, e.g., /ġadaaʔ/ →/ġaddeeʔ/. Some speakers shorten the long vowel /-ee-/ and say /ġade'/ instead. Such words as these are governed by the same rule:

ġadaaʔ	lunch	→	ġadaaya	*my lunch*
			ġadaak	*your (m.s.) lunch*
			ġadaaš	*your (f.s.) lunch*
			ġadaana	*our lunch*
			ġadaah	*his lunch*

etc., etc., etc.

Other examples are: /ʕašaaʔ/ 'dinner', /šagaaʔ/ 'hard work, labor', /waraaʔ/ 'behind', etc.

Nouns ending with -i do not take suffixed pronouns, unless they are very commonly used, e.g. /guuzi/ 'lamb'./guuzi/ 'lamb' takes the following suffixes: /-yih/, -/yhum/, -/yha/, /-yhin/, /-yak/, /-ykum/, /-yisʔ, /-ykin/, /-yi/, and /-yna/. Examples:

guuziyi	*my lamb*
guuziyiš	*your (f.s.) lamb*
guuziyhum	*their (m.) lamb*
guuziykum	*your (m.p.) lamb*

Nouns that are not very commonly used make use of /ḥagg/. Examples:

/ʔal-kitli ḥaggiy/	*my tea kettle*
/ʔat-taaniki ḥaggakum/	*your (m.p.) water tank*
/ʔal-loori ḥaggana/	*our truck*

2. Nouns Ending With /-cc/

Nouns ending with a two-consonant cluster take the helping vowel /-a-/ before suffixes beginning with a consonant. The helping vowel /-u-/ is usually used before -hum. Examples:

bayt	house	→	baytiy	*my house*
			baytiš	*your (f.s.) house*
			baytih	*his house*
		but:	baytana	*our house*
			baytakum	*your (m.p.) house*
			baytahin	*their (f.) house*
			baytahum/baytuhum	*their (m.) house*
ḥagg	belong to	→	ḥggiy	*belonging to me*
			ḥaggiš	*belonging to you (f.s.)*
			ḥaggana	*belonging to us*
			ḥaggahum/ḥagguhum	*belonging to them (m.)*

etc., etc., etc.

3. The nouns /ʔab/ 'father' and /ʔax/ 'brother' take the suffixes /-uuh/, /-uuhum/, -/uuha/, /-hin/, /-uuk/, /-uukum/, /-uuš/, /-uukin/, /-na/, and /-iy/ for /ʔana/ 'I':

ʔabiy	*my father*
ʔabuuna	*our father*
ʔabuuh	*his father*
ʔabuuhum	*their (m.) father*
ʔabuuha	*her father*
ʔabuuhin	*their (f.) father*
ʔabuuk	*your (m.s.) father*
ʔabuukum	*your (m.p.) father*
ʔabuuš	*your (f.s.) father*
ʔabuukin	*your (f.p.) father*

4. Nouns ending with -eh/-ah undergo the following change before the pronominal suffixes:

-eh/-ah	→	-at-	
ḥilbeh	→	ḥilbathum	*their (m.) fenugreek*
	→	ḥilbatiš	*your (f.s.) fenugreek*
	→	ḥilbatih	*his fenugreek*
mareh	→	maratih	*his wife*
	→	maratiy	*my wife*
šamṭah	→	šamṭatha	*her bag*
	→	šamṭathum	*their (m.) bag*
	→	šamṭatiš	*your (f.s.) bag*
jambiyeh	→	jambiyatiy	*my dagger*
	→	jambiyatih	*his dagger*
madaaʕah	→	madaaʕathum	*their (m.) waterpipe*
	→	madaaʕatih	*his waterpipe*
	→	madaaʕatna	*our waterpipe*

Examples of masculine nouns ending with -eh/-ah/:

ʔaṣaaṭiyeh	→	ʔaṣaaṭiyathum	*their (m.) craftsmen*
	→	ʔaṣaaṭiyatna	*our craftsmen*
baḥriyeh	→	baḥriyatna	*our naval fleet*
	→	baḥriyathum	*their (m.) naval fleet*
ṭaraagaʕah	→	ṭaraagaʕathum	*their (m.) thieves*

5. The Dual

It was mentioned in 10.2.2 that /ʔθnayn/ 'two (m.)' or /θintayn/ 'two (f.)' + the plural of the noun are more commonly used than /-ayn/ suffixed to a masculine noun or /-tayn/ suffixed to a feminine noun ending with -eh/-ah. The dual + a suffixed pronoun construction is formed according to the following formula:

ʔal-iθnayn + plural noun + pronominal suffix

or: ʔaθ-θintayn + plural noun + pronominal suffix

My language informants tell me that the reverse order is also possible but not very common.

ʔal-iθnayn ʕyaalak	ʕyaalak al-iθnayn	*your (m.s.) two children*
ʔal-iθnayn buyuutkum	buyuutkum al-iθnayn	*your (m.p.) two houses*
ʔaθ-θintayn banaathin	banaathin aθ-θintayn	*their (f.p.) two daughters*
ʔaθ-θintayn šimiiṭkin	šimiiṭkin aθ-θintayn	*your (f.p.) two bags*

Note that */ʕyaal iθnayn/ 'two children' or */banaat θintayn/ 'two girls' are ungrammatical in SA.

If the dual indicates 'two people or two things from a country', then the construction /ḥagg/ 'belonging to + suffixed pronoun follows /ʔal-iθnayn/ or /ʔaθ-θintayn/:

ʔiθnayn min al-yaman	*two (m.) from Yemen*
ʔal-ʔiθnayn ḥaggiy min al-yaman	*my two (m.) things from Yemen*
θintayn min as-suʕuudiyeh	*two (f.) from Saudi Arrabia*
ʔaθ-θintayn ḥaggiy min as-suʕuudiyeh	*my two (f.) things from Saudi Arabia*

If the dual indicates weight, measurement, or money, then the following formula is used:

definite noun + dual morpheme /-ayn/ + ḥagg + pronominal suffix:

ʔar-raṭlayn ḥaggih	*his two pounds*
ʔar-riyaalayn ḥaggiš	*your (f.s.) two riyals*
ʔal-bugšatayn ḥaggaha	*her two* bugšas

12.3 Demonstrative Pronouns

The main forms of the demonstrative pronouns that indicate near objects or persons are:

masculine singular:	haaða, ðayya	*this (one), that (one)*
feminine singular:	haaðih, tayyih	*this (one), that (one)*
plural (m. or f.):	haaðawla	*these, those*

The main forms of the demonstrative pronouns that indicate distant objects or persons are:

masculine singular:	haaḓaak, ðayyik	*that (one)*
feminine singular:	tayyik	*that (one)*
plural (m. or f.):	haaḓawlaak, ðawliyyik	*those*

It should be pointed out that there are less commonly used forms of demonstrative pronouns, which are used in nearby villages and small towns, such as Wadi Dhar, Al-Rawdha, Ans, Kawkaban, Badan, Sawan, Dhamar, etc. Another form of /haaða/ 'this (m.s.)' is /ða/ or /ha/ prefixed to the following noun. Another form of /haaðih/ 'this (f.s.)' is /haaðiy/. /ðawlaaʔi/ is another form for /haaðawla/ 'these'. In San'a and in neighboring villages and small towns /haaḓakka/ and /tayyikka/ are forms that are less commonly used than /haaḓaak/ 'that (m.s.)' and /tayyik/ 'that (f.s.)', respectively, and /ðawliyyik/ or /haaḓawlakka/ are less commonly used than /haaḓawlaak/ 'these' (m. or f.)'.

The following examples show usages of demonstrative pronouns:

ðayya šaybeh naahi.	*This is a good old man.*
haaða min faḓl al-kariim	*This is from Gods kindness, graciousness.*
tayyik sayyaarah jadiideh	*That is a new car.*
haaða bard gawiy	*This is very cold weather.*
haaðawla naas naahiyiin	*These are good people.*
haaḓawlaak nisaaʔ ḥaaliyaat	*Those are beautiful women.*
haaḓawlaak, maa yištuw?	*Those (people), what do they want?*
haaðawla, kayf jaw?	*These (people), how did they come?*
maa yištayn haaðawla?	*What do these (women) want?*
ðawliyyik ʔayyaam xayr	*Those were good days.*
ʔiddiili tayyih!	*Give me this (one)!*
maa ʔabsartš ðayya	*I did not see this (one).*
haaḓawlaak allaði ʔaštiihum	*Those are the things (m.) I want.*
haaða ʔaaxir al-ʕunguud	*This is the last descendant.*

An independent pronoun may precede the demonstrative pronoun for emphasis:

hin haaðawlaaʔ jayn.	*They (f.) are the ones who came.*
huw ðayya šaybeh naahi.	*It's this (one) who is a good man.*
hiy tayyih mareh ḥaaliyeh.	*It's this (one) who is a beautiful woman.*

Section Thirteen

13. PARTICLES

13.1 Interrogatives

The main interrogative particles in SA are the following:

man	*who*
ʔayn	*where*
kam	*how many; how much*
kayf	*how*
maa	*what (+v, + pron.)*
mata	*when*
limih	*why*
ʔay(ya)	*which (one), what (+n)*
b-	*what (+ /ʔism/ name)*
ʔay(ya) ḥiin	*at what time*

Each of the interrogative particles except for /maa/, /b-/, and /ʔay(ya)/ can be used independently as a one-word question, and in a pre- or post-verbal position:

man?	*Who?*
ʔayn?	*Where?*
kam?	*How many? How much?*
kayf?	*How?*
mata?	*When?*
limih?	*Why?*
ʔay(ya) ḥiin?	*At what time?*
man absart?	*Whom did you see?*
ʔabsart man	*Whom did you see?*
kam tištiy?	*How much do you want?*
tištiy kam?	*How many do you want?*
kayf jiʔt?	*How did you come?*
jiʔt kayf?	*How did you come?*
mata ṣṭabaḥt?	*When did you have breakfast?*
(ʔi)ṣṭabaḥt mata?	*When did you have breakfast?*
limih jiʔt ʔila l-yaman?	*Why did you come to Yemen?*
jiʔt limih ʔila l-yaman?	*Why did you come to Yemen?*

/man/ 'who', /kam/ 'how much', /ʔayn/ 'where', /kayf/ 'how', and /mata/ 'when' can be used in a pre- or post-nominal or pronominal position:

man ʔant?	ʔant man?	*Who are you (m.s.)?*
man ʔantayn?	ʔantayn man?	*Who are you (f.p.)?*
ʔayn al-jihhaal?	ʔal-jihhaal ʔayn?	*Where are the children?*
ʔayn hum?	hum ʔayn?	*Where are they (m.)?*
(bi)kam ʔaṭ-ṭamaaiis?	ʔaṭ-ṭamaaṭiis (bi)kam?	*How much are the tomatoes?*
(bi)kam hum?		*How much are they?*

/ʔay(ya)/ must be used in a pre-nominal position:

ʔay(ya) waaḥid?	*Which one?*
ʔay(ya) waaḥid tištiy?	*Which one do you want?*

It can be preceded by a preposition:

min ʔay(ya) bilaad antayn?	*Which country are you (f.p.) from?*

Note that /*ʔay(ya) bilaad ʔantayn min?/ is ungrammatical.

fi ʔay(ya) šaariʕ tuskun?	*On which street do you (m.s.) live?*

/man/ 'who', /kam/ 'how much; how many', /maa/ 'what', /limih/ 'why', /ʔayn/ 'where', and /kayf/ 'how' can be used as parts of equational sentences (see 14.1):

man ʔabuuk?	*Who is your (m.s.) father?*
maa liš?	*What is wrong with you (f.s.)?*
kam makaan fiih?	*How many rooms are there in it?*
(bi)kam al-mawz?	*How much are the bananas?*
ʔayn al-madaaʕah?	*Where is the waterpipe?*
kayf al-jaww?	*How is the weather?*

/man/ 'who', /kam/ 'how many', /ʔayn/ 'where', /mata/ 'when', and /ʔay(ya)/ 'what, which (one)' can be followed by a preposition:

ʔila man ʔaddaytaha?	*Who did you (m.s.) give it (f.) to?*
bi kam?	*For how much?*
min kam saneh?	*For how many years? Since when?*
min ʔayn hiy?	*Where is she from?*
ʔila mata yištaġil?	*Up to what (time), until when, is he working?*
maʕ ʔay(ya) jaamiʕah?	*With which university?*

/man/ 'who' can be used after the preposition /ḥagg/ to mean 'whose; for whom, to whom':

ḥagg man ðayyih al-bayt?	*Whose is this house?*
ðayyik as-sayyaarah ḥagg man?	*Whose is that car?*

/man/ preceded by a noun expresses the meaning of 'Whose?'

bayt man haaða?	*Whose house is this?*
jihhaal man haaḍawlaak?	*Whose children are those?*

/kam/ 'how much' is optionally preceded by the preposition /bi-/ to mean 'how much is, are?'

(bi)kam al-ḥabḥab?	*How much are the watermelons?*
(bi)kam ar-raṭl?	*How much is the pound?*

Note the following idiomatic uses of /kam/:

kam lak haana?	*How long have you (m.s.) been here?*
kam ʕumrak?	*How old are you (m.s.)?*
ʔibn kam ʔant?	*How old are you (m.s.)?*
bint kam ʔantiy?	*How old are you (f.s.)?*
saaʕat kam?	*At what time?*
kam as-saaʕah?	*What time is it?*

b- 'what' is only followed by the word /ʔism/ 'name':

b-ismak?	*What is your (m.s.) name?*
b-ismiš?	*What is your (f.s.) name?*
b-ismih?	*What is his name?*
b-ismaha?	*What is her name?*

13.2 Prepositions

Almost all prepositions in SA take suffixed pronouns. In most cases the suffixation of pronouns to prepositions is governed by the same rules as nouns. Thus /minniy/ 'from me', /minha/ 'from her,' /ʕalayya/ 'on me,' /miθliy/ 'like me,' /miθlahum ~ miθluhum/ 'like them (m.),' /jambiš/ 'by you (f.s.),' /jambana/ 'by us,' etc. In a few cases the base forms differ on suffixation, which involves /fi/ 'in,' /ʕala/ 'on,' /ṣala/ 'toward', /min/ 'from,' /ʕan/ 'about,' and /maʕ/ 'with'. The only prepositions that do not take suffixed pronouns are /saaʕ/ 'like' and /ḥawaali/ 'about, approximately.' The suffixed pronoun that corresponds to 'I' is /-yya/ after /ʕala/ and /ṣala/. For the rest /ʕala/ and /ṣala/ change into /ʕalay-/ and /ṣalay-/ before syffixation, /-i/ of /-ih/ and /-is/ is dropped. Thus:

ʕalayh	*on him*	ṣalayh	*toward him*
ʕalayhum	*on them (m.)*	ṣalayhum	*toward them (m.)*
ʕalayš	*on you (f.s.)*	ṣalayš	*toward you (f.s.)*
ʕalaykin	*on you (f.p.)*	ṣalaykin	*toward you (f.p.)*
ʕalayha	*on her*	ṣalayha	*toward her*
ʕalayhin	*on them (f.)*	ṣalayhin	*toward them (f.)*
ʕalayk	*on you (m.s.)*	ṣalayk	*toward you (m.s.)*
ʕalaykum	*on you (m.p.)*	ṣalaykum	*toward you (m.p.)*
ʕalayna	*on us*	ṣalayna	*toward us*

The suffixed pronoun that corresponds to 'I' is /-niy/. Thus: /fiiniy/ 'in me,' /fiik/ 'in you (m.s.),' /fiikum/ 'in you (m.p.),' /fiih/ 'in him,' /fiihum/ 'in them,' /fiiha/ 'in her,' etc. Prepositions of the pattern CVC, except for /maʕ/ 'with', change into CVCC- before suffixes with initial -V. Thus: /ʕannih/ 'about him,' /ʕanniš/ 'about you (f.s.),' /ʕannak/ 'about you (m.s.),' but /ʕanhum/ 'about them (m.),' /ʕanha/ 'about her,' /ʕanhin/ 'about them (f.),' /ʕankum/ 'about you (m.p.),' /ʕankin/ 'about you (f.p.),' /ʕanniy/ 'about me,' and /ʕanna/ or /ʕannana/ 'about us.' Similarly /min/ 'from' changes into /minn-/. Examples: /minnih/ 'from him,' /minnak/ 'from you (m.s.),' and /minniš/ 'from you (f.s.),' /minhum/ 'from them (m.),' /minha/ 'from her,' etc.

maʕ/ 'with' has two alternate forms /maʕ/ or /miʕ/ before suffixes with initial -V:

maʕh ~ miʕih	*with him*
maʕiy ~ miʕiy	*with me*
maʕak ~ miʕak	*with you (m.s.)*
maʕiš ~ miʕiš	*with you (f.s.)*

With the other suffixes /maʕ/ changes into /maʕaa-/:

maʕaahum	*with them (m.)*	maʕaaha	*with her*
maʕaahin	*with them (f.)*	maʕaakum	*with you (m.p.)*
maʕaakin	*with you (f.p.)*	maʕaana	*with us*

Prepositions in SA may be divided into the following groups:

A. These are prepositions proper, i.e., they are used only as prepositions and are followed by a noun, a suffixed pronoun, a demonstrative pronoun, or a particle. The following are the most common:

fi: *in; on; within, during; by, among*

kalaam fi kalaam	*prattle, nonsense*
fi ðayyik al-yawm	*on that day*
fi š-šahr al-gaadim	*during next month*
fi ʕišriin saneh	*in twenty years*
xamseh fi sitteh	*five (multiplied) by six*

min: *from; among; belong to; of; ago*

hiy min ṣanʕa.	*She is from San'a.*
min faᶁl-i-llaah	*from Gods favor, benevolence*
min faᶁlak!	*If you please! lit., "from your favor"*
min bayt al-fagiih	*belonging to, from, the Fagih family*
min al-ḥamaadineh	*belonging to, from, the family or tribe of Hamdan*
minhum waaḥid šuuʕ.	*One of (among) them is ugly.*
min waaḥid ʔila waaḥid	*from one to another*
min yawm ʔila yawm	*from day to day*
maa gult min saaʕah?	*What did you (m.s.) say an hour ago?*

ʕala: *on, over, according to (ones taste, liking); against*

ʔas-salaam -u-ʕalaykum!	*Peace be upon you!*
midd rijlak ʕala gadr fraašak.	*prov. As you make your bed you must lie in it. (lit.),"Stretch your (m.s.) leg according to your bed."*
ʕala kulli[72] ḥaal	*in any case; however*
maa ʕalayk (min)	*Never mind! Dont worry about...*
maʕaahum maʕaahum; ʕalayhum ʕalayhum	*with them and against them, for their own good*
ʕala jamb![73]	*lit., "To the side (of the road)." Pull over!*
ʔaṣ-ṣabaaya ʕala ʕammaathin maa hin ʕala ʔummahathin.	*prov. Young girls take after their paternal aunts, not their mothers.*

ʕan: *about; away from*

gal-liy ʕannak.	*He told me about you.*
ġaab ʕan ʔahlih.	*He went away from his folks.*

b-: *with; by means of; for (at the price of)*

štaraah-i-b-zalaṭih.	*He bought it with his money.*
gaṭaʕ al-ḥabḥabeh b-i-s-sikkiin	*He cut the watermelon with a .knife.*
ṭaʕanih b-l-jambiyeh.	*He stabbed him with the dagger.*
saafar b-i-ṭ-ṭayyaarah.	*He traveled by plane.*
baaʕih b-raʔs maalih.	*He sold it for its cost price.*
sirt b-nafsiy.	*I left by myself.*
ʔar-raṭl b-i-ryaalayn.	*A pound is for two riyals.*

bayn: *between; among*

bayniy wa baynak (*bayniy wa ʔant.)	*between me and you (m.s.)*
šallayt waaḥid min baynahum	*I took one from among them.*
bayn ʔixwatak	*among your brothers*

baʕd: after; in

baʕd ġudweh	*after tomorrow*
baʕd að-ðuhr	*in the afternoon*
baʕd saaʕah	*in an hour*

maʕ: *with, in the company of*

sirt maʕ yaḥya.	*I went with Yahia.*
sirt maʕaahum.	*I went with them.*
kam duulaar maʕak?	*How many dollars do you have?*
maʕ baʕðahum al-baʕð̣	*together (3rd pers. mas. p.)*
šii-bih maʕak?	*Do you have anything?*

jamb: *by, near; beside*

gambar jambiy	*He sat by my side.*
ʔal-maktab jamb al-mustašfa	*The office is near the hospital.*
gad kaan jambiy	*He was beside me.*

miθl: *like, similar to; the same as*

miθl ʔabuuh.	*(He is) like his father.*
miθl al-yawm	*the same as today*
miθl ðayya	*like this; in this manner*

saaʕ: synonymous with /miθl/, though more commonly used.

saaʕ al-jamal	*like a camel*
mḥammir saaʕ an-naṣaara	*(He is) red-colored like Christians.*
ḥamal saaʕ al-jinn.	*He ran (away) like jinnis.*

/saaʕ/, unlike /miθl/ does not take suffixed pronouns, but it takes /maa/ + personal pronouns instead:

saaʕ maa-na	*like me*
saaʕ maa-ḥna	*like us*
saaʕ maaʔant	*like you (m.s.)*
saaʕ maa-ntu	*like you (m.p.)*
saaʕ maa hiy	*like her*
saaʕ maa hin	*like them (f)* *etc. etc. etc.*

ʕind: at (the time of); in the possession of; at (someone's place)

ʔal-guuziy ʕind al-jazzaar	*Lamb is at the butchers.*
ʔaḍ̄-ḍ̄ayf ʕindiy.	*The guest is at my place(or with me here).*
ʕind al-buṭuun taḍ̄iiʕ al-ʕuguul	*prov. When we eat, our minds stop thinking.*

l-: 'to have (with suffixed pronoun); to; in the direction of; take after, resemble in character and features

gult la-buuk.	*I told your (m.s.) father.*
laha ʕyaal ṣiġaar.	*She has little children.*
raaḥ la-fawg.	*He went (to) upstairs.*
rijiʕ la-waraaʔ	*He went backwards, in reverse.*
ʔal-walad la-buuh.	*Like father like son.*
kam la-k fi l-yaman?	*How long have you been in Yemen?*

ḥawaali: *approximately, about*

gaʕad ḥawaali saneh.	*He stayed about a year.*
ḥawaali saaʕat sitt	*about six oclock*

ʕala sibb: *because of; due to*

ʕala sibb al-maṭar	*because of the rain*
jiʔt ʕala sibbaha.	*I came because of her.*

B. These are prepositions that can also be used as adverbs and nouns. The following are the most common:

fawg: *over, above; up*

fawg al-bayt	*above, over the house*
huw ṭaaliʕ fawg.	*He is going upstairs.*
fawg afḍal min tiḥt.	*Up (upstairs) is better than down (downstairs).*
raaḥ la-fawg.	*He went upstairs.*

tiḥt: opposite of /fawg/

al-kaatib tiḥt al-mudiir.	*The clerk is under the director.*
jaaʔ min tiḥt.	*He came from below.*

waraaʔ: 'behind; after', usually said with ʔimaalah /waree'/ if followed by pause.

waraaʔ al-matḥaf	*behind the museum*
rijiʕ ʔila l-wareeʔ.	*He went backwards.*
guddaam ʔaḥsan min al-wareeʔ	*The front (e.g., position or place) is better than the back.*

xalf: synonymous with /waraaʔ/.

guddaam: opposite of /waraaʔ/

guddaam al-bank	*in front of the bank*
xuṭiy guddaam	*He walked in front.*
xṭa guddamana!	*Walk (m.s.) in front of us!*

daaxil: *inside, within*

daaxil al-makaan	*inside the room*
min daaxil	*from the inside, from within*

xaarij: opposite of /daaxil/

xaarij baytana	*outside our house*
xaarij al-jaziirah	*outside the (Arabian) Peninsula*
min al-xaarij	*from abroad; from the outside*
fi l-xaarij	*abroad*

gabl: *before, prior to; ago*

gabl aṣ-ṣalaah	*before prayer*
gabl saaʕat sitt	*before six oclock*
gabl saaʕah	*an hour ago*
jeʔ min gabl.	*He came before.*
gad kaan haana min gabl.	*He had been here before.*

Note that nisba adjectives (see 11.5.1.3) can be derived from this group of prepositions, e.g., /fawgaaniy/ or /fawgiy/ 'upper', /tiḥtaaniy/ or /tiḥtiy/ 'lower', /daaxiliy/ 'internal', etc., except for /gabl/. The nisba adjectives from /waraaʔ/ and /guddaam/ are /warraaniy/ and /guddamaaniy/, respectively.

tijaah: *in the direction of; opposite, in front of*

xuṭiy tijaah al-baḥr.	*He walked in the direction of the sea.*
min haaða t-tijaah	*from this direction*
ʔal-baḥr tijaahna.	*The sea is in front of us.*
ʔal-mighaayeh tijaah al-fundug	*The coffee house is in front of the hotel.*

ġayr: other than, except for; (+ article) the others, other people

ʔiddiili ġayr haaðawla!	*Give me some other ones!*
kulluhum jaw ġayr ḥasan	*They (m.) all came except for Hasan.*
yištiy maal al-ġayr.	*He likes what belongs to others.*

ḥagg: *belonging to, for*

ʔat-taayir ḥagg as-sayyaarah	*the tire of the car or: The tire belongs to the car.*
ʔas-sayyaarah ḥaggiy	*my car or: The car belongs to me.*
ḥagg nafsih w-ḥagg ʕyaalih	*for himself and for his children*

Many of the prepositions can be compounded with /min/ 'from' /ġayr/ 'other than,' etc., i.e., compound prepositions can be formed with /min/ or /ġayr/ as the first element.:

min gabl	*before; ago*
min tijaah	*from the direction of*
min ʕind	*from the place, house, of*
min tiḥt	*from below, under*
ġayr tiḥt	*other than below; except for below*
ġayr guddaam	*other than in front; except for in front*

Other examples:

la-fawg	*upwards*
la-waraaʔ	*backwards*
gabl fawg	*before above*
miθl gabl	*like before*
saaʕ mawwal	*like before*
saaʕ maa fawg	*like upstairs*
saaʕ maa gabl	*like before*

13.3 Conjunctions

13.3.1 Coordinating Conjunctions

The main coordinating conjunctions in SA are the following:

wa: /wa/ 'and' has four basic forms, depending upon its environment and the rate of speech. Either /w-/ or /ʔu-/ is used at the beginning of a sentence or a phrase: /w-ḥasan/ 'and Hasan,' /w-ant min ʔayn?/ 'And where are you from?' /w-/ is normally used in a pre-vowel initial position, e.g., /w-ismih/ 'and his name' and medially between two vowels, e.g., /ṣaaliḥ w-ant/ 'Saleh and you.' Otherwise /u-/ is usually used, e.g., /ðamaar u-ṣanʕa/ 'Dhamar and San'a.' Note the use of /wa/ in literary borrowings: /ʔahlan wa sahlan!/ 'Welcome!' (In the transcription employed in this volume, however, this conjunction is always shown as /wa/.)

ʔal-ḥareew wa l-ḥareeweh	*the bridegroom and the bride*
ʔismaha wa ʔism ʔabuuha	*her name and her fathers name*

walla: 'or.' /walla/, like /wa/, may join words, phrases, and sentences:

ʔant walla ʕaṭa?	*You (m.s.) or Ata?*
gabl að̣-ð̣uhr walla baʕd að̣-ð̣uhr	*before noon or afternoon*
jaaʔ walla saar haanaak?	*Did he come or did he go there?*
bi-ysammuunih ʕabd al-gaadir walla wajiih?	*Do you call him Abdulkadir or Wajih?*

In the last example /walla/ is explanatory.74

aw: 'or.' /ʔaw/ is synonymous with /walla/ and is typically used to join sentences:

gaal ʔaw maa gaalš	*(whether) he said or not*

fa: 'and, and then'. /fa/ is usually replaced by /wa/, but it usually implies a quick and logical or natural reaction or consequence. It approaches the meaning of 'and (my) reaction, or the reaction called for by the situation ...' /daʕaaniy fa-sirt lih/ 'He called me, and I then went to him.'

ʔimma-willa: *neither...nor*

ʔimma haana willa haanaak	*either here or there*
ʔimma tji willa tsiir	*either you come or go*

la-wala: *neither ... nor*

la lih wala ʕalayh.	*Nobody owes him anything and he does not owe anybody anything.*
la giri wala štaġal.	*He neither studied nor worked.*
la tiḥmil wala tibṭiy!	*Do not run and do not walk slowly!*

laakin: *but; however*

jiʔt laakin maa ʔabsartih.	*I came but I did not see him.*
laakinnih ḥaami šwayyeh.	*but he is running a low temperature*

13.3.2 Subordinating Conjunctions

A. Temporal

lawma: *until; while; when*

raaʕayt lih lawma jaa?	*I waited for him until he came.*
ḥaakaytih lawma gaal ṭayyib.	*I talked with him until he.said, "Fine, O.K."*
lawma kunt xaaṭiy ?absart ḥsayn.	*While I was walking, I saw Hussein.*
lawma wuṣul raaḥ al-ḥakiim.	*When he arrived, he went to.the doctor.*
?addayt-a-lih al-waragah lawma jaa?	*I gave him the piece of paper when he came.*

gablama: *before*

gablama sirt al-jaamiʕ	*before I went to the mosque*

lamma: *when* /lawma/ is more commonly used.

lamma daxal sallam ʕalayna.	*When he entered, he greeted us.*

baʕdama: after (opposite of /gablama/)

yawmma: *the day when; when*

yawmma absarthum tḥaakayt maʕaahum.	*When I saw them (m.), I spoke to them.*
yawmma maat	*the day when he died*

w-: while, when. As a temporal conjunction, /w-/ precedes an independent pronoun:

?absartih w-huw raakib saykal.	*I saw him while he was riding a bicycle.*
w-aana kunt saayir	*while I was leaving*
w-hiy kaanat tigra?	*while she was reading*

tijaahma: 'before.' Synonymous with /gablama/, though less common.

ʔakal tijaahma gaabalak ʕams.	*He ate before he met you yesterday.*

ḥiin: *when; during the time that*

ʕa-yisbir kull šay ḥiin tijiy.	*Everything will be ready when you come.*

B. Conditional[75]

laa: 'if.' Variants of /laa/ are /ʔin/ and /ʔiða/. /ʔin/ is not very common.

laa wugiʕ maṭar š-axruj aḥriθ.	*If it rains, I will go out to plough.*
laa ja ḥsayn guuluulih...	*If Husain comes, tell (m.s.) him that ...*
laa taġawfal ad-dimm tagambaʕ al-faʔr	*(lit. "If the cat is inattentive, the mouse will jump out of joy.") (Meaning: 'When the cat's away, the mouse will play.'*
laa ʕirif al-gabiili baab daarak galabt al-madaggah.	*(lit. "If the gabiili knows the door to your house, turn your door knocker upside down.") (Meaning: 'Give him an inch and he will take a mile.')*

ʔin: *if*

ʔin garayt najaḥt.	*If you study, you will succeed.*
ʔin jaaʔ al-xayr fa-ḥna niʕtaadih wa ʔin jaaʔ al-balaaʔ fa-ḥna ʔawtaadih.	*(lit., "If wealth and abundance come, we are used to them; and if misfortune comes, we are its stakes [against it].") (Meaning: Be prepared!)*

ʔiða: *if*

ʔiða kaan ṣaaḥibak ʕasal laa tilḥasih kullih.	*(lit., "If your friend is honey, do not lick all of it.") (Meaning: 'Don't use up your credit all at once.')*
ʔiða kaθurat al-ʔadyaak taxarrab al-layl.	*(lit., "If there are too many roosters, the night will be spoiled.") (Meaning: 'Too many cooks spoil the broth.')*

law: *if*

law miʕi zalaṭ la-štarii-li bayt.	*If I had money, I would buy myself a house.*
law intabah maa ṣadam.	*If he had been careful, he would not have had an accident.*
law giriy ʔinnu najaḥ.	*If he had studied, he would have succeeded.*

lawla: *had it not been for.* /lawla/ can also be used as a preposition with the meaning of 'without.'

lawlaaha ʔinnani maa jiʔt.	*Had it not been for her, I would not have come.*
lawla yaḥya kaan maatuw.	*If it had not been for Yahia, they would have died.*

C. Purpose

min mayd: *so that, in order that*

jaaʔ min mayd yitkallam miʕi.	*He came so that he might talk to me.*

ʕala sibb: Synonymous with /min mayd/, but more commonly used.

jaaʔ ʕala sibb yištaġil.	*He came in order to work.*

/min mayd/ and /ʕala sibb/ can also be used as prepositions. See D. Others below.

D. Others

kaʔann-: /kaʔann-/ is used with suffixed pronouns; it has the meaning of 'as if...was, were' as if...had.'

kaʔannaha ʔummaha	*as if she were her mother*
kaʔanniš ʔamiirah	*as if you were a princess*
kaʔannih raʔiis al-wuzaraaʔ	*as if he were the prime minister*

It is usally followed by a noun or a noun phrase, as the above examples show.

li?ann: *because*

yišti yišrab li?annahuw ʕaaṭiš.	*He wants to drink because he is thirsty.*
li?annahum majaaniin	*because they are insane*

min mayd: Either /min mayd/ or /ʕala sibb/ can be used as prepositions. They govern nouns or suffixed pronouns. The meaning is 'because of'.

ji?t min maydiš. ji?t ʕala sibbiš.	*I came because of you (f.s.)*

li?ajl: *for the purpose of, in order to*

b-yištaġil li?ajl lugmat al-ʕayš.	*He works in order to make (eke out) a living.*

?inn-: This conjunction is usually used with suffixed pronouns and introduces a direct or an indirect speech clause; it has the meaning of 'that':

gaal innahum gabaayil.[76]	*He said that they were mountaineers.*
maa gultš inniš xuṭiitiy.	*I did not say that you had walked.*

miθlama: 'in the same manner (way) as; according to; as'

miθlama gult-a-lak	*as I have told you*
miθlama yguul al-maθal	*as the proberb says, according to what the proverb says*
jaa? miθlama saar.	*He came (back) in the same way he left. (Meaning: 'He has achieved nothing.')*

?aynama: *wherever*

?aynama saarat	*wherever she went*

walaw: *even if; although*

walaw ?addayt-a-li maal ad-dunya	*even if you gave me the wealth of the whole world*
walaw kaan abuuhum	*although he was their father*

13.4 Adverbs

Adverbs are words or phrases that modify verbs, adjectives, or other adverbs. The following are the main groups of adverbs and adverb phrases with some examples.

A. Time

ʔams: *yesterday*

wuṣul ʔams.	*He arrived yesterday.*
ʔams ar-rubuuʕ.	*Yesterday was Wednesday.*

ʔal-yawm: *today; nowadays*

ʔal-yawm al-iθnayn.	*Today is Monday.*
ʔal-yawm al-maʕiišeh ġaaliyeh.	*Nowadays the cost of living is expensive.*

ġudweh: *tomorrow*

ʕa-yijiy ġudweh.	*He will come tomorrow.*

gabl ams: *(The day) before yesterday*

gabl ams al-xamiis.	*Before yesterday was Thursday.*

ðalḥiin: *now; at this moment*

ʔayn b-tištaġil ðalḥiin?	*Where are you (m.s.) working now?*

la ðalḥiin: *up to now*

zaarathiin: *sometimes*

yxazzin zaarathiin	*He chews qat sometimes.*

zaarat yawm:	*some day*
zaarat ʕaši:	*some evening*
zaarat saaʕah:	*some hour*

min baʕd: *later on*

> gad jeʔ min baʕd.   *He came later on.*

> tayyik as-saaʕah: *then (lit. "that hour.")*
> ?al-ʕaši: *at night, in the evening*
> ?aṣ-ṣubḥ: *in the morning*
> ?uð̣-ð̣uhr: *at noon(time)*
> ?aš-šahr al-maað̣i: *last month*
> ?al-?usbuuʕ al-maað̣i: *last week*

?awwal: *before, earlier*

> gad jeʔ ?awwal.   *He had come before. He has come before.*
> gad jiit haana ?awwal.   *I have been here before.*

> gabl usbuuʕ: *a week ago*
> baʕd usbuuʕ: *in a week's time*
> gabl šahr: *a month ago*
> baʕd šahr: *in a month's time*
> gabl saneh: *a year ago*
> baʕd saneh: *in a year's time*
> gabl að̣-ð̣uhr: *before noon (time)*
> baʕd að̣-ð̣uhr: *in the afternoon*

B. Place

haana: *here* (var. /hnayya/). /hnayya/ is less common.

haanaak: (pron. /hæænaak/): *there, over there*
> haana walla haanaak   *here or there*

min haana: *from here*

min haanaak: *from there*
> min haana la-haanaak   *from here to there*

tijaah: *in the direction of*

min ðayya t-tijaah	*from this direction*

/fawg/ *up; upstairs,* /tiḥt/ *below; downstairs*

/guddaam/ *in front,* /gafa/ *behind,* (var./waraaʔ/), /tiḥt/ *behind,* etc.[77]

C. Others

fiisaʕ: *fast, quickly; immediately*

dala-dala: (usually pronounced with ʔimaalah: dala-dale) *slowly*

la-waḥd-:	*by (ones) self*
haakaða:	*like this, in this manner*
saaniy:	*straight, straight ahead*
ṭayyib:	*well, fine; all right*
tamaam:	*exactly, perfectly*
jamʕah:	*together*
kaθiir:	*a lot, a great deal*
šwayyeh:	*a little*
šwayyeh ġaaliy:	*a little expensive*
š(u)wayyeh-š(u)wayyeh:	*little by little*

farṣ: *only*

bi-ybiiʕ saaʕat farṣ	*He sells watches only.*

yamneh: *to the right, on the right*

ʔuʕṣur yamneh!	*Turn to the right!*
ʔal-maktab yamneh.	*The office (will be) on the right.*

yasrah: *to the left, on the left*

gawiy: *very.* This adverb modifies only adjectives, e.g.,

/naahiy gawiy/ '*very good*'

giyaam: *immediately*

saar giyaam.	*He left immediately.*

sunub: *standing up*(There was standing room only.)

ʔabsarna l-film sunub.	*We saw the film standing up.*

marra: *once, one time*

marratayn: *twice*

saaʕah: one hour

/saaʕatayn/	*two hours*
/saaʕat xams/	*at five o'clock*
/saaʕat θintayn/	*at two o'clock, etc.*

ʔawwalan:	*firstly, first of all*
θaaniyan:	*secondly*
ʔaxiiran:	*lastly, at last*
blaaš:	*free (of charge)*
b-al-ġaṣb:	*by force, by hook or by crook*

b-al-guwwah: Synonymous with /b-al-ġaṣb/.

b-al-galb: *incorrectly, in a wrong way*

ṣallaḥ as-saaʕah b-al-galb.	*He repaired the watch incorrectly.*

13.5 Other Particles

Among particles are also words or phrases that serve other functions, such as interjections and exclamations. A few belong to special grammatical categories with no English equivalents. Also included here are negative particles.

Some of these words and phrases have already been explained in Yemeni Arabic I and Yemeni Arabic II by the same author. The reader is referred to their meanings and usages, which are usually in NOTES ON TEXT in the individual lessons. Polite formulas, impolite formulas, curses, etc., are included in SAMPLE TEXTS below:

bass: *enough! only*

bass! uskut!	*Enough! Be quiet! Enough! Shut up!*
ʔaddii-li sukkar bass!	*Give me sugar only!*
bass ðayya	*only this one*

ya: oh (vocative particle)

  ya mḥammad! *Muhammad!*

ya rayt: *would that*

  ya raytani fi ṣanʕa. *I wish I were in San'a.*
  ya raytahum jaw. *I wish they had come.*

labbayk: *Here I am! At your service!* /labbayk/ is from literary Arabic /labbayka/ with the same meaning. It has a further use in SA, which is similar to English 'I beg your pardon! Excuse me!' in a conversation between two people. However, it is not commonly used in SA.

wal̤l̤a: *honestly; by golly!*

wal̤l̤aahi: This has a similar meaning to /wal̤l̤a/, but it is more emphatic. (UNIT 9)

naʕam: *yes; right* (UNIT 8)

ʔaywa: *yes; right,* used in free variation with /naʕam/.

la: *no,* in an answer to a question. [læʔ](/la/ + imperfect signals a negative command).

maa: (neg. part.) negates a verb.

miš: (neg. part.) negates a noun, an adjective, an adverb, or a phrase. (var., but less commonly used than /maaš/.

ḥaaḍ̣ir: *yes (sir), certainly.* More polite than /naʕam/.

t(a)faḍḍal: Please! /t(a)'faḍḍal'/ is here the imperative form of the Form V verb /t(a)'faḍḍal'/ to be so good as to do s.th. As an imperative it means please! It is said when s.o. is offered s.th., e.g., coffee, food, etc., or a seat or when urging s.o. to go first, e.g., through a door.

tfaḍḍal išrab! *Please drink (m.s.)!*

tfaḍḍaliy! *Please!Go ahead (f.s.)! Please! Come in (f.s.)!*

ṭayyib: *all right, O.K., I agree*

tamaam: *right (you) are; exactly.* /tamaam/ is usually used in the phrase /b-it-tamaam wa l-kamaal/ 'precisely'.

bi-xayr: *fine; in good health* (UNIT 2)

naahiy: *fine; in good health* (UNIT 2)

la-ši: 'if ... s.th.' (var. /la-šayʔ/)

ʔibsir la-ši bih riiḥ xaarij! 'Look (and see) if there is wind outside!'

bih: *there is, there are*78

bih xubz. *There is bread.*

šii-bih xubz? *Is there bread?*

maabiš xubz. *There isn't (any) bread.*

maaši: *no.* /maaši/ is more commonly used than /la/.

yaʕni: *that is to say, namely*

maa lak: *What's wrong with you (m.s.)?*

maa bih: *What's the matter?*

ʕaad: *yet; still; anymore; already*

maa ʕaadanaaš ṭayyib.	*I am not yet healthy. (I am no longer healthy.)*
ʕaadana l-mudiir.	*I am still the director.*
ʕaad huw xaaṭiy.	*He is still walking.*
ʕaadana xazzant.	*I have already chewed qat.*
ʕaad miʕi zalaṭ.	*I still have money.*

gad: *already*

gad huw haana.	*He is (already) here.*
gad hiy saarat.	*She has (already) left.*
maa gadanaaš ṭayyib.	*I am not healthy.*
maa gad biš miʕi zalaṭ	*I do not have any money.*

kawd-: *barely, hardly.* /kawd-/ is always used with a suffixed pronoun.

kawdakum xarajtuw.	*You (m.p.) have just gone out.*
kawdiš xaaṭiyeh.	*You (f.s.) have just walked.*

yimkin: *perhaps*, usually followed by /ʔinn-/ that.

yimkin innaha haana.	*Perhaps she is here.*

xayraat: *a lot of, a whole lot of.* It may precede or follow a noun.

gad maʕaana xayraat jihhaal.	*We have a lot of children.*
ʕindana gaat xayraat.	*We have a lot of qat.*

laazim: *must, should, have to*

laazim ysiir.	*He must go.*
laazim tsaaʕid ʔahlak.	*You have to help your folks.*

baahir:	/ʕiis/ is a synonym of /baahir/.	*well done! bravo!*
	Both /baahir/ and /ʕiis/ can be used as adjectives meaning *fine, good.*	
marḥaba:	(expression of acceptance) Yes; it's all right; that will do.	
	ruuḥ al-madraseh!	*Go (m.s.) to school!*
	marḥaba.	*Yes, I will.*
	ʔar-raṭl b-ʕišriin ryaal.	*Twenty riyals a pound.*
	marḥaba.	*O.K. (I will buy.)*
maa ʕalay-:	(with a suffixed pronoun expresses refusal). It implies a negative idea.	
	maa ʕalayya minnih.	*It (m.s.) does not concern me.*
	maa ʕalyak!	*Never mind! Do not worry!*
miš naahiy:	(expresses disapproval)	
hayya:	*come on! let's go! now then!*	
	ḥsayn! hayya!	*Husain! Let's go!*
	hayya maa gult?	*Now then! What did I say? (Speak up! What do you think I have said?*
ʔaaḥ(ḥa):	(expresses pain)	
yooh:	(expresses fear)	
yih-yih:	(expresses joy)	
yaʕaaw:	(expresses loss)	

ʔuṣṣ:	silence! shut up
kuss:	(used to drive away a dog.) It is repeated twice at least: /kuss .. kuss /
biss:	(used to drive away a cat.) It is repeated twice at least: /biss ... biss .../. Some say: /bišš ... bišš/.
ḥaaw:	used to bring animals, especially mules and donkeys, to a halt.). It is repeated twice at least: /ḥaaw ... ḥaaw/
sir:	(used to make animals walk.) It is repeated twice at least: /sir ... sir/
nanneh:	(said by a child who wants bread.)
baa-bowh:	(said by a child who wants water.)
šit ...šit:	(used as a left turn command to an animal.)
yim ... yim:	(used as a right turn command to an animal.)

FOOTNOTES

1. See, for example, John Macdonald, *"The Arabic Derived Verb Themes: A Study in Form and Meaning,"* Islamic Quarterly 7, 1963, pp. 96-116.
2. /f/, /ʕ/, and /l/ throughout this study refer to the first, second, and third radicals of the verb, respectively.
3. As in /faaš as-sirr/ 'the secret was revealed (or known)', /faašat al-ʔaxbaar/ 'the news spread,' /faašu l-jihhaal/ 'the children dispersed'.
4. This verb is usually said with ʔimaalah, i.e., /jeeʔ/ or shortened to /jeʔ/.
5. sannab might be related to the adverb /sunub/ 'standing (upright)' as in /bsar al-film sunub/ 'he saw the film standing'.
6. /jarras/ might be related to the noun /jaras/ 'bell'.
7. /xazzan/ might be related to the verb /xazan/ 'he stored, put s.th. in storage'.

8. /ṭallab/ might be related to the verb /ṭalab/ 'he requested'.

9. /tafruṭah/ stands for women's gatherings, sessions, including qat chewing sessions.

10. Instead of /tmaaraḍ̣/.

11. Instead of /tmaawat/.

12. /tabaarak/, rather than /tbaarak/, is literary.

13. A reduplicated quadriliteral verb is one in which the first two radicals are repeated, e.g., /lamlam/ 'he gathered'.

14. From now on the third person masculine singular form of the perfect will be used as the citation form of the verb, i.e. the gloss will always be 'to ...' rather than 'he...'.

15. See 4.4 Pausal Diphthongization.

16. Verbs of Forms VII and IX do not occur in SA.

17. For the definition of weak verbs, see 6.1.2 above.

18. From now on imperfect stems are cited between hyphens, e.g., -rgud- 'to sleep' as opposed to the perfect stem /ragad/ 'to sleep', which is the third person masculine singular form.

19. Historically, however, the quality of the vowel may have been determined semantically. See Wright, op. cit., pp. 29-47.

20. Peter Abboud, *"On Ablaut in Cairo Arabic"*, Afro-Asiatic Linguistics, Vol. III, Issue 9 (December 1976) p. 2. For a more recent and scholarly study see Michael Brame, "Arabic Phonology: Implications for Phonological Theory and Historical Semitics." MIT Unpublished Ph.D. Dissertation, 1970.

21. Note that /wulid/ is both active and passive, e.g., /wulidat bint/ 'She gave birth to a girl,' and /wulid fi ṣanʕa/ 'He was born in San'a'.

22. For the definition of weak verbs see 6.1.2 above.

23. /(ʔi)tka/ is a corruption of literary Arabic /ʔittakaʔ/ 'to lean'.

24. /(ʔi)šta/ is a corruption of literary Arabic /ʔištaha/ 'to want, desire'. The perfect /(ʔi)šta/ is rarely used in SA; /kaan yišti/ is very commonly used.

25. Hollow verbs of Form IV are rare in SA; they are mainly borrowings from literary Arabic or 'pan-Arabic' koine forms.

26. The order in which the patterns appear is not proportional to their frequency.

27. See 9.4 below for the occurrence of /-eh/ and /-ah/.

28. The former pattern for the formation of the dual, i.e., /θintayn/ + the sound feminine plural is more commonly used in SA. See 10.2.2 below for more details.

29. See footnote 27 above.

30. /ḥabbeh/, /ḥšarah/, and /guḥṭah/ as the first terms in construct phrases change into /ḥabbat/, /ḥšarat/, and /guḥṭat/. See 11.1 Construct Phrases below.

31. If /r/ or /g/ precedes -eh/-ah, -ah is usually used, e.g., /ṭayyaarah/ 'airplane', /sayyaarah/ 'car', /ṭaagah/ 'window', etc., but /mareh/ 'woman' and /šiigaareh/ 'cigarette' are more commonly used than /marah/ and /šiigaarah/.

32. /balas/ usually means 'prickly pears', but sometimes it is also used to mean 'figs'. If the meaning is only "figs" then /balas ʕarabi/ is usually used.

33. See 11.5.3 Nisbah Adjectives below.

34. See Footnote 27 above.

35. See Footnote 27 above.

36. See 9.4 for some more examples.

37. See 9.2 for some more examples.

38. See 9.3 for some more examples.

39. See 9.3 for some more examples.

40. See 11.5.1.3 below.

41. See 9.6 below.

42. See 9.9 above.

43. See 9.4 above for the occurrence of /-eh/ and /-ah/.

44. A /gabiili/ is an uncouth, ill-mannered peasant or mountaineer. He may carry firearms and work as a bodyguard. Note that the plural of gabiileh 'tribe' is also /gabaayil./

45. See 9.7 above.

46. See 9.8 above.

47. See 9.6 above.

48. For the occurrence of -eh/-ah see 9.4 above.

49. Construct phrases in this section are restricted to noun and elative constructs. Numeral, Non-Numeral, and Ordinal constructs appear under Quantifiers below.

50. "Treated as definite" means that if the first element has an attribute, then the attribute shows definite agreement by having the article prefix /ʔal-/, as the examples show.

51. N is the noun head.

52. See 11.4 below.

53. The elative form of the adjective is of the pattern /ʔafʕal/, e.g., /ʔaḥsan/ 'better', /ʔaṭwal/ 'taller'. See 11.5.1.4 Elative Adjectives.

54. See the handling of this phenomenon by Verma, Manindra, "A synchronic Comparative Study of the Noun Phrase in English and Hindi." Unpublished Ph.D. dissertation, University of Michigan, 1966.

55. If the noun following the numeral is a unit of money or a foreign noun of measurement, it is usually singular:

xamseh dulaar	*five dollars*
θalaaeh jneeh	*three pounds*
sitteh ryaal	*six riyals*
ʔarbaʕah mitr	*four meters*
ʕašarah ṣanti	*ten centimeters*

but:

ʕašarah ʔaðruʕ	*ten cubits*
θalaθ ʔašbaar	*three spans (of the hand)*

56. var. /θalatt/.

57. Ibid.

58. Ibid.

59. Ibid.

60. For the forms of /wa/ 'and' see 13.3.1 below.

61. I have also heard /θiliθ/ and /θulθ/.

62. I have also heard /rubiʕ/.

63. See 12.3 Demonstrative Pronouns below.

64. See Footnote 24 above.

65. The dual is not usually used; the plural is used instead (see 18.1.1.1A).

66. From defective verbs the passive participle pattern is /mafʕiy/ as in /madʕiy/ 'called; invited' from /daʕa/ 'to call; to invite.' From hollow verbs the pattern is /mafyuul/ as in /makyuul/ 'weighed' from /kaal/ 'to weigh'.

67. From Form II defective verbs the passive participle pattern is /mfaʕʕa/ as in /mxalla/ 'left' from /xalla/ 'to leave.' From Form III defective verbs the pattern is /mfaaʕal/ as in /mḥaaka/ 'spoken to' from /ḥaaka/ 'to speak to s.o.'

68. Note that /baarid/ 'cold' as used in this section applies to animate nouns with the meaning of 'undergoing a cold spell.' It is also used with inanimate nouns with the meaning of 'cold', e.g., /šaahi baarid/ 'cold tea.'

69. See 9.3 above.

70. /ʔanha/ is very infrequently used. Many of my language informants rejected /ʔanha/. /ʔaḥsan/ from literary /ḥasan/ 'good' is used instead.

71. See 18.1.1A below.

72. This is a literary borrowing. /-i/ in /kulli/ is a case ending.

73. This phrase is typically said by a passenger to the driver when he wants to get out of the car.

74. I said, "explanatory" because people whose names are, e.g., /ʕabd al-ʕaziiz/, /ʕabdaḷḷa/, /ʕali/ 'Ali', /ʕabd ar-raḥmaan/ 'Abd Al-Rahman', /mḥammad/ 'Muhammad', /ḥamuud/ 'Hamoud', etc., are also called /wajiih/, /faxri/, /jamaali/, /wajjiih/, /ʕizzi/, /ð̣iyaaʔ/, etc., respectively.

75. See 14.5 below.

76. See Footnote 44 for the description of /gabiili/.

77. For these, other prepositions, and prepositional phrases used as adverbs, see 13.2 Prepositions.

78. See 14.2 C.

Part Three

The Syntax of Yemeni Arabic

Section Fourteen

14. MAJOR SENTENCE TYPES

14.1 Nominal Sentences

A nominal sentence is one that does not have a finite verb. The subject may be a noun or a pronoun (with or without modifiers); the predicate may be a noun, an adjective, an adverb of place, or a prepositional phrase. The equivalent of such a sentence in English contains a form of the verb to be in the present (am, is, or are):

1.	waalidih baggaal.	*His father is a greengrocer.*
2.	huw jazzaar min ʔibb.	*He is a butcher from Ibb.*
3.	ʔantu ḥaḍaarimeh?	*Are you (m.p.) from Hadhramaut?*
4.	ʔal-yawm aθ-θaluuθ.	*Today is Tuesday.*
5.	tayyih ṭabiineh.	*This (f.) is a second wife.*
6.	ðawlaaʔi ṣanʕaaniyiin.	*These are from San'a.*
7.	yaḥya ḥaḍramiy.	*Yahia is from Hadhramaut.*
8.	ḥna ðamaariyiin.	*We are from Dhamar.*
9.	ʔal-bint ḥaaliyeh.	*The girl is beautiful.*
10.	at-taaniki marmiy.	*The (storage) tank is thrown away.*
11.	ðayya ġayr naahiy.	*This (m.) is not good.*
12.	ʔantu ṭayyibiin?	*Are you (m.p.) fine (i.e., in good health)?*
13.	ʔas-sabbaak haana.	*The pipe fitter is here.*

Sentences 1-8 show predicates of different kinds of nouns and 9-12 are examples of adjectival predicates. Sentence 13 has an adverbial predicate. The subject may also be expressed by a pronominal suffix attached to certain particles:

kawduhum mxazziniin.	*They (m.) have chewed qat.*
ya raytani haanaak.	*I wish I were there.*
kawdana xaaṭiyiin.	*We have just walked.*

Note that when the predicate is an interrogative, it may precede the subject:

ʔayn al-mafraj?	*Where is the (qat chewing) reception hall?*
(bi) kam aṭ-ṭamaaṭiis?	*How much are tomatoes?*
man ʔant?	*Who are you (m.s.)?*
kayf al-jihhaal?	*How are the children?*
b-ismiš?	*What is your (f.s.) name?*
saaʕat kam ṣalaat aṣ-subḥ?	*When is the morning prayer?*

The particle /gad/ may precede an independent pronoun functioning as the subject of a nominal sentence for emphasis (see 12.1.1).Appropriate stem changes may occur:

gad huw taaʕib.	*He is tired.*
gadaani ʕaaṭiš.	*I am thirsty.*
gad hin ḥaaliyaat.	*They (f.) are beautiful.*
gadak daariy.	*You (m.s.) know.*

The independent pronoun may occupy a position between /maa gad/ and the negative particle /-š/.

maa gadanaaš taaʕib.	*I am not (yet) tired.*
maa gadantš baaliġ.	*You (m.s.) are not (yet) an adult.*
maa gadinḥaaš ʔaṣaaṭi.	*We are not (yet) craftsmen.*

/ʕaad/ 'yet; still; anymore; already' has a syntactic function similar to /gad/ in nominal sentences (see 13.5).

ʕaadana l-mudiir.	*I am still the director.*
maa ʕaadaniiš ṭayyib.	*I am no longer in good health.*

A special kind of nominal sentence called 'equational sentence' is included in this section. An equational sentence is here defined as one in which the subject and the predicate are interchangeable, or can be switched. In an equational sentence the subject and the predicate are definite:

14.	ʔabuuhum mahdiy. mahdiy ʔabuuhum.	*Their (m.) father is Mahdi.* *Mahdi is their (m.) father.*
15.	raʔiis al-jumhuuriyah l-yamaniyah ʕali ʕabdaḷḷa ṣaalih	*The president of the Republic of Yemen is Ali Abadalla Salih.*
	ʕali ʔabdaḷḷa ṣaalih raʔiis al-jumhuuriyah l-yamaniyah.	*Ali Abdalla Salih is the president of the Republic of Yemen.*
16.	ʕabd al-ʕaziiz gaaḍ̱iihum. gaaḍ̱iihum ʕabd al-ʕaziiz.	*Abd Al-Aziz is their judge.* *Their judge is Abd Al-Aziz.*

Elatives and ordinals as parts of construct phrases (see 11.2 and 11.3.2.1.2) may be found in equational sentences:

17.	haaðawlaaʔ ʔaḥla bintayn. ʔaḥla bintayn haaðawlaaʔ.	*These are the (two) most beautiful girls.* *The (two) most beautiful girls are these.*
18.	ʔaḥsan-ma ʕindi ðayya. ðayya ʔaḥsan-ma ʕindi.	*The best (thing) I have is this(m.).* *This (thing) is the best I have.*
19.	ʔawwal muʔaððin huw. huw ʔawwal muʔaððin.	*The first muezzin is he.* *He is the first muezzin.*

Other Examples:

20.	tayyik al-madaaʕah ʔaġla wa ʔaḥsan madaaʕah.	*That waterpipe is the most expensive and best waterpipe.*
21.	ʔaḥsan-ma fi s-suug al-yawm al-gaat.	*The best (thing) in the market today is qat.*
22.	ʔagdam suug fi ṣanʕa suug al-milḥ	*The oldest market in San'a is the Salt Market.*

23.	ʕadan θaaniy madiinah.	*Aden is the second city.*
24.	ʔaaxir al-ḥayaa l-mawt.	*Death is the end of life.*
25.	ʔaθgal-ma ʕindi ʔaxaff-ma ʕindak.	*My heaviest (i.e., most serious) matter is your lightest (i.e., least serious) matter.*
26.	ʕabd al-gaadir ṣadiigiy.	*Abd Al-Kadir is my friend.*
27.	ʕabd al-gaadir kafiiliy.	*Abd Al-gaadir is my guarantor.*
28.	ʔabuuh fi ʕadan.	*His father is in Aden.*
29.	ḥaanuutih jamb al-mustašfa.	*His store is near the hospital.*
30.	huw miʕi.	*He is with me.*
31.	ʔal-xitaan baʕd ġudweh.	*Circumcision is after tomorrow.*
32.	raṭl aṭ-ṭamaaṭiis b-ʕišriin.	*A pound of tomatoes is for twenty riyals.*

Sentence 26 is considered here an equational sentence, though the reverse, /ṣadiigiy ʕabd al-gaadir/, implies that Abd Al-Kaadir is my only friend, which is not normally implied by /ʕabd al-gaadir ṣadiigiy/. Sentence 27, on the other hand, is an equational sentence, as there is usually one person, at one time, that is responsible for someone else, i.e., a host for a guest, a car owner for a hired cab driver or chauffeur, etc. Sentence 32 is used in pricing. Other examples of sentence 32 are: /darzan il-mawz b-xamsa ryaal/ 'five riyals per a dozen bananas,' /kiis al-mraysi b-miʔat ryaal/, one hundred riyals per a sack of sugar,' etc. Either the subject or the predicate of the above cited sentences can be used with modifiers:

waalidih al-kabiir baggaal.	*His big (or old) father is a greengrocer.*
ʔal-baʕiid ʕan al-ʕayn baʕiid ʕan al-galb.	*Out of sight out of mind. (lit., "The one far away from the eye is far away from the heart.")*
tayyih al-mareh ṭabiineh.	*This woman is a second wife.*
ðayya naahiy gawiy.	*This (m.) is very good.*

14.2 Pseudo-Verbal Sentences

A. /ʕind/, /maʕ/ and /l-/

The prepositions /ʕind/, /maʕ/, and /l-/ are used with suffixed pronouns to form verb-like constructions with the general meaning of 'to have; to own.' Examples:

1.	ʕindana jihhaal kaθiir.	*We have many children.*
2.	ʕindiy θintayn sayyaaraat.	*I have two cars.*
3.	ʕindakum ʕaadaat muxtalifeh?	*Do you (m.p.) have different customs?*
4.	maa ʕindahum jihhaal.	*They do not have any children.*
5.	maa ʕindiš ðahab?	*Don't you (f.s.) have gold?*
6.	ʔað̣-ð̣ayf ʕindiy.	*The guest is at my place (or with me here).*
7.	kam duulaar maʕak?	*How many dollars do you (m.s.) have?*
8.	šii-bih maʕiš?	*Do you (f.s.) have anything?*
9.	maʕha θnayn ʔawlaad.	*She has two boys.*
10.	šii-bih maʕkum zalaṭ?	*Do you (m.p.) have money?*
11.	laha ʕyaal ṣiġaar.	*She has little children.*
12.	kam lak haana?	*How long have you (m.s.) been here?*

The noun possessed or owned is usually indefinite and almost always follows the prepositional pseudo-verbs as in the examples above; if the noun is definite, pseudo-verbs cease to have a verb-like quality as in sentence 6; they form part of an equational sentence. /l-/, however, always has the meaning of 'to have'.:

13.	ʕindahum al-jihhaal. ʔal-jihhal ʕindahum.	*The children are with them (m.); the children are at their place.*
14.	maʕna l-bugšeh. ʔal-bugšeh maʕna.	*The purse is with us.*
15.	lahum as-sayyaaraat. ʔas-sayyaaraat lahum.	*The cars are theirs; they own the cars.*

A prepositional pseudo-verb is negativized by the particle /maa/, which negates verbs[1] as in examples 4 and 5. Examples 13 and 14, on the other hand, are negativized by /miš/ (or less commonly used /maaš/:

16.	miš ʕindahum al-jihhaal. ʔal-jihhaal miš ʕindahum.	*The children are not with them.*
17.	miš maʕna l-bugšeh. ʔal-bugšeh miš maʕna.	*The purse is not with us.*

B. /ḥagg/

/ḥagg/, whether used with a suffixed pronoun or not, always indicates possession, alienable or inalienable:

18.	ʔal-gaat ḥaggana. ḥaggana l-gaat.	*The qat belongs to us,* *the qat is ours.*
19.	ʔal-bilaad ḥaggana. ḥaggana l-bilaad.	*The country is ours, the country* *belongs to us.*
20.	ʔat-taayir ḥagg as-sayyaarah. ḥagg as-sayyaarah t-taayir.	*The tire belongs to the car.*
21.	ðayya ḥagg nafsih. ḥagg nafsih ðayya.	*This (m.) is for himself.*

C. /bih/

The particle /bih/ 'there is; there are' is also a pseudo-verb[2]; it cannot be used in an equational sentence:

22.	bih xubz. *xubz bih.	*There is bread.*
23.	bih ḥawaaniit haanaak. *ḥawaaniit haanaak bih.	*There are stores there.*

The negative of /bih/ is */maabihš/ →/maabiš/:

24.	maabiš xubz.	*There isn't (any) bread.*
25.	maabiš ḥawaaniit haanaak.	*There are no stores there.*

14.3 Verbal Sentences

A verbal sentence[3] is here defined as a sentence that contains a finite verb with or without modifiers. The subject may be a noun or a pronoun with or without modifiers. There are two types of verbal sentences:

A. If the subject of the sentence is indefinite, it normally follows the verb:

1.	kaan ʕindiy madaaʕah.	*I had a water pipe.*
2.	kaan bih ðibbaal.	*There was a wedding celebration.*
3.	kaan maabiš gahwa.	*There was no coffee.*
4.	ja sittat ʔanfaar.	*Five people came.*
5.	wuṣulni risaaleh minneh.	*I received a letter from him. (lit., "A letter came to me from him.")*
6.	maa ḥaal šayʔ.	*Nothing happened.*
7.	maa yišti šayʔ ġayr gafaṣ šigaayir.	*He does not want anything except a package of cigarettes.*
8.	wugiʕ maṭar kaθiir.	*A lot of rain fell.*
9.	ʕuṭus waaḥid minhum.	*One of them sneezed.*
10.	faaš sirr min al-ʔasraar.	*One of the secrets was revealed (or known).*
11.	surug minnih zalaṭ.	*(Some) money was stolen from him.*
12.	jaaʔahum walad sammuuh ʔibraahiim.	*They had a baby boy (whom) they named Ibrahim. (lit., "A baby boy whom they named Ibrahim came to them.")*

Sentences 1-3 have /kaan/ 'to be' as the verb. Note that /kaan/ followed by /bih/ 'there is; there are' expresses the meaning of 'there was; there were.' For stylistic purposes an indefinite subject may precede the verb, unless the verb is /kaan/ followed by /bih/ as in sentence 2. /madaaʕah kaanat ʕindiy/ 'I have a water pipe' is acceptable but it is very rare. In sentence 4 the verb may be inflected for gender, i.e., /jaw/. If the noun precedes, however, gender agreement is compulsory: /sittat ʔanfaar jaw/.

B. If the subject is definite, it may either precede or follow the verb, although it has a tendency to precede the verb. Examples: Definite Subject + Verb

13.	ʔal-banaat jaaʔayn.	*The girls came.*
14.	ʔaz-zawaaj yikallif kaθiir.	*Getting married costs a lot.*
15.	ʔal-ḥareew yijahhiz kull šayʔ.	*The bridegroom provides everything.*
16.	ʔaz-zalaṭ txarrij al-jinn mrabaṭṭiin.	*Money talks. (lit., "Money drives away jinnis in shackels.")*
17.	w-baʕdah yiṭlaʕ al-ḥareew la-baab al-makaan.	*And later on, the bridegroom goes to the door of the room.*
18.	hin saarayn al-madraseh bir-rijl.	*They (f.) went to school on foot.*
19.	hum ʕa-yxazzinuw ġudweh.	*They (m.) are going to chew qat tomorrow.*
20.	hiy tsiir la-bayt al-ḥareew aṣ-ṣubḥ.	*She goes to the bridegroom's house in the morning.*

Examples: Verb + Definite Subject

21.	laa yinfaʕak maa maʕ ʔaxuuk wala siraajeh yḍ̣ii?-lak.	*Depend on yourself. (lit. "What your brother has is of no avail to you; neither will his lantern give you light.")*
22.	ʔiða kaθurat al-ʔadyaak taxarrab al-layl.	*Too many cooks spoil the broth. (lit., "If there are too many roosters, the night will be spoiled.")*
23.	maa yigṣidš al-mudiir ʔaððiyyat al-muwaaṭiniin.	*The director does not intend to harm the citizens.*
24.	gatalni l-jašaʕ.	*Greed killed me.*
25.	rtafaʕ siʕr as-sukkar.	*The price of sugar went up.*
26.	ykayyis al-mukayyis b-l-kiis wa l-liifeh.	*The masseur rubs with a bag-shaped luffa.*
27.	yišti l-walad yitzawwaj.	*The boy wants to get married.*
28.	ʔasʕadaḷḷaah masaaʔakum!	*(Response to good evening!) It literally means, "May God make your evening happy!"*
29.	ʕaafaakum aḷḷaah!	*(Said by s.o. wishing somebody else a speedy recovery.) lit., "May God cure, heal you!"*

30.	ʕaafaakum aḷḷaah bi ṣ-ṣiḥḥa wa l-ʕaafiyeh	*(Same as the above, but more polite.) lit., "May God restore health and well-being to you!"*
31.	ḥayya ḷḷaah man jaaʔ!	*(Said by a host to a guest.) lit., "May God grant a long life to the one who came!"*
32.	ʕazzaakum aḷḷaah!	*(Said by s.o. offering condolences to the family of a dead person.) lit., "May God comfort, console you (for the loss of)...!"*
33.	šalluuk al-jinn!	*(Said when cursing s.o.) lit., "May jinn, demons take you away!"*

The subject may precede the verb in sentences 21-27. Sentences asking for a blessing from God or good (or bad) wishes for s.o. almost always have /ʔaḷḷaah/ 'God' as the subject preceded by a past-tense verb as in sentences 28-33.

14.4 Topical Sentences

A topical sentence is made up of two main parts: a topic which is usually a noun or a pronoun, with or without modifiers, and a comment on the topic; the comment is either a nominal sentence (see 14.1) or a verbal sentence (see 14.3). The comment includes a pronoun suffixed to the noun or particle in a nominal sentence or pseudo-verbal sentence or suffixed to the verb or preposition in a verbal sentence. The referent of the suffixed pronoun is the noun or pronoun in the topic. In the following examples the referent and the suffixed pronoun are italicized.

1.	ʔanwar ʔabuuh jazzaar.	*Anwar's father is a butcher.*
2.	ḥna bilaadna l-yaman.	*Our country is Yemen.*
3.	ʔas-sabbaak ʕamalih miš naahiy.	*The pipe fitter's work is not good.*
4.	ʔal-banaat maa ʕindahin zalaṭ.	*The girls do not have any money.*
5.	ṣanʕa ʔahlaha ṭayyibiin.	*The people of San'a are good-natured.*
6.	jaarana ʕindih ʔiθnayn ḥawaaniit.	*Our neighbor has two stores.*
7.	hum ʕindahum zalaṭ kaθiir.	*They (m.) have a lot of money.*

8.	ʔal-gabaayil4 lahum tariix ṭawiil.	*Mountaineers have a long history.*
9.	ṣanʕa fiiha ḥammaamaat min zaman al-ʔatraak.	*San'a has public baths (dating) from the time of the Turks.*
10.	ʔan-nisaaʔ maʕhin al-jihhaal.	*The children are with the women.*
11.	saarah tištiiha ʔummaha tzawwijha waaḥid ġaniy.	*Sarah's mother wants to marry her to someone rich.*
12.	ʔaš-šamṭah šalluuha min al-maṭaar.	*They (m.) stole the suitcase from the airport.*
13.	ʔal-ʔawlaad mḥaaziihum ʔabuuhum.	*The children's father has told them an anecdote.*
14.	ʔal-gabiili šalluw minnih al-jambiyeh.	*They took away the mountaineer's dagger.*
15.	ʔal-banaat sirna wiyyaahin.	*We went with the girls.*

In sentences 1-5 the comment is a nominal sentence in which the pronoun is suffixed to the subject; in 6-10 the comment is a pseudo-verbal sentence with a pronoun suffixed to a preposition; in 11 and 12 the comment is a verbal sentence with a pronoun suffixed to the verb; in 13 the pronoun is suffixed to the active participle /mḥaaziy/ 'having told an anecdote,' which has the function of a verb; and in 14 and 15 the pronoun is suffixed to a preposition in the verbal sentence which is the comment.

Note that the suffixed pronouns in sentences 1-5 indicate possession; those in 11-13 function as objects either of the verbs /tištiy/ 'she wants' and /šalluw/ 'they stole' or the active participle /mḥaaziy/ 'having told an anecdote.' Either the topic or the comment can be used with modifiers. In the following examples the modifiers are in parentheses:

16.	ʔanwar (ʔal-muhandis) (min ʕadan) ʔabuuh (ʔal-ġaliiḍ) jazzaar.	*Anwar (the engineer) (from Aden) – His old father is a butcher.*
17.	tagiyyeh (ʔakbar-bint) mgarriyeh (fi l-maḥwiit).	*Tagiyeh (the oldest girl) is a teacher (in Mahwit).*

14.5 Conditional Sentences

A conditional sentence in SA is one which consists of an if-clause and a result or main clause, which may occur in either order. The if-clause is introduced by such particles as /ʔiða/, /ʔin/, /laa/ and /law/. Conditionals in SA are of three types:

14.5.1 Open Conditionals

In open conditionals, sometimes known as real conditions, the verb usually expresses possibility, i.e., a condition that may or may not be fulfilled. The verb in the if-clause may be either perfect or imperfect, depending upon the meaning; in the result clause it may be perfect, imperfect or imperative. The particles used in open conditionals are usually /ʔiða/, /ʔin/, and /laa/. /ʔin/ is infrequently used. Yemeni sayings and proverbial phrases abound with conditional sentences. Examples:

1.	ʔiða daxalt blaad al-ʕuuraan ʔiʕwir ʕaynak.	*When in Rome do as the Romans do. (lit.,. "If you enter the country of the blind, blind your eye.")*
2.	ʔiða ḥalag ʔibn ʕammak ballayt.[5]	*When the wind is fair, hoist your sails.*
3.	ʔiða ṣaaḥibak ʕasal laa tilḥasih kullih.	*Don't use up your credit all at once. (lit,. "If your friend is honey, do not lick him up all at once."*
4.	ʔiða ʕugir aθ-θawr kaθurat as-sakaakiin.[6]	*All lay hands on the willing horse.*
5.	ʔiða jaaʔ ḥsayn ʔasallim ʕalayh.	*If Hussain comes, I will shake hands with him.*
6.	ʔiða kaθurat al-ʔadyaak taxarrab al-layl.	*Too many cooks spoil the broth. (lit., "If there are too many roosters, the night will be spoiled.")*
7.	ʔiða šaddat ad-dawleh ragadt.[7]	*(lit., "If the goverment prepares for travel, i.e., if it wants to do something, e.g., paving a street, I will go to sleep.")*
8.	laa ʕaraf al-gaabiili baab baytak galabt al-madaggah.	*Give him an inch and he will take a mile.8*
9.	laa taġawfal ad-dimm tagambaʕ al-faʔr.	*When the cat's away, the mice will play. (lit., "If the cat is inattentive, the mouse will jump out of joy.")*

10.	laa wugiʕ maṭar š-arjaʕ b-ḥiin.	*If it rains, I will return quickly.*
11.	laa yuugaʕ maṭar al-gabaayil yišġabu l-maal.	*If it rains, mountaineers will plough the fields.*
12.	laa ʔabsart flaan xabbirni.	*If you see Mr. so-and-so, tell me.*
13.	laa tiji miʕi ġudweh ʔaḥsan.	*If you come with me tomorrow, it is better.*
14.	ʔin jaaʔ al-xayr fa-ḥna niʕtaadih wa ʔin jaaʔ al-balaaʔ fa-ḥna ʔawtaadih.	*Be prepared! Be ready. (lit., "If wealth and abundance come, we are used to them; and if misfortune comes, we are its stakes [i.e., against it].")*
15.	ʔin kaan maʕak zalaṭ ʔištarii-lak bayt.	*If you have money, buy yourself a house.*

14.5.2 Unlikely Conditionals

In unlikely conditionals, the verb usually expresses a condition which presumably cannot be fulfilled now. The verbs in the if-clause are in the perfect tense and the particle is usually /law/ if.

16.	law jiʔt ʕindi la-gult lak.	*If you came to me, I would tell you.*
17.	law garayt najaḥt.	*If you studied, you would succeed.*
18.	ʔas-sirr miθl al-ḥamaami; law falat min yaddi ṭaar.	*lit., "A secret is like a pigeon; if it slipped away from my hand, it would fly away."*

14.5.3 Unreal Conditionals

Unreal conditionals express a contrary-to-fact or rejected condition. The verb in the if-clause is usually perfect with or without the verb /kaan/ 'to be' and in the main clause it is perfect preceded by /inn-/ with a suffixed pronoun or preceded by /kaan/ to be. /kaan/ is uninflected in such constructions. The /kaan/ + perfect-tense verb construction is equivalent to the English conditional perfect, i.e., would or should have + past participle:

19.	law giriy ʔinnih najaḥ.	*If he had studied, he would have succeeded.*
20.	law intabaht ʔinnak maa ṣadamt.	*If you had been careful, you would not have made an accident.*

21.	law wugiʕ maṭar ʔinnani ḥaraθt.	*If it had rained, I would have ploughed.*
22.	law ʔabsartih kaan gult-lih.	*If I had seen him, I would have told him.*
23.	law ḥamal ʔinnih wuṣul fiisaʕ.	*If he had run, he would have arrived quickly.*
24.	law kaan fiih xayr kaan maa ramaaḥ aṭ-ṭayr.	*It is a worthless thing. (lit., "If it had been of any use, the bird (of prey) would not have discarded it.")*
25.	law simʕtiy al-xabar ʔinnš ṭirtiy min al-faraḥ.	*If you (f.s.) had heard the news, you would have been overjoyed.*
26.	law kaan miʕi zalaṭ ʔinnani štarayt-li bayt.	*If I had had money, I would have bought myself a house.*

In all of the above cited conditional sentences, the if-clause has a verb except for example 3, which has an equational sentence after /ʔiða/. The if-clause may also have a pseudo-verbal construction (see 14.2):

27.	ʔiða miʕiy zalaṭ ʔaštarii-li bayt.	*If I have money, I will buy myself a house.*
28.	laa ʕindi gaat xazzant.	*If I have qat, I will chew.*
29.	laa minnih maa ʔaštiih.	*If it is from him, I don't want it.*
30.	iða lahum duyuun ʕalayk ʔidfaʕha.	*If you owe them money, pay it back.*

A participle is occasionally used in the if-clause, especially in unreal conditionals.

31.	ʔiða mistaʕjil xuð taxi.	*If you are in a hurry, take a taxi.*
32.	law kaanuw msabbiriin al-ġadaaʔ ʔinnana jiʔna.	*If they had prepared lunch, we would have come.*
33.	law kunt mibsirih kaan ʔaʕṭaytih hisaabih.	*If I had seen him, I would have given him his due.*
34.	law gaayil-li kaan maa xallaytih yxazzin.	*If you had told me, I would not have let him chew qat.*

The negative particle /laa/ 'no; not' is sometimes used with the effect of a conditional particle. The verb in the main clause is also negated by /laa/ and expresses a negative command:

35.	laa tusrug wa laa tixaaf.	*If you do not steal, you won't have anything to fear.*
36.	laa tsibb an-naas wa laa ysibbuuk.	*If you do not call people bad names, they won't call you bad names.*

/lawla/ is another particle used in unreal conditionals with the meaning of 'had it not been for; if ... not.' It may be used with suffixed pronouns:

37.	lawlaaha maa jiʔt.	*If it had not been for her, I would not have come.*
38.	lawla yaḥya kaan ʔinnahum maatuw.	*Had it not been for Yahi, they would have died.*
39.	lawla l-murabbiy maa ʕaraft rabbiy.[9]	*Lit., "Had it not been for the educator, I would not have known my God."*
40.	lawla l-kassaar maa ʕaaš al-maddaar.[10]	*(lit.,"If it had not been for the one who breaks (pots), the potter would not have lived.")*

Sometimes the main clause in a conditional sentence is not stated, but it is implied. Such conditional sentences express an impossible state of affairs. The implied main clause is equivalent to English What you have said (or what you plan to do) will, under no circumstances, take place. An impossibility is expressed in English by such sentences as: When elephants fly. Not in this lifetime.

Examples:

law tʕammir ʕumr nuuḥ	*lit., "If you live as long as Noah lived."*
law tuðrub al-meʔ lamma yiḥma.	*lit., "If you hit water until it warms up."*
law tiṭlaʕ aš-šams min al-maġrib.	*lit., "If the sun rises in the west."*

The if-clause is always introduced by /law/.

Section Fifteen

15. CLAUSES

15.1 Noun Clauses

A noun clause has the function of a noun. It may serve as:

A. the subject of a sentence:

1.	yimkin ša-ruuḥ ġudweh.	*It is possible that I will go tomorrow.*
2.	yimkin ʔinna ṭ-ṭamaaṭiis miš naahiy.	*It is possible that the tomatoes are not good.*
3.	miš ṣaʕb ʕalayk tiji maʕanna?	*Isn't it difficult for you to come with us?*
4.	miš naahiy tiddiilhum ryaalayn bas.	*It is not good (for you) to give them only two riyals.*
5.	miš ṣaḥiiḥ maabiš ḥuut al-yawm?	*Isn't it true that there is no fish today?*
6.	bidaayat al-miil xaṭweh, tamaam?	*The first step is always the hardest, isn't it (true)?(lit., "The beginning of a mile is a step, isn't it (true)?"*
7.	ʔal-jaar gabl ad-daar, tamaam?	*A man is known by the company he keeps, is't it (true)?*[11]

B. the object of a verb:

8.	gaal maabiš xawf.	*He said there was no fear (or concern).*
9.	gult numt ṭuul al-layl.	*I said I had slept throughout the whole night.*
10.	ʕaraft ʔinnih rajjaal galiil al-ḥayaaʔ.	*I knew that he was a shameless, impudent man.*
11.	smiʕt ʔinnahum ʕa-yirfaʕu siʕr as-sukkar.	*I heard that they were going to raise the price of sugar.*
12.	rafaḍayn yijayn miʕi.	*They (f.) refused to come with me.*

C. the object of a preposition

13.	staraddaytih min allaði šallih.	*I got it back from the one who stole it.*
14.	ðayya ḥagg allaði gad kaan jambiy.	*This belongs to the one who was (seated) beside me.*
15.	tayyik as-sayyaarah ʔaḥṣan min alli štaraytaha.	*That car is better than the one you have bought.*

Noun clauses functioning as objects of prepositions are usually introduced by the relative /ʔallaði/ (see 15.2) below.

15.2 Relative Clauses

A relative clause modifies a noun, a proper name or a pronoun (including a demonstrative pronoun). The noun, proper name, or pronoun modified by a relative clause is called the antecedent. If the antecedent is definite, the relative clause is introduced by the relative particle /ʔallaði/.[12] If the antecedent is indefinite, /ʔallaði/ is not normally used in SA, although some speakers do rarely use it in this way. A relative clause is either verbal or nominal (see 14.1 and 14.3).

Examples of definite relative clauses:

1.	haaða r-rajjaal allaði jeeʔ.	*This is the man who came.*
2.	man al-mareh ʔallaði jaaʔat?	*Who is the woman who came?*
3.	ʔayn al-gaat allaði štaraynaah?	*Where is the qat we have bought?*
4.	ʔaš-šugaah allaði saaruw	*the workmen who left*
5.	ʔas-saarig alli šall as-saaʕah	*the thief who stole the watch*
6.	ʔal-jihhaal ali ragaduw	*the children who fell asleep*
7.	ʔas-saykal alli štaraytih	*the bicycle (which) I bought*
8.	ʔan-nisaaʔ ali ġannayn	*the women who sang*
9.	suug að-ðahab alli fi baab al-yaman	*the gold market (which is) in Bab Al-Yaman*
10.	ʔal-ḥaanuut allaði ʕala l-yamiin	*the shop (which is) on the right*

The antecedents in the above examples, /r-rajjaal/ 'the man', /al-mareh/ 'the woman,' /al-gaat/ 'the qat,' /ʔaš-šugaah/ 'the workmen,' etc., are definite and also the subjects of the relative clauses. The relative clauses in 1-8 are verbal, while those in examples 8-10 are nominal.

Examples of Indefinite Relative Clauses

11.	ʔabsart waaḥid yibuul.	*I saw someone who was urinating.*
12.	ʔašti sayyaarah maa tkallif kaθiir.	*I want a car that does not cost a lot.*
13.	sawwa šayʔ maa yraḍḍi ʔaḥad.	*He did something that did not please anyone.*
14.	šamṭah maa tinšaal	*a bag that cannot be lifted*
15.	šaagi yištaġil naahi gawiy	*a workman who works very well*
16.	bayt fiih daymeh	*a house that has an old Yemeni kitchen*
17.	šaariʕ ywaddi t-taḥriir	*a street that leads to the Tahrir Square*

If the antecedent is the object of the relative clause, the verb in the relative clause has a suffixed pronoun referring to the antecedent and agreeing with it in gender and number; if the relative clause has a verb + preposition, the suffixed pronoun is attached to the preposition:

18.	ʔal-gaat allaði xazzanuuh	*the qat (which) they chewed*
19.	ʔal-banaat allaði ʔabsartahin	*the girls (whom) I saw*
20.	ʔal-ʔakl alli sabbarannih	*the food (which) they (f.) prepared*
21.	ʔal-kalaam ali tguuliih	*the words (which) you are saying*
22.	ḥareeweh tazawwajha	*a bride (whom) he married*
23.	ʔar-rijaal allaði kallamtahum	*the men (whom) I spoke with*
24.	ʔaṭ-ṭali allaði ðabaḥnaah	*the lamb (which) we slaughtered*
25.	šayʔ taʕawwadt ʕalayh	*something (which) I got used to*

26.	huw allaði jiʔt maʕaah.	*He is the one (whom) I came with.*
27.	ʔal-jaamiʕ allaði ṣallayt fiih	*the mosque (which) I prayed in*
28.	ʔad-daar alli sakanna fiiha	*the house (which) we lived in*
29.	ʔal-banaat allaði takallamt maʕaahin	*the girls (whom) I talked to*
30.	ʔal-fundug ali numt fiih	*the hotel (which) I slept in*

Another type of relative clause in SA is one in which a suffixed pronoun referring to the antecedent is attached to a noun. Such a relative clause is similar to an English relative clause introduced by whose, of which, etc., as shown in the examples below.

31.	ʔal-walad allaði ʔismih zaki	*the boy whose name is Zaki*
32.	ʔal-bint alli šaʕraha ṭawiil	*the girl whose hair is long* *the girl with the long hair*
33.	ṣadiig ʔaxuuh taajir	*a friend whose brother is a merchant*
34.	sayyaarah moodeelha gadiim	*an old model car*
35.	ʔal-bayt allaði makaanaatih waasiʕah	*the house whose rooms are big* *the house with the big rooms*
36.	bayt ḥammaamih franjiy	*a house with a Western-style bathroom*
37.	bint ʕyuunha ḥaaliyaat	*a girl whose eyes are beautiful* *a girl with beautiful eyes*
38.	maṭʕam ʔaklih naḍ̱iif	*a restaurant that has clean food*
39.	ṭabiineh jihhaalha xamseh	*a second wife who has five children*
40.	šaybeh liḥyatih bayḍ̱ee?	*an old man whose beard is grey* *an old man with a grey beard*

Relative Clauses as Nouns

Another type of relative clause that does not modify a noun, a pronoun, or a pronoun occurs in SA. Such a relative clause has the function of a noun, i.e., it may function as the subject or predicate of a sentence, or the second term of a noun construct, or the object of a verb or a preposition. /ʔallaði/, in a relative clause functioning as the subject of a sentence, has an indefinite meaning corresponding to 'he who,' 'the one who,' 'those who,' 'whoever,' 'that which,' etc. The verb of the relative clause is third-person masculine singular. This type of relative clause is frequently found in proverbial and idiomatic phrases:

41.	ʔali maa yijiiš maʕ al-ḥareeweh maa yijiiš baʕdaha.	*(lit., "What does not come with the bride will not come after her, i.e., after she is no longer a bride.")*[13]
42.	ʔalli maat faat.[14]	*Don't cry over spilled milk. Let bygones be bygones.(lit., "What has died has gone.")*
43.	ʔalli ma yiʕrifkš maa yθamminkš.	*(lit., "Those who do not know you do not appreciate your worth.")*
44.	ʔali maa yidriiš yguul balas.	*Sour grapes.(lit., "He who doesn't know says, "It's cactus.")*
45.	ʔallaδi maa lih ʔawwal maa lih ʔaaxir.[15]	*(lit., "He who has no beginning has no end.")*
46.	ʔallaδi maa yxaaf aḷḷaah xaaf minnih.	*(lit. "Beware of those who do not fear God.")*
47.	ʔali yišti l-ʕasal yaṣbir ʕala gabṣ an-nuub.	*(lit., "Those who want honey will have to bear calmly the biting of bees.")*
48.	ʔalli maa ysaaʕidš nafsih maḥḥad ysaaʕdih.	*(lit., "Nobody will help those who do not help themselves.")*

The relative clauses in examples 41-48 function as subjects of the sentences.

Other examples of relative clauses as nouns:

49.	ʔanwar allaδi saar.	*Anwar is the one who left.*
50.	ʔal-mudiir alli xazzan.	*The director is the one who chewed qat.*
51.	ʔal-musabbireh ʔalli jaaʔat.	*The caterer (f.) is the one who came.*
52.	ʔal-gabiili llaδi ʔabsarnaah.	*The mountaineer is the one we saw.*
53.	ya wayl allaδi maa yṣalliy.	*Woe unto the one who doesn't pray.*

54.	haaða jazaaʔ alli yšill.	*This is the punishment of the one who steals.*
55.	haaði taḥiyyat allaði yxaaf aḷḷaah.	*This is the greeting of the one who fears God.*
56.	ʔaddii-li llaði tištiih.	*Give me what you like.*
57.	xuð alli haana!	*Take (m.s.) what is here!*
58.	ʔidfaʕ allaði ʕalayk!	*Pay (m.s.) what you owe!*
59.	ligyat ali tištiih.	*She found what she wanted.*
60.	gul-lana lli tiʕrifih!	*Tell (m.s.) us what you know!*

In examples 49-52 the relative clauses function as predicates of the sentences; in examples 53-55, they are used in construct with the nouns /wayl/ 'woe,' /jazaaʔ/ 'punishment,' and /taḥiyyat/ 'greeting.' In examples 56-60, they function as direct objects of the verbs /ʔaddi/ 'give,' /xuð/ 'take,' /ʔidfaʕ/ 'pay,' /ligyat/ 'she found,' and /gul/ 'tell.' In the following examples the relative clauses are governed by the prepositions /ḥagg/ 'belonging to,' and /saaʕ/ 'like, similar to':

61.	ðayya ḥagg allaði kaan haana.	*This belongs to the one who was here.*
62.	yuxṭi saaʕ allaði ltabaj.	*He walks like the one who has been hit.*

In the following examples the relative clauses have participles instead of verbs:

63.	ʔal-ʔadiib alli kaatib haaða l-magaal	*the writer who has written this article*
64.	ʔali msawwi nafsih mudiir	*the one who has made himself director*
65.	ʔat-taniki l-matruus meeʔ	*the tank which is full of water*

15.3 /ḥaal/ clauses

A /ḥaal/ clause is a clause of manner or circumstance; it describes, for example, the manner in which one did something, the manner how something happened, one's condition when something happened, etc. A /ḥaal/ clause can be:

A. a nominal sentence (see 14.1) introduced by /wa/ 'and':

1.	daxalat wa galbaha ṭaayir min al-faraḥ.	*She entered with an overjoyed heart. (lit., "She entered and her heart was flying from joy.")*
2.	jaaʔ wa huw raakib ḥimaar.	*He came riding a donkey. (lit., "He came and he was riding a donkey.")*
3.	ʔabsartih wa huw xaaṭi fi baab al-yaman.	*I saw him and (or while) he was walking in Bab Al-Yaman.*
4.	gad-li muddeh tawiileh wa ʔana msannib haana jambak.	*I have been standing up here by you for a long while.*
5.	gad-lana muddeh ṭawiileh wa ḥna mirtaḥiin að-ðamiir.	*We have been peaceful of mind for a long time.*
6.	limih sirt al-ʕamal wa ʔant ḥaamiy?	*Why did you go to work while you were running a temperature?*

B. a verbal sentence (see 14.3) introduced by /wa/ followed by an independent pronoun followed by an imperfect verb:

7.	daxal wa huw yišrab šiigaareh.	*He entered smoking a cigarette. He entered while he was smoking a cigarette.*
8.	ʔabsartahin wa hin yurguṣayn fi l-ʕurs.	*I saw them (f.) dancing in the wedding.I saw them (f.) while they (f.) were dancing in the wedding.*

C. a pseudo-verbal sentence (see 14.2) introduced by /wa/:

9.	saafar wa ʕindih zalaṭ kaθiir.	*He traveled, having acquired a lot of money.*
10.	jayn wa maʕaahin jihhaal xayraat.	*They (f.) came with many children.*
11.	jiʔna l-yaman wa fiiha xayr kaθiir.	*We came to Yemen and (i.e., at the time when) it had a lot of wealth.*
12.	ʔaxaðt al-madaaʕah wa maa kaanš fiiha titin.	*I took the waterpipe and (i.e., at the time when) there was no tobacco in it.*

D. a verbal sentence introduced by an imperfect verb. The same sentences under B above can be used without /wa/ with the same meaning.

13. daxal yišrab šiigaareh.
14. ʔabsartahin yurguṣayn fi l-ʕurs.

Section Sixteen

16. MAJOR PHRASE TYPES

16.1 Noun Phrases

A noun phrase consists of a noun and one or more modifiers. For this section of noun phrases, see 11. NOUN MODIFIERS above.

Below are the major kinds of noun phrases in SA:

16.1.1 N + N (+N+N...)

ṭagat al-makaan	*the window of the room*
ṭaagat makaan al-bayt	*the window of the room of the house*
ṭaagat makaan bayt zaki	*the window of the room of Zaki's house*

The construct phrases above can also be used with /ḥagg/ 'belonging to' with the same meaning.

ʔaṭ-ṭaagah ḥagg al-makaan
ṭaagat al-makaan ḥagg al-bayt

or: ʔaṭ-ṭaagah ḥagg makaan al-bayt
ṭaagat makaan al-bayt ḥagg zaki

or: ṭaagat al-makaan ḥagg bayt zaki
or: ʔaṭ-ṭaagah ḥagg makaan bayt zaki
or: ʔaṭ-ṭaagah ḥagg al-makaan ḥagg bayt zaki

16.1.2 N (+N) + Adj. (+Adj....)

dimm kabiir	*a big cat*
ʔad-dimm al-kabiir	*the big cat*

If two adjectives or more are used to modify the noun-head, usually there are no restrictions on the order of those adjectives:

dimm ʔaswad kabiir — *a big black cat*
dimm kabiir ʔaswad

Both adjectives /ʔaswad/ 'black' and /kabiir/ 'big' modify the head, /dimm/ 'cat'.

Sometimes the last string in a series of attributive adjectives may apply to the whole preceding phrase. This occurs mainly in set phrases, titles, or proper names:

ʔal-bank al-waṭani l-yamani	*the National Bank of Yemen (lit., "the Yemeni National Bank")*
ʔal-mustašfa l-ʕaskari l-jadiid	*the new Military Hospital*

As has already been mentioned in Construct Phrases (see 11.1), an adjective coming after a noun construct may modify either noun, depending on sense and agreement. Thus, the following patterns of modification are established:

1. N N Adj Adj

	suug ḥuut kabiir raxiiṣ	*the market of*
or:	suug ḥuut raxiiṣ kabiir	*cheap big fish*
	mabna s-safaarah ʔal-ʔamriikiyeh ʔal-jadiideh	*the building of the new American embassy*
or:	mabna s-safaarah ʔal-jadiideh ʔal-ʔamriikiyeh	

2. N N Adj Adj

	suug al-ḥuut al-jadiid an-naðiif	*the clean new fish market*
or:	suug al-ḥuut an-naðiif al-jadiid	
	taaniki l-maaʔ al-kabiir al-jadiid	*the big new water tank*
or:	taaniki l-maaʔ al-jadiid al-kabiir	

3. N N Adj Adj

makaatib aš-šarikah ʔal-yamaniyah ʔal-jadiideh	*the new offices of the Yemeni company*
gaṣr al-ʔimaam al-ʕaadil al-baʕiid	*the distant palace of the ruler*

but /*gaṣr al-ʔimaam al-baʕiid al-ʕaadil/ is ungrammatical. In other words, the pattern N N Adj Adj is ungrammatical. The directions of modification are parallel, i.e., either the two adjectives modify the same noun, or the first adjective modifies the second noun in the construct and the second modifies N, the noun-head. Of the three logical possibilities of the modification patterns above, the third one is rare.

16.1.3 Quantifier + N

The position of quantifier can be filled by Numeral (cardinal[15] or ordinal), Non-Numeral (partitive, fraction, intensifier, or demonstrative),[16] or Elative Adjective (see 11.5.1.4). Examples:

sitteh ʔawlaad	*six boys*
saadis walad	*the sixth boy*
baʕḍ̱ al-ʔawlaad	*some (of the) boys*
xums al-ʔawlaad	*one-fifth of the boys*
kull al-ʔawlaad	*all (of the) boys*
ʔawlaaʔik al-ʔawlaad	*those boys*
ʔaḥsan walad	*the best boy*
ʔaḥsan al-ʔawlaad	*the best (of the) boys*

The noun-head, N, can be the first element in a noun construct, giving the phrase N N, e.g. /mudallik al-ḥammaam/ 'the bath masseur.' The plural form of this noun construct, i.e., /mudallikiin al-ḥammaam/ 'the bath masseurs,' may be modified by a pre-nominal non-numeral.:

muʕḍ̱am mudallikiin al-ḥammaam	*most of the bath masseurs*
baʕḍ̱ mudallikiin al-ḥammaam	*some of the bath masseurs*
nuṣṣ mudallikiin al-ḥammaam	*half (of) the bath masseurs*
kull mudallikiin al-ḥammaam	*all (of) the bath masseurs*

The non-numeral is obligatorily pre-posed, either to a noun construct, as shown above, or to an elative construct:

kull ʔaḥsan mudallikiin al-ammaam	*all (of) the best bath masseurs*

The last phrase can be modified only post-nominally by cardinals, ordinals, and all the subclasses of positive adjectives. There are no restrictions on the order of those post-nominal modifiers:

kull mudallikiin al-ḥammaam	| al-xamseh at-taaʕibiin | at-taaʕibiin al-xamseh	*all (of) the five tired bath masseurs*

The number of possible phrases can be worked out by a mathematical progression. Let M stand for a post-nominal modifier, and M1, M2, M3, etc., stand for the first, the second, the third modifiers ... etc. If three modifiers are used, we can have the following six possible phrases:

$$M_1\ M_2\ M_3 \quad M_1\ M_3\ M_2 \quad M_2\ M_3\ M_1$$
$$M_2\ M_1\ M_3 \quad M_3\ M_1\ M_2 \quad M_3\ M_2\ M_1$$

If four modifiers are used, we can have 24 possible phrases; if five are used, we can have 120, etc. If n stands for the number of modifiers, then the number of logical possibilities is:
n(n-1)(n-2)(n-3), etc.

If coordinate modifiers are used, they behave as one unit syntactically, i.e., the coordinate modifiers as a unit can precede or follow other modifiers. Word order within coordinate modifiers is free:

mu?assaseh | tijaariyeh wa ?igtiṣaadiyeh / yamaniyeh
| ?igtiṣsaadiyeh wa tijaariyeh
a Yemeni commercial and economic establishment

or:

mu?assaseh yamaniyeh | tijaariyeh wa ?igtiṣaadiyeh
| ?igtiṣaadiyeh wa tijaariyeh

16.1.4 N + Adj. + N

The construction N + Adj. + N is common in SA. Noun phrases of such a construction are descriptive clichés or stereotyped expressions. The whole construction functions as an adjective: the second term, which is always a definite noun, restricts or specifies the item of reference of the adjective, the first term. Such phrases are known as false /?iḍaafah/ constructions in literary Arabic.:

ḍ̱ayyig aṣ-ṣadr	*easily annoyed; impatient*
waasiʕ aṣ-ṣadr	*open-minded; patient*
waasiʕ ar-raḥmeh	*abounding in mercy (usually said of God)*
murtaaḥ aḍ̱-ḍ̱amiir	*peaceful of mind, undisturbed by scruples*
maksuur al-galb	*broken-hearted*
kaθiir aṭ-ṭamaʕ	*very greedy*
galiil al-ḥayaa?	*shameless; impudent*
ṣaġiir an-nafs	*mean-spirited, base-minded*
kabiir an-nafs	*high-minded, proud*
ṭawiil al-lisaan	*long-tongued*
?aʕma l-galb	*blind of heart*
?abyaḍ̱ al-wašš	*white-faced*

16.1.5 N + Participle + N

daliil mṭawwif al-ḥijjaaj	*a guide who takes, has taken pilgrims around (the Ka'ba)*
ʔibn ʕaaṣi l-waalidayn	*a son who disobeys, has disobeyed his parents*
ʔal-gaššaam ar-raafiʕ siʕr aṭ-ṭamaaṭiis	*the greengrocer who has raised the price of tomatoes*
al-walad al-laabij ʔaxuuh	*the boy who has hit his brother*
rajjaal msabbir al-ʔakl	*a man who prepared, has prepared the food*
ṭabiineh gaasiyat al-galb	*a hardhearted, callous second wife*
rajjaal maʕruuf ʔaṣlih	*a man whose descent, lineage is known*
bayt mġallagaat ṭiigaanih	*a house whose windows are closed*

16.1.6 N + Prepositional Phrase

rajjaal min bayt al-fagiih	*a man from, belonging to the Fagih family*
xayr min faðl-i-llaah	*a blessing from God's favor*
θintayn min ʕadan	*two (f.) from Aden*
bilayzig min ðahab	*a gold bracelet*
ṣabaaya ʕala ʕammathin	*young girls who take after their paternal aunts*
rajjaal saaʕ al-jinn	*a man who is like jinnis*
ʔal-gumgumi ḥagg as-sayyaarah	*the car motor oil can*
ʔal-kitli ḥagg aš-šaahiy	*the tea kettle*
madaaʕah ġayr tayyih	*a waterpipe other than this; another waterpipe*

16.2 Adjective Phrases

An adjective can be modified by such particles as /kaθiir/ 'a lot, a great deal,' /gawiy/ 'very,' /šwayyeh/ 'a little'. Only /šwayyeh/ may either precede or follow the adjective:

xayyir kaθiir	*very charitable*
ḥaali kaθiir	*very beautiful; very sweet*
naahi gawiy	*very good, very nice*
šuuʕ gawiy	*very ugly*
ġaali šwayyeh/šwayyeh ġaaliy	*a little expensive*
jaawiʕ šwayyeh/šwayyeh jaawiʕ	*a little hungry*

No other adjective modifiers have been recorded.

16.3 Adverb Phrases

16.3.1 Time

Among adverb phrases of time are those that are introduced by an adverbial particle of time (see 13.4.A).:

ʔabsartih gabl ams.	*I saw him (the day) before yesterday.*
ʕa-nsiir baʕd ġudweh.	*We will leave after tomorrow.*
ša-ruuḥ zaarat yawm.	*I will go some day.*
ʔabsarnaah tayyik as-saaʕah.	*We saw him then. (lit., "We saw him that hour.")*
gad jeʔ min baʕd.	*He came later on.*
yġallig saaʕat xams.	*It closes at five o'clock.*

Others are made up of two nouns compounded together, e.g., /ṣabaaḥ ʔams/ or /ʔams aṣ-ṣubḥ/ 'yesterday morning,' /ʔams al-ʕaši/ or /ʔams fi l-layl/ 'last night,' etc. Some others are made up of the demonstrative /ha-/ and a noun, e.g., /ha-lwagt/ 'now, this time,' or the particle /la/ 'up to, until,' and the adverb /ðalḥiin/ 'now.' A few are made up of N + Adj., e.g., /ʔaš-šahr al-maaḍi/ 'last month,' /ʔas-saneh al-maaḍiyeh/ 'last year,' etc.

16.3.2 Place

Adverb phrases of place are usually introduced by an adverbial particle of place (see 13.4.B). Examples:

xuṭiit min haana.	*I walked from here.*
raaḥ min haana la-haanaak b-r-rijl.	*He went from here to there on foot.*
wugaf guddaam al-boosṭah.	*He stopped in front of the post office.*

16.3.3 /ḥaal/[18]

yxazzin dala-dala.	*He chews qat slowly.*
yxazzin la-waḥdih.	*He chews qat alone.*
zawwajha b-al-ġaṣb	*He married her off by force.*
xaraj b-al-guwwah.	*He went out by force.*
ṣallaḥ as-saaʕah b-al-galb.	*He repaired the watch incorrectly.*

Section Seventeen

17. VERB PHRASES

This section deals with verbs and verbal auxiliaries from the point of view of meaning and function. Included in this section are verb strings of two, sometimes three or more, verbs with the same subject and active participles (see 11.4.1), which often have a verb-like function.

17.1 /kaan/

/kaan/ 'to be', in this section, functions as an auxiliary. It precedes a perfect or an imperfect form of the verb, or an active participle. The most common possible combinations are below.

17.1.1 /kaan/ + perfect verb

The perfect of /kaan/ followed by a perfect verb occurs mainly in the result clause of conditional sentences (see 14.5). In such cases /kaan/ is invariable, but the main verb agrees with the subject. Examples:

law miʕi zalaṭ kaan štarayt-a-li bayt.	*If I had money, I would have bought a house.*
law giriy kaan najaḥ.	*If he had studied, he would have succeeded.*

17.1.2 /kaan/ + imperfect verb

In phrases consisting of the perfect of /kaan/ and a verb in the imperfect, both /kaan/ and the main verb agree with the subject. Verbs that have a punctual aspect, e.g., /wuṣul/ 'to arrive,' /ʕaraf/ 'to know,' /waʕad/ 'to promise,' /ragad/ 'to fall asleep,' etc., usually express a habitual action in the past, if used with /kaan/. Such verb phrases often correspond to English 'used to do' something. Examples:

kaan yuuṣul saaʕat xams.	*He used to arrive at five.*
kunt ʔaʕrif ḥaarathum.	*I used to know their quarter.*
kaanat tuuʕidni.	*She used to promise me.*
kaanu yurqudu fiisaʕ.	*They (m.) used to fall asleep fast.*
kaan ramaḏ̣aan yuugaʕ fi ṣ-ṣayf.	*Ramadhan used to be (lit., "take place") in the summer.*
kunt ʔaxruj fi l-layl.	*I used to go out at night.*

Verbs that have a durative aspect, e.g., /xazzan/ 'to chew qat,' /ġallag/ 'to close, shut,' /ʔibsar/ 'to see; to watch,' /ʃirib/ 'to drink,' /xatan/ 'to circumcise,' etc., usually express both a habitual action in the past or an action in progress at a certain time in the past, if used with /kaan/. Such verb phrases often correspond to the English construction made up of a past form of the verb to be plus an /-ing/ form.:

kunna nxazzin saaʕat xams yawm al-xamiis.	*We used to chew qat at five on Thursday. We were chewing qat at five on Thursday*
kunt ʔabsir al-film.	*I was watching the movie.*
kunt ʔabsir ðawlaaʔi l-ʔaflam.	*I used to see these movies.*
ḥiin ibsartih kaan yigraʔ.	*When I saw him, he was reading.*
kaan yigraʔ fi l-layl.	*He used to read at night.*
kunna nišrab bunn.	*We used to drink Yemeni coffee. We were drinking Yemeni coffee.*

17.1.3 /kaan/ + active participle

Verb phrases consisting of /kaan/ plus an active participle usually refer to a situation in the past which resulted from some previous action, or to an action in progress at some time in the past. English translations vary with the context. /kaan/ agrees with the subject like a verb and the active participle like an adjective:

ḥiin ʔabsartih kaan mxazzin.	*When I saw him, he had (already) chewed qat.*
kaan gaarir b-ðanbih.	*He had (already) confessed to his crime.*
kunt mitwaḍḍi gablama sirt al-jaamiʕ.	*I had (already) performed ablution before I went to the mosque.*
ḥiin wuṣult ad-daymeh kaanat misabbireh kull šayʔ.	*When I got to the (Yemeni) kitchen, she had prepared everything.*

In the case of verbs that have both a punctual and a durative aspect, /kaan/ + active participle usually refers to actions of the durative type in progress at some time in the past, and the English equivalent is generally was/were with an /-ing/ form:

yawmma ʔibsarnaah kaan ḥaamil ladaatih ʕala ḍahrih.	*When we saw him, he was carrying his personal effects on his back.*
kaanat laabiseh gunṭuratha l-jadiideh.	*She was wearing her new shoes.*

17.2 Other Verb Phrases

Other major verb phrases consist of a string of two (sometimes three or more) verbs with the same subject. The first verb may be perfect, imperfect or the active participle form, and may be modified by a form of /kaan/. It may be an auxiliary verb, e.g.,/badaʔ/ 'to start to do s.th.,' or another kind of verb that expresses a desire, e.g., /štaaʔ/[19] 'to want, to do s.th.,' an ability or capability, e.g., /gidir/ 'to be able to do s.th.,' or continuation, e.g., /bigiy/ 'to continue to do s.th.' etc., as shown below.

17.2.1

/bigiy/[20]	*to remain, continue to do s.th.*
/ṣaar/	*to become, turn into s.th.*

Examples of verb strings with /bigiy/:

A. Perfect + Imperfect

1. bigi yiʕmal maʕaana.	*He continued to work with us.*
2. bigyat tigraʔ.	*She continued to read, study.*
3. bigyu yxazzinuw.	*They (m.) continued to chew qat.*
4. bigyayn yilʕabayn.	*They (f.) went on playing.*
5. bigiit ʔaṣalli fi ðayya l-jaamiʕ.	*I continued to pray in this mosque.*
6. bigi yisrig.	*He continued to steal.*
7. bigiina njurr al-maʕaaš.	*We continued to get our salary.*

B. Perfect + Imperfect + Imperfect

8. bigi yišti yištaġil.	*He continued to have a desire to work.*
9. bigiina ništi nigraʔ.	*We continued to have a desire to study.*
10. bigi yḥaawil yirhan bilayzig maratih.	*He kept on trying to pawn his wife's bracelet.*
11. bigiit ʔasiir agraʔ.	*I continued to go to study.*
12. bigi yigdar yigraʔ.	*He continued to have the ability to study.*

The verbs in such a string, as those in any other string in this section, have one subject and agree with it in gender and number. The meaning expressed by the imperfect verb /ʔagraʔ/ in sentence 11 above is purpose. The sentence can be paraphrased to read: I continued to go so as to study, or for the purpose of studying. In SA this meaning of purpose is expressed by all imperfect verbs after a verb of motion. Other examples are given below.

Examples of verb strings with /ṣaar/:

13. ṣaar yitmayraḏ̣.	*He got to the point where he pretended to be sick.*
14. ʔal-bank ṣaar yġallig saaʕat xams.	*The bank got to the point where it closed at five.*
15. ṣirna nsiir nigraʔ.	*We got to the point where we would go to study.*
16. ṣaarat tḥaawil tigraʔ.	*She got to the point where she tried to study.*
17. ṣaarat tḥaawil tijiy tigraʔ.	*She got to the point where she tried to come to study.*

/kaan/ can be prefixed to any verb string to switch it from a present to a past time frame:

ysiir	*he leaves*	kaan ysiir	*he used to leave*
saar	*he left*	kaan saar	*he would have left*

Other examples:

18. kaan yišti yiji yištaġil.	*He wanted to come to work.*
19. kunt ʔaḥaawil ʔajiy ʔaštail.	*I was trying to come to work.*
20. kaan saar.	*He would have left.*
21. kaan sirt.	*I would have left.*
22. kaan garaʔna.	*We would have studied.*

/kaan/ in such strings is invariable. The meaning expressed (in 18-22) is that of a result clause in a conditional sentence (see 14.5 and 17.1).

23. kaan jaaʔ garaʔ.	*He would have come and studied.*
24. kaan gaam ragad.	*He would have gone (lit., "stood up") and slept.*
25. kaan jaaʔ yigraʔ.	*He would have come to study.*
26. kaan gaam yurgud.	*He would have gone (lit., "stood up") to go to bed.*

Examples 23 and 24 can be paraphrased: /kaan jaaʔ wa kaan garaʔ/ and /kaan gaam wa kaan ragad/, respectively. The imperfect verbs in 25 and 26 express purpose.

Among the verbs in this section, only invariable /kaan/ can be followed by a perfect verb. The imperfect of /kaan/, /yakuun/, is not used as a first verb in a verb string.

17.2.2

/šta/	*to want, like to do s.th.*
/raad/	*to want to do s.th.; to feel like doing s.th.*
/gidir/	*to be able to do s.th.*
/ḥaawal/	*to try to do s.th.*
/jarrab/	*to try to do s.th.*

Verbs that belong to this subgroup express a desire, an ability, or an effort to do something. Like the verbs in 17.2.1 they can be followed by one, two, or more verbs in the imperfect. Examples:

27. šta yijiy.	*He wanted to come.*
28. šta yiji yigraʔ.	*He wanted to come to study.*
29. šta ygarrir yiji yigraʔ.	*He wanted to decide to come to study.*
30. šta yistaʔðin yijiy yigraʔ.	*He wanted to get permission to come to study.*

/raad/, /gidir/, /ḥaawal/, and /jarrab/ may occur in the same position as /šta/. Unlike /kaan/, these verbs cannot be followed by a perfect form verb:

31. *šta jaaʔ.
32. *šta jaaʔ yigraʔ.

like /bigiy/, the imperfect form of these verbs can be used:

33. yigdar yiji yigraʔ.	*He can come to study.*
34. triid tiji tigraʔ.	*She wants to come to study.*

/ḥaawal/ and /jarrab/ are not used interchangeably in all positions. As far as meaning is concerned, /ḥaawal/ expresses the idea of 'making an attempt to do s.th.'; /jarrab/ expresses the idea of 'making an effort to do something' with the implication of testing or trying it out:

	35. šta yjarrib yigraʔ.	*He wanted to try to study.*
	36. šta yḥaawil yigraʔ.	*He wanted to try to study.*
	37. šta yjarrib al-ʕamal.	*He wanted to try out the job.*
but:	38. *šta yḥaawil al-ʕamal.	

17.2.3

/bada?/	*to begin, start to do s.th.*
/gaam/	*to begin, start to do s.th.*

/bada?/ and /gaam/ express similar meanings. Like /bigiy/, /ṣaar/, /šta/, /raad/, /gidir/, /ḥaawal/, and /jarrab/, they may be followed by one, two, or more verbs in the imperfect tense:

39. bada? (or /gaam/) yigra?. — *He began to study.*
40. bada? (or /gaam/) yḥaawil yigra?. — *He started to try to study.*
41. bada? (or /gaam/) yḥaawil yiji yigra?. — *He started to try to come to.study.*

If followed by a perfect tense verb, /gaam/ ceases to function as an auxiliary; it becomes a finite verb with a different meaning. /bada?/ does not have a similar function.

42. gaam širib. — *He stood up and had a drink.*
43. gaam tafal. — *He stood up and spat.*
44. *bada? širib.

like /šta/ and the verbs in 17.2.2, the imperfect or future of /bada?/ and /gaam/ can be used to imply a state, condition, habitual or future action;

45. yguum yigra? kull yawm. — *He studies every day.*
46. ʕa-yguum yigra? ġudweh. — *He will study tomorrow.*
47. ša-bda? ?agra ġudweh. — *I will start studying tomorrow.*

The progressive meaning is expressed by the present participle of /gaam/, i.e., /gaayim/:

48. gaayim yigra?. — *He is studying.*

Based on the preceding discussion in 17.2.1-17.2.3, we can say that:

1. A perfect tense verb may be preceded by /kaan/; if it is a verb of motion, it may be followed by another verb, in which case the perfect tense verb expresses completed action and the imperfect tense verb expresses purpose:

jaaʔ.	*He came.*
kaan jaaʔ.	*He would have come.*
jaaʔ garaʔ.	*He came and studied.*
kaan jaaʔ garaʔ.	*He would have come and studied.*
kaan jaaʔ yigraʔ.	*He would have come to study.*

2. An imperfect tense verb may be preceded by any combination of the following, but in the following order:

	kaan	modal	auxiliary	imperfect
or:	(kaan)	(modal)	(auxiliary)	imperfect

3. If the imperfect is a verb of motion, it may be followed by an imperfect verb with the grammatical meaning of purpose:

kaan	ṣaar	yišti	yiji	yigraʔ	*He would have begun to want to come to study.*
			X		*He comes.*
		X	X		*He wants to come.*
	X		X		*He got in the habit of coming.*
X			X		*He used to come.*
X		X	X		*He wanted to come.*
X	X		X		*He would have started coming.*
	X	X	X		*He began to want to come.*

Time Marker	Modal	Auxiliary	Main Verb	Complement (after verb of motion)
kaan X			Perfect	Perfect (complement action)
X	X	X	Imperfect	Imperfect (purpose)

Note: The position of main verb on the chart above can be filled by a verb phrase modal + verb, so that we might get a sentence like:

kaan ṣaar yišti yḥaawil yibga yiʕmal. *He would have wanted to try to keep on working.*

kaan ṣaar yigdar yḥaawil yibga yiʕmal. *He would have been able to try to go to work.*

17.2.4 /laazim/

This section deals with verb strings that are formed with the help of the auxiliary /laazim ʕala/. /laazim/ is uninflected and expresses one or more of the following meanings: 'should, must, have to, ought to' if followed by one, two, or more imperfect form verbs. /ʕala/ of /laazim ʕala/ takes a suffixed pronoun which corresponds to the subject of the following verb (see 12.2):

49. laazim ʕalayy asiir ðalḥiin. *I must go now.*

50. laazim ʕalyh ysiir yibsirih. *He has to go to see him.*

51. laazim ʕalayna nibga niʕmal. *We must, have to continue to work.*

52. laazim ʕalaykum tḥaawlu tibgu tiʕmaluw. *You (m.p.) must, have to try to continue to work.*

53. laazim ʕalayš tistaḥi min nafsiš. *You (f.s.) ought to be ashamed of yourself.*

54. ðalḥiin kull waaḥid laazim ʕalayh ysiir al-muʕaskar. *Nowadays everyone must, has to go to the (army) camp.*

The negative form of /laazim ʕala/ is either /maa laazim ʕala/ or /miš laazim ʕala/. The former is more commonly used. The negative form expresses either a negative obligation, i.e., 'shouldn't, mustn't, ought not to' or a lack of obligation, i.e., 'not have to':

55. maa laazim ʕalayk tsiir ġudweh.	*You (m.s.) don't have to go tomorrow.*
56. maa laazim ʕalayh ysiir al-ʕamal ʔiða huw mariiḍ.	*He shouldn't go to work if he is sick.*

If one of the verbs after /laazim ʕala/ is negated, only a negative obligation is expressed:

57. laazim ʕalayh maa yxazzin.	*He shouldn't, mustn't chew qat.*
58. laazim ʕalayk maa tibga tiʕmal.	*You (m.s.) mustn't continue to work.*
59. laazim ʕalayk tibga maa tiʕmal.	*You (m.s.) must continue not to work.*

The phrase /laazim ʕala/ followed by /ykuun/ expresses a deduction or an inference if it is followed by a perfect form of the verb:

60. laazim ʕalayh ykuun saar.	*He must have gone.*
61. laazim ʕalayk tkuun sirt tsallim ʕalayh.	*You (m.s.) must have gone to greet him.*
62. laazim ʕalayha tkuun saarat ragadat.	*She must have gone and went to bed.*
63. laazim ʕalaykum tkuunu sirtu xazzantu ʔams.	*You (m.p.) must have gone and chewed qat yesterday.*

The perfect of /laazim ʕala/ is /kaan laazim ʕala/, in which case /kaan/ is uninflected. The negative of /kaan laazim ʕala/ is made by prefixing the negative particle /maa/:

64. kaan laazim ʕalayh ysiir.	*He had to go.*
65. kaan laazim ʕalayha tsabbir aṣ-ṣabuuḥ.	*She had to prepare breakfast.*
66. maa kaan laazim ʕalayh ysiir.	*He did not have to go.* *He did not need to go.*
67. maa kaan laazim ʕalayha tsabbir aṣ-ṣabuuḥ.	*She did not have to prepare breakfast* *She did not need to prepare breakfast.*

If one of the verbs after /laazim ʕala/ is negated, only a negative obligation is expressed (see examples 57-59 above):

68. kaan laazim ʕalayh maa yxazzin. *He shouldn't have chewed qat.*

69. kaan laazim ʕalayh maa yibga yiʕmal. *He shouldn't have continued to work.*

Based on the preceding discussion, we can have the following verb strings with the auxiliary /laazim ʕala/:

Time Marker	Auxiliary	Verb
		(ykuun) Perfect = Probability
	laazim ʕalayh	
(kaan)		Imperfect: Necessity

1. = laazim ʕalayh (ykuun) saar yigraʔ. *He must have gone to study.*
2. = (kaan) laazim ʕalayh ysiir (yigraʔ). *He had to go to study.*

Section Eighteen

18. CONCORD

The parts of speech that show inflectional agreement are nouns, pronouns (personal and demonstrative), adjectives, and verbs. Nouns are the governing or determining elements, and the other parts of speech are the governed elements.

18.1 Adjectives

18.1.1 Positive adjectives

Positive adjectives are post-posed. They usually agree in gender, number, and definiteness with the noun they modify:

bilayzig jadiid	*a new necklace*
mabsareh jadiideh	*new eyeglasses*
ʔal-bilayzig al-jadiid	*the new necklace*
ʔal-mabsareh al-jadiideh	*the new eyeglasses*

Positive adjectives show either a two-fold distinction or a three-fold distinction for each of the following categories:[21]

a. Gender:	*masculine and feminine*
b. Number:	*singular and plural*
c. Definiteness:	*definite or indefinite*

For these three categories, an inflected adjective has the following forms:

18.1.1.1 Gender-Number

Adj.1 are unmarked; these are masculine singular forms:

rajjaal ṭayyib	*a good man*
walad ʕaaṭiš	*a thirsty boy*

Adj.2 are unmarked; they are feminine singular forms:

mareh ḥaamil	*a pregnant woman*
mareh ʕagiim	*a sterile woman*

It should be noted that in the case of animate nouns the real sex of the referent determines grammatical gender, regardless of the grammatical form of the word, e.g., /rajjaal/ 'man,' /ḥimaar/ 'donkey', /šaybeh/ 'old man,' and /xaliifeh/ 'Caliph,' are all masculine, while /mareh/ 'woman,' /ʔuxt/ 'sister,'/ ʔumm/ 'mother,' and /dimmeh/ 'cat,' are all feminine. As for inanimate nouns and adjectives, grammatical gender serves as a means of indicating agreement between noun and adjective:

maktabat al-jaamiʕ al-kabiireh	*the big library of the mosque, the big mosque library*
maktabat al-jaamiʕ al-kabiir	*the library of the big mosque, the big mosque library*

Examples of unmarked feminine singular nouns are (see 10.1 B.5):

šams	*sun*
yad	*hand*
ḥarb	*war*
gamar	*moon*
ʕayn	*eye*
ʔarð̣	*earth, ground*

Adj.3 are marked by the feminine morpheme -eh/-ah and are feminine singular:

ḥareeweh ḥaaliyeh	*a beautiful bride*
mareh šuuʕah	*an ugly woman*

Adj.4 are sound masculine plural forms. These are marked by the ending /-iin/; the referent is male human:

šugaah ʕaaṭišiin	*thirsty workmen*
rijaal ṭayyibiin	*good men*

Adj.5 are sound feminine plural forms; they are marked by the morpheme /-aat/; the referent is female human:

nisaaʔ ḥaaliyaat	*beautiful women*
banaat jaawiʕaat	*hungry girls*

Adj6 are marked by internal vocalic patterns. They are known as broken plural forms:[22]

ʔawlaad zġaar	*small, young boys*
rijaal hubl	*weak-minded men*

Note the following:

A. Adjectives modifying masculine dual nouns are masculine plural:

	ʔiθnayn buyuut kibaar	*two big houses*
or:	baytayn kibaar	
	ʔiθnayn rijaal naahiyiin	*two good, honest men*
or:	rajjaalayn naahiyiin	
	θintayn banaat ḥaaliyaat	*two beautiful girls*
or:	bintayn ḥaaliyaat	

B. Adjectives modifying non-human plural nouns are usually masculine plural, but may be singular feminine; the latter form is not commonly used:

gawaariir kibaar	or:	gawaariir kabiireh	*big bottles*
ʔagraaṭ ġaaliyiin	or:	ʔagraaṭ ġaaliyeh	*expensive earrings*
jibaal ʕaaliyiin	or:	jibaal ʕaaliyeh	*high mountains*
dimam suud	or:	dimam sawdaaʔ	*black cats*
θalaaθah ṭamaaṭiis ḥumr	or:	θalaaθah ṭamaaṭiis ḥamraaʔ	*three red tomatoes*
jimaal jaawiʕiin	or:	jimaal jaawiʕah	*hungry camels*

18.1.1.2 Definiteness

As for definiteness, all the forms of the adjectives given above may be definite, i.e., marked by the article prefix /ʔal/ or indefinite, i.e., unmarked:

ʔar-rajjaal al-kabiir	*the big, old man*
ʔal-mareh al-ḥaaliyeh	*the beautiful woman*
ʔaš-šugaah at-taaʕibiin	*the tired workmen*
jihhaalana z-ziġaar	*our little children*
maktabat al-jaamiʕ al-kabiir	*the library of the big mosque*
bintiš al-kabiireh	*your (f.s.) old(est) daughter*
ṣanʕa l-gadiimeh	*the old (section of) San'a*

18.1.2 Elative Adjectives[23]

The comparative form of the adjective is not inflected for gender or number.

rajjaal ʔaġlaḍ̱	*a fatter man (m.s.)*
ʔiθnayn rijaal ʔaġlaḍ̱	*two fatter men (m.p.)*
rijaal ʔaġlaḍ̱	*fatter men (m.p.)*
mareh ʔaġlaḍ̱	*a fatter woman (f.s.)*
θintayn nisaaʔ ʔaġlaḍ̱	*two fatter women (f. dual)*
nisaaʔ ʔaġlaḍ̱	*fatter women (f.p.)*

The superlative is formed either by making the comparative definite:

ʔar-rajjaal al-ʔaġlaḍ̱	*the fattest man*

or by putting the comparative in a construct with no concord; this latter pattern has a higher frequency of occurrence in SA and in most other dialects of Arabic:

ʔaġlaḍ̱ rajjaal	*the fattest man*
ʔaġlaḍ̱ mareh	*the fattest woman*
ʔaġlaḍ̱ an-nisaaʔ	*the fattest (of the) women*
ʔaḥsan al-gaat	*the best qat*

18.2 Pronouns and Verbs

There is no gender distinction in the first person pronouns and verb forms; modifiers agree with the referents of /ʔana/ 'I' and /ḥna/ 'we':

ʔana jiʔt.	*I (m. or f.) came.*
ḥna jiʔna.	*We (m. or f.) came.*
ʔana taaʕib.	*I (m.) am tired (m.).*
ʔana taaʕibeh.	*I (f.) am tired (f.).*
ḥna taaʕibiin.	*We (m.) are tired (m.p.).*
ḥna taaʕibaat.	*We (f.) are tired (f.p.).*
ʔana l-mudiir.	*I (m.) am the director (m.).*
ʔana l-mudiireh.	*I (f.) am the director (f.).*
ḥna l-mudaraaʔ.	*We (m.) are the directors (m.p.).*
ḥna l-mudiiraat.	*We (f.) are the directors (f.p.).*

When the second and third person pronouns are used, verbs agree with them in gender and number:

ʔant sirt.	*You (m.s.) left.*
ʔanti sirtiy.	*You (f.s.) left.*
ʔantu sirtuw.	*You (m.p.) left.*
ʔantayn sirtayn.	*You (f.p.) left.*
huw saar.	*He left.*
hiy saarat.	*She left.*
hum saaruw.	*They (m.) left.*
hin saarayn.	*They (f.) left.*

If the subject of a verb is an expressed noun, verb agreement is as follows:

A. If the noun is singular, the verb agrees with it in number and gender, whether it precedes or follows the noun:

ʔar-rajjaal saʔalniy.	*The man asked me.*
uxti saarat al-madraseh.	*My sister went to school.*
ʔal-ḥareew yištari l-ḥilyeh.	*The bridegroom buys the jewelry.*
ʔal-ḥareeweh tištari l-kisweh.	*The bride buys the clothing.*
al-firsik miš ṭayyib ðalḥiin.	*Peaches are not good now.*
aṭ-ṭamaaṭis ġaaliy.	*Tomatoes are expensive.*
haaði l-ḥabḥabeh ḥamreeʔ.	*This watermelon is red.*

B. If the noun is dual or plural and refers to human beings, the verb is plural and agrees with its subject in gender:

ʔiθnayn ʔawlaad gaamuw yigruw.	*Two boys started to study.*
al-ḥareewaat aθ-θintayn ragaṣayn wa ġannayn.	*The two brides danced and sang.*
ʔar-rijaal yziffu al-ḥareew ʔila baytih.	*Men conduct the bridegroom in solemn procession to his home.*
ʔan-nisaaʔ ysabbirayn al-ʔakl.	*Women prepare the food.*
saaru tġaddu al-jihhaal.	*The children went and had lunch.*

C. If the noun is dual and does not refer to human beings, the verb is masculine plural:

ʔal-baabayn ġallaguw.	*The two doors closed.*
ʔaṭ-ṭiigan aθ-θintayn ktasaruw.	*The two windows were broken.*
ftaṭaru l-ʕajalatayn.	*The two tires went flat.*
ʔiθnayn ʔawlaad ltabajuw.	*Two boys were hit.*

D. If the noun is plural and does not refer to human beings, the verb is usually masculine plural, but may be feminine singular.

ʔat-tiniik mtalaʔu/mtalaʔat b-l-meeʔ.	*The (water) tanks were full of water.*
aṭ-ṭiigaan ktasaruw/ktasarat.	*The windows were broken.*
rtafaʕat/rtafaʕu ʔal-ʔasʕaar.	*Prices went up.*
btallat/btallu ʔal-ganaaṭir.	*The shoes were wet.*

If the plural noun refers to animals, a masculine plural form of the verb is normally used, regardless of the gender of the subject:

ʔad-dimam ḥamaluw.	*The cats ran away.*
ʔal-jimaal ʕagguw.	*The camels grunted.*
xamsah ʕaṣfar ṭaaruw.	*Five sparrows flew (away).*
al-kasaakis jaawiʕiin.	*The puppies are hungry.*

Section Nineteen

19. NEGATION

See also 13.5 for the meanings and uses of /laa/, /maa/, /miš/, and /maaši/.

19.1 Negating Verbs

19.1.1 Perfect and Imperfect

The perfect and imperfect forms of the verb are usually negated by /maa/, which always precedes the verb; the verb normally takes the suffix /-š/:

limih maa xazzantš?	*Why didn't you (m.s.) chew qat?*
maa ʔagdar ʔaji saaʕat xams.	*I cant come at five.*
maa sirnaaš aš-šuug al-yawm.	*We didn't go to the market today.*
waḷḷaahi maa fihimtš.	*Honestly, I didnt understand.*
maa yištiiš.	*He doesn't want.*
maa yisbirš.	*It wont work; it is not suitable or proper.*
maa gaalš šayʔ.	*He didn't say anything.*

Imperfect verb forms that denote a passive-potential sense are also negated by /maa -š/:

ðayya maa yitġayyarš.	*This cannot be changed.*
yitgawwa walla maa yitgawwaš?	*Can it be made stronger or not?*
maa yiθθammanš.	*It cannot be priced; it is priceless.*
maa yigtaraʔš.	*It cannot be read.*
maa yistanṭagš.	*He cannot be interrogated.*

Two verbal constructions with a perfect or an imperfect verb joined by /wa/ 'and' are negated by /maa ... wa maa .../ or /maa ... wa laa .../ or /laa ... wa laa/ ... Examples:

maa yistanṭagš wa maa yitḥaakaaš. maa yistanṭagš wa laa yitḥaakaaš.	*He can neither be interrogated nor talked to.*
maa yinfaʕak ma maʕ ʔaxuuk wa laa siraajih yiḍ̣iiʔ lak.	*(lit., "What your brother has is of no avail to you; neither will his lantern give you light.") (Meaning: Depend on yourself.)*
laa sirt wa laa jiʔt. / maa sirtš wa maa jiʔtš.	*I neither went nor came.*

laa ragad wa laa xalla ʔaḥad yurgud.	*He neither slept nor let anybody (else) sleep.*
maa taġaddaaš wa maa taʕaššaaš.	*He didn't have lunch; neither did he have dinner.*
laa ṣalla wa laa ṣaam.	*He neither prayed nor fasted.*

Note that if /laa ... wa laa/ ... is used the particle /-š/ is not used.

In constructions with /ʔilla/ 'except' /maa/ is used to negate the verb. Such constructions have the meaning of 'nothing or nobody ... except' or 'not ... anything or anybody except':

maa bigiy ʔilla ladaatih.	*Nothing remained except his personal effects.*
ma ligiiš ʔilla bagariy.	*He didn't find anything (i.e., any other kind of meat)except beef.*
maa yfarrig as-saḥaab ʔilla l-maṭar.	*There is nothing that disperses clouds except rain.*
maa yijiiš al-xayr ʔilla karrah.	*(God's) blessing comes only once.*
maa tiksir al-ḥajar ʔilla l-ḥajar.	*Nothing breaks a rock except its sister.*
maa ʔibsarhum ʔilla ʕabdaḷḷa.	*Nobody saw them except Abdalla.*
maa ʔibsaruw ʔilla ʕabdaḷḷa.	*They (m.) didn't see anybody except Abdalla.*

/ʔilla/ may be followed by a prepositional phrase:

maa ysiiruw ʔilla fi l-layl.	*They do not go (at any time) except at night.*
maa tibsirišš ʔilla fi baab al-yaman.	*You will not see him except in Bab Al-Yaman.*

/maa/ and /laa/ are used to negate indefinite nouns and express the meaning of 'there isn't; there aren't; you cannot find, etc.' /maa/ is usually used with /ʔilla/ 'except.' Proverbs and sayings abound with such examples:

maa maliiḥ ʔilla fiih ʕayb	*(lit., "There isnt anything good, but there is a defect in it.")*
maa fi d-dunya ʔilla raḥmat aḷḷaah.	*There is nothing in this world except God's blessing.*
maa šayʔ saaʕ šayʔ.	*There is nothing similar to any other thing.*
maa ʔaḥad haana ʔilla yaḥya.	*No one is here except Yahya.*

Examples with /laa/

laa maaʔ yiruub wala gaḥbeh tituub.	*(lit., "No water turns into yogurt, nor does a prostitute repent.") Meaning: You cannot make a silk purse out of a sow's ear. A leopard cannot change his spots.*
laa zġayyir ymayyiz kabiir wala kabiir yirḥam zaġiir.	*(lit., "There isn't a young person who respects an older one, nor is there an old person who has compassion for a young one.")*

In classicisms /laa/ negates indefinite nouns, in which case it has the function of literary Arabic /laa/ of absolute negation:

laa šakk	*no doubt*
laa šukr(a) ʕala waajib.	*(lit., "No thanks for ones duty.")*
laa budd min as-safar.	*Travel is inevitable.*
laa mafarr	*no escape*

19.1.2 Negating Pseudo-Verbs

Prepositional pseudo-verbs (see 14.2) are negated by /maa/:

maa biš gaat haana.	*There isn't any qat here.*
maa ʕindahum jihhaal.	*They dont have any children.*
maa ʕindiš ðahab?	*Don't you (f.s.) have any gold?*
maa ʕalayh duyuun.	*He doesnt have any debts. (lit., "Debts are not on him.")*

Two prepositional pseudo-verbal constructions are usually negated by /laa ... wala .../ or /maa ... wala/ .../ 'neither ... nor.' :

laa lih ʔawwal wala taali.	*(lit., "He does not have a beginning; nor does he have an end.") (Meaning: Everything should have a sound beginning.)*
laa lih dayn wala ʕalayh dayn.	*People do not owe him any money; neither does he owe any money.*
maa ʕindih bayt wala zalaṭ.	*He has neither a house nor money.*

19.1.3 Negating Imperatives

A negative command (or request), which is used to tell s.o. not to do s.th., consists of the negative particle /laa/ followed by the imperfect of the verb.

laa traajim an-naas wa baytak min zujaaj!	*(lit., "Do not throw rocks at people if your house is made of glass." (Meaning: Those who live in glass houses should not throw stones.)*
laa titzawwaj wa ʕaad garguuš ʔummak fi ṭ-ṭaagah.	*(lit., "Do not get married and your mother's cap is still in the window.") (Meaning: Haste makes waste.)*
laa tsiirayn as-suug!	*Don't go (f.p.) to the market!*
laa txazzinu haana!	*Do not chew (m.p.) qat here!*
laa tguuli maa biš.	*Do not say (f.s.): "There isn't."*

Two negative commands are joined by /wa/ 'and':

laa tusrug wa laa txaaf.	*(lit., "Do not steal and do not be afraid!") (Meaning: If you do not steal, you should not be (or you do not have to be) afraid.)*
laa tġaddiihum wa laa tʕaššiihum.	*Do not give them lunch and do not give them dinner!*

19.2 Negating Other Parts of Speech

Nouns, pronouns, adjectives, and verbs, particles, and prepositional phrases are negated by /miš/:

huw miš mgawwit.	*He is not a qat dealer.*
miš ġudweyh, ʔal-yawm	*not tomorrow, today*
miš ab-sabt, al-xamiis	*not (on) Saturday, (on) Thursday*
miš hin, ʔantayn	*not they (f.), you (f.p.)*
ʔana miš jaawiʕ.	*I am not hungry.*
hin miš ðaahinaat.	*They (f.) are not smart.*
huw miš ġaarig.	*He is not mad.*
miš haakaða?	*Isn't it so?*
hin saarayn, miš haana.	*They (f.) left; they are not here.*
ḥna miš mirtaaḥiin haanaak.	*We are not comfortable there.*
miš naahiy?	*Isn't it good?*
miš dala-dale, fiisaʕ	*not slowly, quickly*
miš haakaða	*not in this manner*
miš saaʕat θintayn	*not at two oclock*
miš saaʕ-maa huw	*not like him*
miš ʕala sibbih	*not because of him*
miš min ṣanʕa	*not from San'a*

Either /laa ... wa laa/ or /maa ... wa laa/ is used with the meaning of 'neither ... nor':

laa bayt wa laa zalaṭ	*neither a house nor money*
laa li wala lak	*neither mine nor yours*
laa ʕaaṭiš wa laa jaawiʕ	*neither thirsty nor hungry*
maa šay saaʕ šay? wa laa ṣ-ṣabaaḥ saaʕ al-ʕašiy.	*(There is) nothing like anything else and the morning is not like the evening.*
maa kull sawdeh tamrah wala kull šaḥmeh laḥmeh.	*(lit., "Not every piece of charcoal is a date, and not every piece of fat is meat.") Meaning: Do not judge people by their appearance.*

The negative form of /ʔaḥad/ 'somebody, someone' is /maḥad/ 'nobody, no one' is usually used as the subject of a sentence:

maḥad ʔibsarih.	*Nobody saw it.*
maḥad yudxul haana.	*Nobody enters here.*
maḥad maat min al-juuʕ.	*No one died of hunger.*

but:

maa ʔibsart ʔaḥad. *ibsart maḥad.	*I did not see anybody.*
maa labajtš ʔaḥad? *labajtš maḥad.	*Didn't you hit anybody?*

When /maa/ negates a noun or a phrase and is followed by /ʔilla/ or /ġayr/ 'except' the meaning expressed in English is usually 'there isn't any + N (that can be found) except':

maa fi l-mudun ġayr ṣanʕa.	*There isn't any other city except San'a (i.e., San'a is the best of cities.)*
maa ṣadiig ʔilla saaʕat að̣-ð̣iig	*There isn't any friend except at the time of distress.(i.e., A friend in need is a friend indeed.)*
maa fi l-ḥanaš ʔilla raasih.	*There isn't anything in the snake except its head. (i.e., The head of a snake is its most important part.)*

maa by itself may negate a noun or a phrase and expresses the meaning of 'There isn't any + N':

maa mareh tḥibb mareh.	*There isn't any woman who likes (another) woman*
maa minhum ð̣arar.	*There isn't any harm they can do.*

A negative response to a yes- or no-question is either /laa/ or /ʔabadan/ (lit., "never") or both /laa ʔabadan/ for emphasis:

ʔant txazzin?	*Do you chew qat?*
laa.	*No.*
tišrab šigaayir?	*Do you smoke cigarettes?*
laa ʔabadan.	*No, never.*

The phrase /miš haakaða/ 'isn't it so' is appended to a statement to form what is known in English as a tail question; it is usually known as a question tag; it is invariable. The phrases /miš ṣaḥiiḥ/ and /miš tamaam/ or simply /ṣaḥiiḥ/ and /tamaam/ are also heard but /miš haakaða/ occurs more frequently.:

ʔal-gaat ġaali, miš hakaða?	*Qat is expensive, isn't it?*
ʔal-jihhaal saaru l-madraseh, miš ṣaḥiiḥ?	*The children went to school, didn't they?*
ʕa-yiji ġudweh, tamaam?	*He will come tomorrow, won't he?*
ʔant miš jaawiʕ, ṣaḥiiḥ?	*You are not hungry, are you?*

FOOTNOTES

1. See 19.1.2 below.
2. See 13.5.
3. In literary Arabic "verbal sentence" is used to mean a "sentence beginning with a verb," which is not the meaning intended here. The tendency in literary Arabic for verbal sentences to begin with verbs is not seen in the colloquials where verbal sentences tend to begin with a noun or a pronoun, if any.
4. See Footnote 44 in the Morphology section.
5. Lit., "If your cousin shaves, you (should) moisten your beard." You should be on the lookout and forestall events. Seize the opportunity.
6. A bull or an ox is a symbol of power and strength. If it is wounded or killed, people would come with knives to cut it up (and inflict more wounds or take pieces of its meat.). When a great man falls or makes an error, people will show no compassion for him.

7. Lit., "If the government prepares for travel, i.e., if it wants to do something, e.g., paving a street, I will go to sleep." This proverb is used to describe the slow pace at which the government executes domestic affairs. It describes a person who wavers, hesitates, and takes too long to do anything.

8. Lit., "If a gabiili knows the door of your house, turn your door knocker upside down." This proverb is very similar in meaning and usage to /ʔadxaltih min al-baab fa ʔaxrajak min aṭ-ṭaagah/, which means literally,"You let him enter through the door, but he kicked you out of the window." It is similar to the literary proverb /ʔittaqi šarra man ʔaḥsanta ʔilayhi/, i.e.,"Fear the evil of those whom you have done favors to."

9. This proverb gives credit to educators, such as teachers, religious leaders, etc., who educate people and lead them to the correct path.

10. /al-kassaar/ is the one who breaks pots made of clay or pottery and /ʔal-maddaar/ is the one who makes them.

11. The literal meaning of the proverb is: "(Inquire about) the neighbor before (inquiring about) the house."

12. /ʔallaði/ 'who, whom, which, that' is invariable, i.e., it is not inflected for gender or number in SA. It is often shortened to /ʔali/ or /ʔalli/ in rapid speech.

13. This proverb urges people to seize the opportunity and do things before it is too late. It is similar in meaning to: Make hay while the sun shines.

14. /ʔalli faat maat/ is also possible.

15. This proverb is used, for example, to describe a person who professes loyalty and sincerity after he has proved to be disloyal and unfaithful.

16. Except for /waaḥid/ 'one' and /ʔiθnayn/ 'two'.

17. See 11.3.2 for more examples and the rules governing the pre-posing and post-posing of these modifiers.

18. See 15.3 above.

19. /štaaʔ/ is often reduced to /šta/ or /štaʔ/ in normal speech. It is a Form VIII hollow verb; its imperfect form is /yištiy/. Sometimes /raad/ is used instead of /štaaʔ/ with the same meaning.

20. /bigiy/ and /ṣaar/ may also occur as finite verbs, in which case they may require a complement, which might be nominal, adjectival, or prepositional:

bigiy fi l-bayt.	*He stayed at home.*
ṣaar mudiir.	*He became director.*
ṣaar jaawiʕ.	*He became hungry.*
bigiy naahiy.	*He stayed, continued to be good.*

21. The general rules given in this section are modified by more specific ones given later on.

22. See Major Broken Plural Patterns in 11.5.2 above.

23 See also 11.2 Elative Constructs and 11.5.1.4 Elative Adjectives above.

Part Four

Texts

Sample Texts

Introduction

This part contains a very small portion of the corpus used for the present work. The whole corpus covers a wide variety of subjects of interest. It includes greetings, getting acquainted, appointments, telling time, weather and climatic conditions, directions, days of the week, months and seasons of the year, systems of education, banking, shopping, mailing letters, etc. Anecdotes, tales, plays, songs, etc., suited to the particular needs of prospective students have also been recorded. Some texts and narratives in Yemeni Arabic I and Yemeni Arabic II form another small portion of the corpus. The first text contains some sayings and proverbial phrases. The second, the third and the fourth texts are dialogs; TEXT V, TEXT VI and TEXT VII are narratives. Each saying or proverbial phrase in TEXT I is followed by a literal translation in parentheses, an explanation of the proverb, and an equivalent English proverbial phrase, if any.

TEXT I

ʔamθaal wa ʔagwaal

1. ʔaaxir al-ʕilaaj al-kayy.
2. ʔaaxir al-layl taʔtiik ad-dawaahiy.
3. ʔaaxir al-mawaaʕiid al-ʕiid.
4. ʔal-ʔawwalah lak wa θ-θaaniyah ʕalayk wa θ-θaaliθah laa raddak a̤l̤laah.
5. ʔal-juuʕ yiddi l-gawzabeh wa š-šibaʕ yiddi l-gambaʕah.
6. ʔal-jaar gabl ad-daar.
7. ʔal-yahwadah fi l-guluub maa hiy b-ṭuul az-zanaaniir.
8. ʔal-ʔaʕwar fi bilaad al-ʕumyaan faakihah.
9. ʔana ʔamiir wa ʔant ʔamiir man yasuug al-ḥamiir?
10. ʔar-rabḥ fi ʕayn ʔummih ġazaal.
11. ʔal-balaaš ṭiʕiim.
12. ʔaz-zalaṭ txarrij al-jinn mrabbaṭiin.
13. ʔaθ-θaʕl θaʕl lo yirkab ʔummih miyat ðiib.

14. ʔal-ġaayib ḥijjatih maʕih.
15. ʔas-sirr miθl al-ḥamaami laa falat min yaddi ṭaar.
16. ʔaṣ-ṣadiig wagt aḏ̣-ḏ̣iig.
17. ʔahda hadiyyeh wa nafsih fiiha.
18. ʔadxaltih min al-baab fa ʔaxrajak min aṭ-ṭaagah.
19. ʔahli wa ʔin kasaru ḏ̣ahriy.
20. ʔallaði maa yajiiš maʕ al-ḥareeweh maa yajiiš baʕdaha.
21. ʔarbaʕah šallu jamal wa l-jamal maa šallahum.
22. ʔašti laḥm min kabši wa ʔašti kabši yamšiy.
23. ʔibn as-saneh ṭabiib nafsih.
24. ʔibn ʔarbaʕiin nahaar maa yiʕwir ʕaynih.
25. ʔibliis maa yxarrib daymatih.
26. ʔibʕid ʕan ʔahlik yḥibbuuk wa jiiraanik yafgiduuk.
27. ʔiða ḥalag ʔibn ʕammak ballayt.
28. ʔiṣrif maa fi l-jayb yaʔtiik maa fi l-ġayb.
29. ʔitġadda bih gablima yitʕašša bik.
30. ʔiθnayn biiḏ̣ xayr min šaahid ʕadl.
31. ʔiθnayn maa yimšiiš bihim markab.
32. ʔiða jiit bilaad al-ʕumyaan ʔiʕwir ʕaynak.
33. ʔiða kaθurat al-ʔadyaak taxarrab al-layl.
34. ʔiða ṣaaḥibak ʕasal laa tilḥasih kullih.
35. ʔiða šaddat ad-dawleh ragadt.
36. ʔiða ʕugir aθ-θawr ḥaḏ̣arat as-sakaakiin.
37. "ʔuḥlub!" gaal: "huw tays!"
38. b-yitʕallam li-ḥsaaneh fi ruus al-guḏ̣ʕaan.
39. b-yabni ʕala xayš.
40. b-yuxlug min al-ḥabbeh gubbeh.
41. baaʕ al-bayyaaʕ wa stawfa θ-θaman.
42. baddal ḥareewatih b-ʕuḏ̣miy.
43. bagarat al-muzayyin maa txaaf min aṭ-ṭaaseh.
44. bard xabba wala gummal xidaar.
45. barguug ya ʔahl as-suug.
46. bayḏ̣at diik.
47. baʕdima šayyab xatanuuh.
48. bidaayat al-miil xaṭweh.
49. bugšatak wa s-suug.
50. buulu ya ʕyaali gadaani raayḥa s-saayileh.
51. ḥaaki r-raṭl yifham wagiyyeh.

52. jaarak al-gariib wala ʔaxuuk al-baʕiid.
53. jalasat jalasat wa ʔaddat bint.
54. jaraadeh fi ṣurri wala barbari fi ṣ-ṣuraab.
55. jirbeh mugaameh wala waadi ṣalb.
56. laa meʔ yiruub wala gaḥbeh tituub.
57. laa taġawfal ad-dimm tagambaʕ al-faʕr.
58. laa titzawwaj wa ʕaad garguuš ʔummak fi ṭ-ṭaagah.
59. laa traajim an-naas wa baytak min zujaaj.
60. laa yinfaʕak maa maʕ ʔaxuuk wala siraajih yḏ̣iiʔlak.
61. laa ʕaraf al-gabiili baab baytak galabt al-madaggah.
62. law tigliilih fi yaddak.
63. maa fi l-mudun ġayr ṣanʕa wa fi l-bawaadi ruṣaabah.
64. maa yḥinn ʕala l-ʕuud ʔilla gišrih.
65. man fi yaddih al-faʔs ligi l-ḥaṭab.
66. man lagaṣih al-ḥanaš ftajaʕ min as-salabeh.
67. man taġadda b-kiðbeh maa taʕaššа b-ha.
68. man xabbaʔ min ʕašaah ʔaṣbaḥ yirah.
69. nuṣf aṭ-ṭariig maʕgim al-baab.
70. raʕs kabši wala ġiraarat jaraad.
71. šakaru ad-dimm xiri fi ṭ-ṭaḥiin.
72. taḥt as-sawaahi dawaahi.
73. tazkiyat an-nafs gabiiḥah.
74. walad ʕaaṣi wala maabiš.
75. yibtariʕ janb aṭ-ṭaaseh.

TRANSLATION I

Proverbs and Sayings

1. (The last remedy is cauterization.)When everything else fails, use force. There is no other remedy.

2. (At the end of the night you will be beset by calamities.) The intoxication has passed away and anxiety has come. The glory of an hour is gone in a second. No good thing lasts forever. In the late afternoon and at the beginning of the night people in Yemen socialize, chew qat and have a good time. At the end of the night all forms of merriment go away and people start to think of problems. This proverb urges people to be prepared for what the future holds. Equivalent to: Be prepared! Take precautions!

3. (The last, i.e., the worst, the most impractical appointment is the feast day.) Do not promise more than you can deliver. Equivalent to: Do not give false promises! If you promise something, make sure that you can keep your promise or put it into effect.

4. (The first time is for you; the second time is against you; the third, may God not protect you from harm.) If you make a mistake once, you are forgiven. If you make the same mistake twice, it is against you. If you make the same mistake for the third time, go to hell.

5. (Hunger leads to being seated in a submissive manner and satiation leads to jumping out of joy.)

6. (Inquire about the neighbor before inquiring about the house.) A man is known by the company he keeps.

7. (Piety is in the heart; it is not by the length of side curls.) Equivalent to: Fair without and foul within.

8. (The one-eyed in the country of the blind is fruit.)The one-eyed in the country of the blind is king.

9. (I am a prince and you are a prince. Who is going to drive the donkeys?) Each one has his own responsibility.

10. (A monkey, in the eyes of its mother, is a gazelle.)Beauty is in the eye of the beholder.

11. (Anything that is free of charge is delicious.)Anything free is delicious and people are desirous of having more of it.

12. (Money drives away jinnis in shackles.) Money talks.

13. (A fox is a fox even if a hundred wolves had sexual intercourse with its mother.) A leopard can not change his spots. This proverb is used in a derogatory sense.

14. (The absent person has his own excuse.) Equivalent to: The absent party is not at fault.

15. (A secret is like a pigeon which, if released, will fly away.) Keep the secret! Do not reveal it!

16. (A friend is for difficult times.) A friend in need is the friend indeed.

17. (He gave a gift, but he wanted to take it back.) This proverb describes a person who is niggardly, or who gives grudgingly. Equivalent to: You cannot eat your cake and have it, too.

18. (You let him enter through the door, but he kicked you out of the window.) Give him an inch and he will take a mile. There are people who will turn against you if you do favors for them. This proverb is equivalent to /ʔadxaltih b-yaddak fa ʔaxrajak b-rijlih/ or to literary /ʔittaqi šarra man ʔasanta ʔilayhi/.

19. (They are my folks, even if they break my back.) This proverb urges people to stick to their tribes and clans. Blood is thicker than water.

20. (What does not come with the bride will not come after her, i.e., after she is no longer a bride.) This proverb urges people to seize the opportunity and do things before it is too late. Equivalent to: Make hay while the sun shines.

21. (Four people can carry a camel but a camel cannot carry them.) This proverb calls for cooperation. What you cannot do singly can be done with others. Numbers overpower the brave. One hand does not clap. Strength is in numbers. In union there is strength.

22. (I want meat from my ram and I want my ram to walk.) This proverb is similar in meaning and usage to Proverb No. 17 above.

23. (A one-year-old is his own doctor.) No one knows you better than you yourself. Similar to Proverb No. 25 and similar to: /ʔibn ʔarbaʕiin nahaar ma yiʕwir ʕaynih/ (A forty-day-old will not blind himself in the eye.)

24. (A forty-day old will not blind himself in the eye.) No one does harm to oneself.

25. (Satan does not destroy his kitchen.) If Satan, the devil, does not do harm to himself and does not ruin his possessions, what about you (who are not Satan)? Equivalent to: No one does harm to oneself.

26. (If you keep your distance, your folks will love you and your neighbors will miss you.) Keep your distance! Familiarity breeds contempt. Better go around than fall into the ditch.

27. (If your cousin shaves, you should moisten your beard.) You should be on the lookout and forestall events. Seize the opportunity. This proverb is similar in meaning and use to No. 29 below. When the wind is fair, hoist your sails.

28. (Spend what is in your pocket and you will be compensated by the invisible, i.e., God.) This proverb urges people to give alms to the poor. Equivalent to: Spend and God will send.

29. (Have him for lunch before he has you for dinner!) Be on the lookout! Forewarned is forearmed.

30. (Two white, i.e., two silver riyals are better than a court witness.) /biiḍ/ 'white (p.)' here refers to the color of the silver riyal, the Maria Theresa silver riyal. This proverb is said during times of bribery. Two silver riyals, i.e., money, will buy a judge and make him twist the testimony of a witness.

31. (A ship does not set sail with two captains.) (Two cannot steer a ship.) Too many cooks spoil the broth.

32. (If you are in the country of the one-eyed, blind yourself in the eye.) When in Rome, do as the Romans do.

33. (If there are too many roosters, the night will be spoiled.) Too many cooks spoil the broth.

34. (If your friend is honey, do not lick him up all at once.) Equivalent to: Don't use your credit all at once.

35. (If the government prepares for travel, i.e., if it wants to do something, e.g., paving a street, I will go to sleep.) This proverb is used to describe the slow pace at which the government executes domestic affairs. It is used to describe a person who wavers, hesitates, and takes too long to do anything.

36. (If a bull is maimed, knives will increase.) A bull or an ox is a symbol of power and strength. If it is wounded or killed, people would come with knives to cut it up (and inflict more wounds or take pieces of its meat). When a great man falls or makes an error, people will show no compassion for him. Equivalent to: All lay hands on the willing horse.

37. ("Milk him!" He said, "He is a bull.") This proverb is used to describe a person who is so dense that he cannot see an impossible thing, or who argues for an impossible thing. Equivalent to: Be reasonable! Do not ask for the impossible! You cannot squeeze blood out of a turnip.

38. (He learns a barber's trade by shaving the heads of the bald.) This proverb is used to describe a person who uses his skill to take advantage of the poor and the weak.

39. (He builds on canvas.) Canvas cannot be a foundation for a building. Equivalent to: He builds castles in the air. He is building a house on sand.

40. (He creates a dome from a grain.) Equivalent to: He makes a mountain out of a molehill.

41. (The seller has already sold the commodity and has been paid in full.) It's too late! This proverb is equivalent to proverb 47 below. 'After he became an old man they circumcised him.'

42. (He exchanged his bride for a bone.) This proverb describes a person who exchanges a valuable thing for a worthless thing.

43. (A barber's cow is not afraid of the drum.) In the olden times in Yemen, especially in the villages, a barber, in addition to cutting hair, performed circumcision and did other kinds of jobs such as beating the drums during the month of Ramadhan and at weddings. His cow was used to hearing the beating of drums; it was not afraid of the drums. This proverb is used to describe a person who does not heed threats because he is used to them. Do not think that you can threaten me.

44. (The cold of Khabba and not the fleas of Khidar.) xabba is a place known for its cold weather and xidaar is a place known for its many fleas. If you are in a position where you have to make a choice of two evils, choose the lesser of them. You're between a rock and a hard place.

45. (It's apricots, shoppers!) It's crystal clear; it does not need any proof. It's clearer than day.

46. (A rooster's egg!) A rooster does not lay eggs; but if it does, it will be a rare event, and will be once in a lifetime; it cannot be repeated. It is usually used for a very pleasant event or occurrence.

47. (After he became a very old man, they circumcised him.) This proverb is equivalent to another Yemeni proverb, i.e., /baʕdima šayyab, daxxaluu l-miʕlaameh/. 'After he became very old, they sent him to school.' You cannot teach an old dog new tricks.

48. (The beginning of a mile is a step.) The first step is always the hardest.

49. (Your money and the market.) This proverb is said by a seller to a buyer who thinks the seller will charge him too much. The seller is telling him, "It's your money; go haggle! Depend upon your skill."

50. (Urinate, my children! I am going to the stream.) The mother is going to the stream to wash her dirty clothes. She asks her children to urinate (in their clothes) so that she might wash her clothes and their clothes. She wants to kill two birds with one stone.

51. This proverb describes a person who is not worth his salt, because he is stubborn.

52. (Your close neighbor and not your distant brother.) Out of sight out of mind.

53. (She waited and waited and gave birth to a girl.) She waited for a long time, hoping that she would give birth to a baby boy, but she gave birth to a baby girl; she disappointed her husband and other people. This proverb describes a person who is expected to fare well but disappoints people.

54. (A grasshopper in my bag and not a billy goat in the fields.) Similar in meaning and usage to No. 70.

55. (A cultivated piece of land and not a barren valley.) Prefer a small arable piece of land to a whole barren valley. Equivalent to: Quality is better than quantity.

56. (Water does not curdle, nor does a prostitute repent.) Equivalent to: You cannot make a silk purse out of a sow's ear. A leopard cannot change his spots.

57. (If the cat is inattentive, the mouse will jump out of joy.) Equivalent to: When the cat's away, the mice will play.

58. Haste makes waste. (Do not get married and your mother's cap is still in the window!) /garguuš/ is a cap that covers the whole head except for the eyes and the mouth; it is worn by children in winter. If your mother's /garguuš/ is still in the window, your mother is still very young. Haste makes waste.

59. (Do not throw rocks at people if your house is made of glass.) Those who live in glass houses should not throw stones.

60. (What your brother has does not benefit you; neither will his lantern give you light.) Depend on yourself.

61. (If a gabiili knows the door of your house, turn your door knocker upside down.) Give him an inch and he will take a mile. This proverb is very similar in meaning and usage to /ʔadxaltih min al-baab fa ʔaxrajak min aṭ-ṭaagah/.

62. (Even if you fry something for him in your hand.) This proverb describes a person who is too difficult to please. He is very stubborn.

63. (There is no other city except San'a, and there is no other farm land except Rusaba.) San'a is the best of cities and Rusaba is the best of farm lands.

64. (There is nothing that sympathizes with a stick, except its bark.) Your relatives will give you support. Nobody can do one's work as well as oneself.

65. (He who has an ax in his hand will find wood.) Equivalent to: Where there is a will there is a way.

66. (He who has been bitten by a snake fears a rope.) Once bitten twice shy.

67. (He who has a lie for lunch, will not have it for dinner.) The truth will out.

68. (He who saves something from his dinner will see it in the morning.) Be economical! Save for a rainy day!

69. (Half the road is the threshold.) This proverb is similar to proverb 48 above. 'The beginning of a mile is one step,' i.e., the first step is always the hardest.

70. (The head of my ram and not a bag of grasshoppers.) One today is better than two tomorrow. A bird in the hand is worth two in the bush.

71. (They thanked the cat and he defecated on the flour.) Equivalent to: Do not bite the hand that feeds you!

72. (In quiet, inattentive people you will find smart, intelligent people.) Do not judge people by their appearance! Equivalent to: Still water runs deep. You can't judge a book by its cover.

73. (Self-praise is disdainful.) Equivalent to: Self-exaltation is the fool's paradise.

74. (A disobedient son is better than nothing.) Something is better than nothing.

75. (He dances next to the drum.) He beats around the bush.

ʔal-xitaan

ḥasan: ya ʔax ʕali! gul-li maa huw al-xitaan law samaḥt!

ʕali: ʔal-xitaan huw at-taṭhiir. ʔiða gaalu fulaan taxatton yaʕni taṭahhar.

ḥasan: ʔal-xitaan farḍ fi l-ʔislaam?

ʕali: fi l-ḥagiigah huw sunneh wa ʔaṣbaḥ waajib fa tibsir kull an-naas yitbaʕuuha.

ḥasan: man allaði ysabbir al-xitaan?

ʕali: fi z-zamaan al-gadiim kaan allaði yguum bih ʔal-muzayyin wa huw al-xaatin walaakin ðalḥiin gad gaamu n-naas yaʕxuðuun aṭ-ṭifl ʔila ṭ-ṭabiib ʔaw fi mustašfa l-wilaadeh.

ḥasan: kam yikuun ʕumr al-walad lamman yaxtinuu?

ʕali: b-ḥasb guwwat aṭ-ṭifl. ʔal-ʕaadeh l-gadiimeh kaanu yaxtinu l-walad wa huw kabiir walaakin ðalḥiin muʕḍam an-naas yaxtinu ṭ-ṭifl baʕd ʔusbuuʕ min al-wilaadeh.

ḥasan: b-yaxtinu l-ʔinθa?

ʕali: haana maaši, laakin fi tuhaamah bas ʕala sibb yikuun al-jimaaʕ ʔagall ʕind al-mareh, wa haaði ʕaadeh mawjuudeh fi muṣr, tamaam?

ḥasan: tamaam. gul-li ʔayš yisabbiru n-naas yawm al-xitaan?

ʕali: ʔal-xaal huw allaði yatakaffal b-kull maṣaariif al-xitaan wa yakuun ʔawwal al-ḥaaḍiriin. ysabbiru ṣabuuḥ saaʕat sabʕ wa yakuun ʕaadatan yawm al-jumʕa. yatakawwan aṣ-ṣabuuḥ min ʔanwaaʕ min al-xubz miθl al-luḥuuḥ wa l-gafuuʕ wa maluuj aš-šaʕiir. ʔal-gafuuʕ huw xubz ðira maʕ ʕadas. baʕḍ an-naas ysabbiru ḥlbeh wa daggah wa marag wa guuzi ʕala l-ġadaaʕ, wa ziyaadeh ysabbiru ḥalawiyaat miθl al-muḥallabiyeh wa l-mulawwazeh wa t-tunfaaš wa l-kunaafeh.

Circumcision

Hasan: Brother Ali! Tell me what circumcision is, please!

Ali: Circumcision is cleansing or purging. If they say someone was circumcised, they mean he was cleansed.

Hasan: Is circumcision obligatory in Islam?

Ali: In fact, it is a habitual practice, but it became an obligation which all people adhere to.

Hasan: Who performs circumcision?

Ali: In the old times, the one who performed circumcision was the barber, but now people take the child to a doctor or to the maternity hospital.

Hasan: How old would a child be when he is circumcised?

Ali: It depends on the strength of the child. People used to have a child circumcised when he was mature, but now they have him circumcised when he is one week old.

Hasan: Are girls circumcised?

Ali: Not here, but they are circumcised in Tihama so that women might be less desirous of sexual intercourse. This is a custom practiced in Egypt, isn't it?

Hasan: Right. Tell me: What do people do on the day of circumcision?

Ali: The maternal uncle is the one responsible for all the expenses of circumcision and he should be the first to come. People prepare breakfast, usually on Friday morning at seven. The breakfast is made up of kinds of bread, /gafuu9/ and barley bread. /gafuu9/ is corn bread mixed with lentils. Some people prepare fenugreek, chopped up beef stew, meat broth, roasted lamb and lamb stew for lunch. In addition, they have sweets, such as jelly, almond jelly, popcorn, and kunaafa.

bayn zawj w-zawjatih
(ṣuurah min al-waagiʕ)

ʔaz-zawj:	hayya maališ mugazzazeh al-yawm?
ʔaz-zawjeh:	gaal-lak mugazzazeh! gad ana ʔašti ʔagðif.
ʔaz-zawj:	ʔaʕuuðu billaah min aš-šayṭaan ar-rajiim! limih?
ʔaz-zawjeh:	wa ʕaadak bi-tguul limih. ya rajjaal gad-li šahrayn wa ʔana ʔaṭlubak tištarii-li zannah.
ʔaz-zawj:	zannah! kaθiira ʕalayna ðalHiin. laakin....
ʔaz-zawjeh:	ʕa-tirjaʕu tguuluu-li ʔinnakum madyuuniin wa l-murattab galiil w-l-ʔasʕaar ġaaliyeh. gad ana daariyeh b-ḥijajkum kullaha. waḷḷaah maa ʕa-tijzaʕ ʕalayy waaHideh. laakin al-yawm jarrayt al-maʕaaš?
ʔaz-zawj:	maa ʕabbih?
ʔaz-zawjeh:	maa ʔašti zannah bass. ʔašti baʕdah sikarbiil wa ʔiθnayn maṣarraat, wa ʔašti ʔilla llaði gult lakum wala maa ʕaad ʔajlis lakum fi bayt.
ʔaz-zawj:	ʕind ʔabuuš ʔaḥsan?
ʔaz-zawjeh:	bayt ʔabi ʔaʕazz-a-li.
ʔaz-zawj:	wa min mayd az-zannah maa yguulu lana an-naas?
ʔaz-zawjeh:	yguulu ma yištu. maabiš ʔilla ʔana llaði b-tuṭlub zawjaha?
ʔaz-zawj:	laakin kull waaḥid b-gadrih. ʔana wa ṭuul haaði l-muddeh wa maa ḥassayti b-ḥaalati wa maa ʕarafti maa ʔaštakiiliš. gult-liš madyuun madyuun.

(abdaḷḷa ydagdig ʕala l-baab)

ʔaz-zawj:	man?
ʕabdaḷḷa:	ʔiftaḥ ya ḥsayn! ʔana ʕabdaḷḷa.
ʔaz-zawj:	ʔahlan! tafaḍḍal!
ʕabdaḷḷa:	laa ʔana mustaʕjil bass ʔaštiik tiji maʕi la-bayt ʕammak ʕala sibb nitḥaaka min muškilatkum ʔant wa zawjatkum.
ʔaz-zawj:	ya ʔaxi gad ana gaaniʕ min haaði l-ḥayaah wa l-mareh jannanatni.
ʕabdaḷḷa:	ma yhimmakš. ðalHiin gad nsiir la-ʕind ʕammak wa ʔana gad taḥaakayt maʕ ʕammak wa laagaytih mutafaahim la-l-mawḍuuʕ.

Between Husband and Wife
(A Picture of the Real World)

Husband: Hey, what are you so grumpy about, today?

Wife: He says, "Grumpy"! I could throw up.

Husband: God save me from Satan! Why?

Wife: You're still asking why? Look, Mister! I have been asking you to buy me a dress for two months.

Husband: A dress! We can't afford it now, but . . . .

Wife: You are going to tell me again that you are in debt, your salary does not go far, and prices have gone up. I am well aware of all your excuses, none of which, rest assured, will go unnoticed by me. Today you have been paid, haven't you?

Husband: What else is there?

Wife: What I would like to get is a dress only. I also would like to have shoes and two scarves. I don't want anything except what I've told you; otherwise I won't stay in your home.

Husband: Is it better at your father's?

Wife: My father's home is dearer, nicer for me.

Husband: Over a dress? What will people say about us?

Wife: Let them say what they like. Isn't there any other woman who asks her husband for anything?

Husband: Yes, but each one has one's own means. All this time you haven't sympathized with me (my situation) and you haven't understood what I have been complaining to you about. I have told you so many times that I am in debt, in debt.

(Abdalla knocks at the door)

Husband: Who is it?

Abdalla: Open! Open! Husayn! It's me, Abdalla.

Husband: Hi! Please come in!

Abdalla: No, thanks. I'm in a hurry. I just want you to come with me to your father-in-law's house in order to talk about the problem between you and your wife.

Husband: Brother! I'm fed up with this life and my wife has driven me crazy.

Abdalla: Don't worry! We will go to your father-in-law's and I have found him to be understanding and aware of the subject.

ʔal-ḥaaḍir yiʕlim al-ġaayib

ʔal-walad: ḥaayyaak aḷḷa ya ʕamm ṭaaha!

ʕamm ṭaaha: laa ḥayyaak wala gawwaak aḷḷa ya ġurraab aš-šuum! haakaða tifʕal-bi fiʕlatak wa tsiir!

ʔal-walad: maa huw ya bih? maa gad ḥaṣal minni?

ʕamm ṭaha: nisiit maa gad faʕalt al-yawm al-ʔawwal ḥiin laagaytani wa ʔana xaaṭi fi s-suug wa gulta-li ʔinna siʕr as-sukkar gad rtafaʕ wa xallaytani ʔaḥmil b-saaʕati ila l-ḥaanuut ʕala mayd ʔabiiʕ baagi s-sukkar allaði miʕi fi l-mixzaan wa baʕda ḥaṣal-li maa ḥaṣal. kullih min taḥt raʔsak ya kabiir ar-raʔs!

ʔal-walad: ya kabiir al-karš kaθiir aṭ-ṭamaʕ! gul-li ya ʕamm ṭaha wala yhimmak ʔana ša-tḥammalak liʔannak miθl ʔabi laakin al-gaanuun wa n-niḍaam maa yiḥmiiš al-ʔaġbiyaaʕ miθl ʔamθaalak wa ʔant guʕt ġabi liʔannak ṣaddagtani. ʔana gult ʔinna baʕḍ an-naas hum allaði ʔašaaʕu ʔinna siʕr as-sukkar gad rtafaʕ wa ʔant taʕrif man hum baʕḍ an-naas; ʔant wa ʔamθaalak min al-jašiʕiin wa l-muġaaliyiin hum allaði bi-yifʕalu haaði l-ʔišaaʕah ʕala sibb yirfaʕu ʔasʕaar as-silaʕ. nisyu ʔinna bih gaanuun yaḥmi l-muwaaṭin al-miskiin min al-mubalbiliin haaðawla. nisiit ʔagul-lak ʔinni fi nafs al-yawm sirt al-jamʕiyyah ʔal-ʔistihlaakiyyah wa štarayt kiis as-sukkar b-nafs as-siʕr al-muḥaddad.

ʕamm ṭaha: hayya smaʕ! ʔismaʕ! hayya ngaliʕ min gubaali! galaʕu ʕaynak! maabiš minnak ʔilla l-xasaarah!

ʔal-walad: ʔana naṣaḥtak ya ʕamm ṭaaha. nisiit titʕaalaj min al-maraḍ allaði fiik.

ʕamm ṭaha: ʔay maraḍ! muriḍat ʕaynak! ʔana saaʕ al-jamal wa ṣiḥḥati ʔaḥsan min ṣiḥḥatak ya ʕuudi! hayya maa gult?

ʔal-walad: maraḍak huw maraḍ al-jašaʕ. ʔant maa ganaʕt b-r-ribḥ al-maʕguul allaði maa yḍurrš b-l-muwaaṭin al-miskiin wala yxaalif gawaaniin ad-dawlah wa ʔanḍimatha.

TRANSLATION IV

Those Attending Will Inform Those Who Are Absent

Boy: May God preserve your life, Uncle Taha!

Taha: May God not preserve your life! You are a bird (crow) of evil omen! Why had you done this to me and left me?

Boy: What is it? What have I done?

Taha: You forgot what you had done to me yesterday when you met me while I was walking in the marketplace. You told me that the price of sugar had gone up, and made me go right away to my store in order to sell the rest of the sugar I had in the storeroom. You were the cause of all that happened to me, you fathead!

Boy: You are a very greedy man. Call me anything you want, Uncle Taha! I will be patient with you because you are like my father, but the law does not protect stupid people like you. You are stupid because you believed me. I said that some people had spread the rumor that the price of sugar had gone up. You know who those people are; they are greedy, just like you. They have forgotten that there is law that protects poor people from those who cause confusion and disorder. I forgot to tell you that on the same day I went to the Consumer Association and bought a sack of sugar at the same fixed price.

Taha: Hey, listen! Listen! Get out of my sight! The hell with you! There is nothing you cause, except loss.

Boy: I have advised you, Uncle Taha. You have forgotten to get medical treatment for the illness you have.

Taha: What illness? You are ill. (Lit., "May your eyes become ill!") I am as strong as a camel and my health is better than your health, you skinny little thing! What do you think?

Boy: Your illness is that of greed. You have not been satisfied with reasonable profit that does not harm poor people and does not violate the law of the land and its systems.

TEXT V

ʔal-ḥammaamaat

bih ḥammaamaat fi Ṣanʕa wa fi kull manaaṭig al-jumhuuriyyah. bih ʔakθar min θamanṭaʕšar ʔaw ʕišriin ḥammaam. ʔahamm al-ḥammaamaat fi Ṣanʕa ḥammaam aṭ-ṭawaaši wa ḥammaam šukr wa ḥammaam as-sulṭaan wa ḥammaam an-naʕiim wa ḥammaam al-mydaan wa ḥammam suug al-bagar. ʔal-ḥammaamaat gadiimeh gawi wa ʔaṣlaha faarisiyyeh gabl al-ʔatraak. ʔaḥsanha ʔagdamha.

kull ḥammaam lah θalaaθat madaaxil. fi kull madxal darajeh muʕayyaneh min al-ḥaraarah. fi l-madxal al-ʔawwal yaxlis al-ʔinsaan θiyaabih wa yilbas ʔizaar walla manšafeh. bih magʕad wa naafuurah fi l-madxal al-ʔawwal. ʔal-madxal aθ-θaani mutawassiṭ bayn al-ḥaraarah wa l-buruudeh. tagʕud ʕala sibb yuxruj al-ʕarag min jismik. ʔal-madxal aθ-θaaliθ nsammiih aṣ-ṣadr wa ṣ-ṣadr haaða bih ʔaḥwaaḓ min al-meʔ al-baarid wa l-meʔ al-ḥaamiy. ʔal-ʔinsaan yastaʕmil al-meʔ b-l-gadr allaði ḥasb ṭabiiʕat jismih. fi kull makaan tagʕud fatrah muʕayyaneh. fi l-makaan aθ-θaaliθ ya-tiik al-mukayyis. ʔal-mukayyis huw allaði ykayyis b-l-kiis wa l-liifeh. ʔat-tadliik yaxtalif ʕan at-takyiis. ʔat-tadliik b-l-ḥajar; ʔal-ʔinsaan yguum bih b-nafsih.

ʔal-ḥammaamaat allaði fi l-yaman taxtalif ʕan al-ḥammaamaat fi l-ʕiraaq. ʔal-ḥammaamaat haana taḥt saṭḥ al-ʔarḓ baynama l-ḥammaamaat fi baġdaad ʕala saṭḥ al-ʔarḓ.

TRANSLATION V

Public Baths

There are public baths in San'a and in all the other regions of the Y.A.R. There are more than eighteen or twenty public baths. The most important public baths in San'a are Al-Tawashi Bath, Al-Naim Bath, Al-Maydan Bath, and the Cattle Market Bath. These public baths are very old; they are of Persian origin--before the Turks. The oldest of them are the best.

Each bath has three entrance halls. At each place there is a certain degree of temperature. At the first place people take off their clothes and wear waist-wrappers or towels. There are a bench and a fountain at this first place. The second place has average (between hot and cold) temperature. You sit there in order to perspire. We call the third place the Sadr, which has basins of hot and cold water. People use the amount of hot or cold water that they can stand, i.e., in accordance with their physical make-up. In each place you sit for a certain period of time. At the third place a masseur will come to you. A masseur is the one who rubs with a bag-shaped luffa. /tadliik/ is different from /takyiis/. The former, /tadliik/, is rubbing with a pumice stone, which is performed by the person himself.

Baths in Yemen are different from those in Iraq. Baths here are below the surface of the earth, whereas those in Baghdad are at the ground level.

ʔal-ʕurs

ʔiðа l-walad yišti yizzawwaj gaaluu-lih: "šeeʔ zalaṭ?" gaal: "ʔii." tsiir ʔummih walla xaalatih la-bayt fulaan. yibsirayn al-bint, hiy ḥaaliyeh ʔadiibeh ... law jayn wa maaš hiy ḥaaliyeh wa ʔadiibeh ysiirayn la-bayt fulaan yibsirayn al-bint an-naahiyeh; laa hiy naahiyeh ysiirayn yguulayn la-l-ʔab: "ligiina bint fulaan ʔadiibeh naðiifeh kaamileh." yguul la-waaḥid min al-jiiraan: "ʔamaaneh[1] guul la-fulaan ʕa-niji ʕindih ʕala sibb nuxṭub al-bint la-ʔibnana." wa ysiiru fi l-yawm al-mawʕuud, yšillu gaat wa madaaʕah wa zalaṭ. ysiiru yitku wa baʕda yitḥaaku wa l-mutawassiṭ yguul: "ya fulaan jiʔna nuxṭub bintakum la-ʔibn fulaan." yguul: "marḥaba!" yguuluw: "ništi šarṭ." yguul: "maa huw maṭluubakum?" yguuluw: "sirwaal ḥaraazi[2] wa gamiiṣ wa ṣummaaṭah wa ..." yguul: "marḥaba! haaða š-šarṭ maḥmuul."
yawm að-ðibbaal ḥagg al-ḥareew

ysiiru yawm θaani yjurru l-kisweh wa yitlaagu yawm al-miiʕaad baʕd aṣ-ṣalaah. yimliku wa yuktub waaḥid fagiih waragat al-milkeh wa yawm θaani yitṣarrafu maṣaariif al-ʕurs.
wa baʕda tsiir ʔumm al-ḥareew la-l-buyuut tguul: "fulaaneh! ʕindana l-yawm al-fulaani ðibbaal." wa tsiir taḥlif ʕala bayt al-ḥareeweh wa yijayn baʕd al-ġadaaʔ b-faarix. yitimmayn at-tafruṭah[3] wa yruuḥayn kull waaḥideh la-baytaha.

yawm að-ðaal Hagg al-ḥareeweh

ʔumm al-ḥareeweh tsiir taḥlif ʕala l-jiiraan wa llaði taʕrifhum wa bayt al-ḥareew wa tguul: "jaw[4] ʕindana ðibbaal!" ysiirayn baʕd al-ġadaaʕ b-faarix gahwah wa yitfarraṭayn wa yġannayn fi l-ḥareeweh wa ʔummaha wa fi ʔabuuha wa baʕda ysiirayn buyuutahin.

ḥammaam wa nagš

tsiir ʔumm al-ḥareeweh ʔaṣ-ṣubḥ la-bayt al-ḥareew wa tguul: "jaw ʔal-ḥammaam wa n-nagš!" yguuluw: "marḥaba!" ysiiru la-ḥammaam an-nisaaʔ maʕ al-ḥareeweh wa hiy tilbis aθ-θiyaab. yiksirayn bayðah5 wa tudxul al-ḥareeweh titḥammam wa ni-nisaaʔ yudxulayn yitḥammamayn wa yiksiru bayðah ʕindima tuxruj al-ḥareeweh min al-ḥammaam. fi l-bayt gad hum ysabbiru l-ġadaaʔ. tudxul al-ḥareeweh min baab bayt ʔabuuha wa yiksiru bayðah. baʕda yilgannaha b-l-mazaamiir wa θ-θurayya wa yziffu al-ḥareeweh min ad-dahliiz la l-makaan. yguumayn yitġaddayn wa yirjaʕayn yitgahwayn wa l-ḥareeweh tajlis hiy wa l-muzayyineh tangušha.

laylat az-zaffeh

fi l-yawm ar-raabiʕ yijlisu min aṣ-ṣubḥ la wagt al-ġadaaʔ wa l-musabbireh trakkib aṭ-ṭabiix wa tguum taxbiz. saaʕat ḥdaʕšar wa nuṣṣ yguumu yitʕaššu wa gabl al-ʕišaaʔ ysiiru l-ḥammaam wa l-ḥareew ysiir yitḥammam maʕ ar-rijaal wa baʕda yuxruj al-ḥareew min al-ḥammaam wa yziffuu b-ṭ-ṭaaseh wa l-ʔitriikaat wa ygarriḥu b-l-girriiḥ.

baʕda tuxruj al-ḥareeweh wa yrakkibha ʔabuuha fawg al-baǧleh[6] wa ysiiru ʕašarah min bayt al-ḥareew wa ʕašarah min bayt al-ḥareeweh la-bayt al-ḥareew. tudxul al-ḥareeweh wa yiksiru bayðah ʕala l-baab wa yṭalliʕuuha ʔabuuha wa ʕammaha wa yruuḥu lahum. baʕda yuxrujayn an-nisaaʕ wa tibga l-muzayyineh wa r-rijaal yziffu l-ḥareew la-baab al-makaan wa yinzilu; yudxul al-ḥareew la-ʕindaha wa yiddi l-ftšee'[7] wa tuxruj al-muzayyineh.

Notes

1. The literal meaning of /ʔamaaneh/ is 'reliability' or 'trustworthiness'. The speaker entrusts the person he is speaking to with news that he is to convey to other people. The general meaning is: "I hope; I beg of you."
2. Characteristic of Haraz, a town in Yemen famous for making /saraawiil/ 'baggy pants'.
3. /tafruṭah/ stands for women's gatherings, sessions, including qat chewing sessions.
4. /jaw/ here means /taʕaaluw/ 'come (m.p.)'.
5. Breaking an egg in this context is a sign of good omen.
6. This is an old custom.
7. /ftšee'/ is money a bridegroom gives to his bride on the wedding night.

TRANSLATION VI

The Wedding

If a boy wants to get married, they ask him: "Do you have any money?" He says: "Yes." His mother or his maternal aunt goes to so-and-so's home. They take a look at the girl to see whether she is beautiful, well-mannered, etc. If she wasn't beautiful and they came back, they go to somebody else's home to see a beautiful girl. If she is beautiful, they go to the (boy's) father and say: "We have found so-and-so's daughter to be well-mannered, clean, and refined. He (the father) says to one of the neighbors: "Will you please tell so-and-so that we will go to him in order to ask for the girl's hand in marriage for our son." They go on the appointed day, take qat, a water pipe and money with them. They go to chew qat and, later on, talk with one another and the go-between says: "Mr. so-and-so! We came to ask for your girl's hand in marriage for so-and-so's son." He says: "You are welcome!" They say: "We have some conditions." He says: "What is your request?" They say: "A pair of baggy pants from Haraz, a shirt, a headdress, ..." He says: "Yes, your conditions are accepted."

The Bridegroom's Day of Celebration

On the second day they go and take the clothes with them. They meet one another on the appointed day after prayer. They contract the marriage and a learned man writes the marriage contract and on the following day they pay for the wedding expenses.
Later on, the bridegroom's mother goes to houses and says on such a day they have a wedding celebration. She goes to invite the bride's folks. They (the bride's folks) come after lunch and bring an urn of coffee. They chatter, chew qat and each one goes home.

The Bride's Day of Celebration

The bride's mother goes to invite the neighbors, her acquaintances, and the bridegroom's folks and says: "Come! We have a wedding celebration." They go after lunch and bring with them a large coffee pot. They chater, chew qat and sing the praises of the bride and her parents and then go home.

The Bath and (Henna) Dyeing

The bride's mother goes to the bridegroom's home and says: "Come to the (public) bath and (henna) dyeing." They say: "Yes." They go to the women's bath with the bride and she puts on (her) clothes. They break an egg; the bride and the women go inside to bathe. They break an egg when the bride comes out of the bath. At home they prepare lunch. The bride enters from the door of her father's room and they break an egg. Later, they meet her with wood-wind instruments and candelabras and conduct her in solemn procession from the hallway to the room. They start to sing and come back to drink coffee, and the bride sits with the beautician who dyes her with henna.

The Night of the Wedding Ceremony

On the fourth day, people sit from the morning until lunch time; the (woman) caterer places the food on the stove and starts baking bread. At 11:30 p.m. they start dinner and before the evening prayer they go to the (public) bath. The bridegroom goes to bathe with the men, and then the bridegroom comes out of the bath and they conduct him in solemn procession with drums and lanterns and they set off firecrackers.

The bride comes out and her father helps her mount a female mule. Ten from the bridegroom's relatives and ten from the bride's relatives walk to the bridegroom's house. The bride enters and they break an egg on the door. Her father and her paternal uncle lead her out. Later, the women go out and the beautician remains. The men conduct the bridegroom in solemn procession to the room and leave; the bridegroom enters, approaches her and gives her the /ftšee'/. The beautician leaves.

ðamaari b-ṣanʕaaniyyayn[1]

kaan bih waaḥid ðamaari wa ʔiθnayn min ṣanʕa gaamu tasaayaru, wa l-ʔiθnayn min ṣanʕa yištu yziidu ʕala ṣaaḥib ðamaar[2] b-ḥiðguhum. ʔawwal-maa ykuun ðabaḥu lahum dajaajeh wa ṭabaxuuha ḥatta ḥaṣṣa luuha. fa gaalu ʔahl ṣanʕa: "man ʕa-yiddi ʔaayeh min al-gurʔaan jarr waṣleh." fa l-ʔawwal min ʔahl ṣanʕa gaal: "fakku ragabah"[3] wa ʔakal ragabeh. wa θ-θaani gaal: "maa yṭiir aṭ-ṭayr ʔilla b-janaaḥih,"[4] wa ʔakal al-janaaḥ. ṣaaḥib ðamaar gaal: "ʔiða laffat as-saag b-s-saag yawmaʔiðin rabbuka li-l-masaag,"[5] wa ʔakal ad-dajaajeh b-kullaha.

min baʕd faʕalu lahum taʕzibeh wa jamaʕu ṭ-ṭali wa l-birr wa s-samn. taġaddu ʕala l-birr wa s-samn wa ṭ-ṭali faʕaluuh la ṣ-ṣubḥ. gaalu: "man traaya r-raʕy aṭ-ṭayyib gaam yaʕkul aṭ-ṭali." ʔal-waʕd baynahum la-ṣ-ṣubḥ. fa min baʕd gaamu ṣ-ṣubḥ.

ṣaaḥib ṣanʕa gaal la-ʔaxuuh: "maa traayayt?" gaal: "traayayt ʔinni ʕarajt as-samaaʔ." ʔaxuuh gaal: "ʔana traayayt ʔinni daxalt al-janneh." ṣaaḥib ðamaar gaam yaʔkul. gaalu: "maa traayayt ya ṣaaḥib ðamaar?" gaal: "ʔana traayayt waaḥid ʕaraj as-samaaʔ wa waaḥid daxal al-janneh fa gumt ʔakalt aṭ-ṭali gablima yaʕtiini malak al-mawt!"[6]

Notes

1. /ðamaari/ is a person from Dhamar and a person from San'a is /ṣanʕaani/.
2. /ṣaaḥib ðamaar/ is the one from Dhamar or the Dhamari.
3. The reference here is to Sura XC, Verse 13 of the Quran. Freeing the enslaved person is one of the three specific deeds that are given in this Sura for treading the difficult path of virtue. There is a play upon words in /ragabah/.
4. The reference here is to Sura VI, Verse 38 of the Quran. The San'ani who said this verse (or part of Verse 38) changed the words and thus changed the meaning of the verse. The verse literally means: 'There is not an animal on the earth, nor a being that flies ... and all life is subject to the Plan and Will of God.'
5. The reference here is to Sura LXXV, Verses 29-30. The two verses mean: When the soul has departed, the legs of the body are placed together. On that day everyone will have to go before the Throne of Judgment.
6. /malak al-mawt/ is Azrael, the angel of death.

TRANSLATION VII

One Dhamari Is Worth Two San'anis

There were one from Dhamar and two from San'a who were walking and became friends with each other. The two San'anis wanted to outwit the Dhamari. First of all, they killed a chicken for themselves and cooked it until it was ready to be eaten. The two San'anis said: "He who cites a verse from the Quran will eat a piece of the chicken." The first San'ani said: "Freeing the bondman," and ate the neck. The second San'ani said: "A bird does not fly except by its wings," and ate the wings. The Dhamari said: "If one leg is joined with another, that day will be to thy Lord," and he ate the whole chicken.

Later on, they went on a picnic. They brought a lamb, wheat, and butter. They cooked them and ate the wheat (cooked in butter) for lunch and kept the lamb for the morning. They said: "He who dreams a pleasant dream will eat the lamb." The appointed time they set (for themselves) was early morning. They woke up in the morning and one of the San'anis said to his friend: "What did you dream?" He said: "I dreamed that I ascended to heaven." His friend said, "I dreamed that I entered paradise." The Dhamari began to eat. They (the San'anis) said: "What did you dream?" He said: "I dreamed that one ascended to heaven and (another) one entered paradise; for that reason I went and ate the lamb before the angel of death (Azrael) comes to me!"

Bibliography

Arabic

Al-Akwa', Ismail. ʔal-ʔamθaal al-yamaaniyya. Dar Al-Maarif, Cairo, 1968.

Al-Maqalih, Abd Al-Aziz. šiʕr al-ʕaammiyya fi l-yaman. Dar Al-Awda, Beirut, 1978.

Al-Nami, Yahya. "min al-lahajaat al-yamaniyya al-ḥadiiθa" *Cairo University Journal of the College of Arts 8* (1946): 69-84 and 15 (1953): 103-113.

Amer, Abdalla Bin Ahmad. min aš-šiʕr al-ḥamiini aṣ-ṣanʕaani. Dar Maktabat Al-Hayaa, Beirut, 1973.

Anan, Zaid Ali. ʔal-lahja al-yamaaniyya fi n-nukat wa l-ʔamθaal aṣ-ṣanʕaaniyya. Al-Saada Press, Cairo, 1980.

Muhammad, Asma'. ʔamθaal ṣanʕaaniyya. Dar Al-Kalima, San'a, 1990.

Sharaf Al-Din, Ahmad. lahajaat al-yaman qadiiman wa ḥadiiθan. Al-Jabalawi Press, Cairo, 1970.

Western

Abboud, Peter. "On Ablaut in Cairo Arabic." *Journal of Afro-Asiatic Linguistics* 3 (1976): 168-187.

Brame, Michael K. *Arabic Phonology: Implications for Phonological Theory and Historical Semitics.* MIT unpublished dissertation, 1970.

Cowell, Mark W. *A Reference Grammar of Syrian Arabic.* Georgetown University Press, 1964.

Critchfield, David. *Yemeni Arabic* (mimeographed, 1970).

Diem, Werner. *Skizzen Jemenitischer Dialekte.* Beirut, 1973.

Greenman, Joseph. "A Sketch of the Arabic Dialect of the Central Yamani Tihamah." *Journal of Arabic Linguistics* 3 (1979) 47-61.

Ingham, Bruce. "Some Characteristics of Meccan Speech" *BSOAS* 34 (1971): 273-279.

Jastrow, Otto. "Zur Phonologie Und Phonetik Des Ṣanʕanischen." *Entwicklungspvozesse in der Arabischen Republic Jemen,* 1984

Macdonald, John. "The Arabic Derived Verb Themes: A Study in Form and Meaning" *Islamic Quarterly* 7 (1963): 96-116.

Qafisheh, Hamdi A. *A Short Reference Grammar of Gulf Arabic.* University of Arizona Press, 1977.

-------------------- *Yemeni Arabic I.* Librarie du Liban, 1990.

Renaud, Etienne. *An Introduction to Yemeni Spoken Arabic* (mimeographed, 1977).

Rossi, Ettore. "Appunti di dialettologia del Yemen." *Rivista degli Studi Orientali* 17 (1938): 230-265 and 460-472.

-------------------- L'Arabo Parlato a Ṣanʔā. Instuto Per L'Oriente, Roma, 1939.

Serjeant, R.B. and Lewcoct, Ronald (ed.). *San'a, An Arabian Islamic City.* London: World of Islam Trust Fund, 1983.

Shaaban, Kassem Ali. *The Phonology of Omani Arabic.* University of Texas unpublished Ph.D. dissertation, 1977.

Wright, W. *A Grammar of the Arabic Language,* 3rd Edition. Cambridge University Press, 1967.